T0163285

New Religions in a Postmodern World

RENNER Studies on New Religions

General Editor
Armin W. Geertz, Department of the Study of Religion, University of
  Aarhus

Editorial Board
Dorthe Refslund Christensen, Institute of Philosophy and the Study
  of Religions, University of Southern Denmark
Annika Hvithamar, Department of the History of Religions, Univer-
  sity of Copenhagen
Hans Raun Iversen, Department of Systematic Theology, University
  of Copenhagen
Viggo Mortensen, Department of Systematic Theology, Centre for
  Multi-Religious Studies, University of Aarhus
Mikael Rothstein, Department of the History of Religions, University
  of Copenhagen
Margit Warburg, Department of the History of Religions, University
  of Copenhagen

RENNER Studies on New Religions is an initiative supported by the
Danish Research Council for the Humanities. The series is established to publish books on new religions and alternative spiritual
movements from a wide range of perspectives. It includes works of
original theory, empirical research, and edited collections that
address current topics, but will generally focus on the situation in
Europe.

The books appeal to an international readership of scholars, students, and professionals in the study of religion, theology, the arts,
and the social sciences. And it is hoped that this series will provide a
proper context for scientific exchange between these often competing
disciplines.

NEW RELIGIONS IN
A POSTMODERN WORLD

Edited by Mikael Rothstein
& Reender Kranenborg

AARHUS UNIVERSITY PRESS

Copyright: Aarhus University Press, 2003
Printed in Denmark by Narayana Press, Gylling
ISBN 87 7288 748 6

AARHUS UNIVERSITY PRESS
Langelandsgade 177
8200 Aarhus N
Denmark
Fax (+ 45) 8942 5380

73 Lime Walk
Headington, Oxford OX3 7AD
United Kingdom
Fax (+ 44) 1865 750 079

Box 511
Oakville, Conn. 06779
USA
Fax (+ 1) 860 945 9468

www.unipress.dk

Preface

The articles in the present volume were presented at a conference held in Amsterdam in August 1997. This conference was co-hosted by the Vrije Universiteit Amsterdam and CESNUR, the Torino based Center for the Study of New Religious Movements. Following the conference it was decided to publish a number of contributions, and the *Research Network on New Religions* (RENNER) in Denmark took on the task. Due, however, to a number of unfortunate — and certainly unexpected — circumstances (lack of funding being the most important), the publication was continuously delayed. Fortunately, though, just as we were about to give up, things changed. Obviously, as editors, we realize that much time has passed and that the contributions to the book may, in certain ways, be a little out of tune with the latest developments in the study of new religions. On the other hand, the articles certainly contain descriptions and analysis that are highly relevant. In short, we found it worthwhile to continue with the project, and we are very relieved now to finally place the volume at the reader's disposal.

Asking for the reader's understanding is one thing. Asking for the authors' obliging cooperation is something very different in such a situation, but in this regard we have been most fortunate. The contributors have been more than patient with us, for which we owe them our sincere thanks. A few contributions have, with our approval, been published elsewhere in the meantime.

The theme for the conference in which the papers were read was 'Magic, Millennium and New Religious Movements'. The contributions, though, focused not only on these issues but covered many different fields. As we edited the articles we therefore decided to abandon the framework of the conference and, more in tune with the material, structure the book according to a number of other themes. Hence the reader will find 'Esotericism', 'Millennialism and Eschatology', 'Religious Leaders', and 'Social Aspects of the New Religions' to be the general section titles. As it has become commonplace to see new religions in the light of post-modernism, we decided accordingly to name our volume 'New Religions in a Postmodern World'.

Scholarly studies of new and emerging religions are, by and large, facing the same challenges in 2003 as in 1997. We need more concrete knowledge on the empirical level, and more sophisticated means for analysing our data on the theoretical and methodological level. This, however, is the order of things: The strictly academic perspectives are constantly being refined and developed. At the same time scholars in this field of research will often find themselves directly or indirectly involved in public debates or legal discussions on new religions. The scholars' societal situation, therefore, also makes it necessary to consider how and why one should — or should not — engage in the public debates. These and many other topics are touched upon in the following disparate *bouquet* of articles.

Financial support from The University of Aarhus Research Foundation, the University of Copenhagen, Landsdommer V. Gieses Legat and RENNER, has made it possible to publish this book. We express sincere gratitude for this support. Finally we wish to extend our thanks to Mary Lund of the Aarhus University Press, who helped the project through numerous difficulties.

Mikael Rothstein and *Reender Kranenborg*
Copenhagen and Amsterdam
April, 2003

Contents

Part III: Religious Leaders

Part IV: Social Aspects of the New Religions

Part I:

Esotericism

CHAPTER 1

Lectorium Rosicrucianum: A Dutch Movement Becomes International

Massimo Introvigne

Methodology

The Lectorium Rosicrucianum (LR), a movement born in the Nether-lands, enjoys today a remarkable international following. There are more than 15,000 pupils and 'members' in the world. (The 'members' are those awaiting admission as a pupil). More than half are in Europe, but the movement is also well established in countries out-side Europe, including Brazil.

In order to study new religious movements (NMR) and those that I suggest be called 'new magical movements',[1] three methods are normally proposed. First, there is the 'religionist' approach, as Dutch scholar Wouter Hanegraaff calls it. It consists in assuming from the outset that a religious or spiritual doctrine is 'true' and in examining from this point of view what are the 'errors' and 'deviations' from the 'truth' contained in all other currents and movements.[2] The 'reli-gionist' approach, applied respectively to the author's own group, or to others, results in apologetics or heresiology. Second, there is the 'anti-cult' approach. It is a secular version of the 'religionist' ap-proach. It often claims to be interested in deeds, not in creeds. In fact, however, it compares each movement with the basic values of mod-ernity such as rationality, conceived in a rather positivist manner;

1. See Introvigne 1990.
2. See Hanegraaff 1996.

and democracy, regarded as applicable to all fields of human life. If the movement deviates too much from these values it becomes a 'cult', labelled as 'destructive' or 'totalitarian' and stigmatized by an image of subversion. Scholars, on the other hand, try to adopt in most cases a 'value-free' approach. They try not to compare the values of a spiritual movement with those of the researcher or of the society at large, but only to analyse its main features within the appropriate context.

Of course the 'religionist' and the 'anti-cult' approach are not illegitimate in themselves. They can contribute to the debate and even address interesting questions. Yet, they cannot be accepted when they claim to present themselves as universal points of view. They also become dangerous when they ask the State to protect a majority religion, or a supposedly dominant ideology. The 'value-free' approach is of course conscious that it is ultimately impossible to present a position totally separated from all values. It accepts that the observer influences the perception of the observed phenomenon. However at least it tries, although it never succeeds completely, to present each religious movement from the standpoint of its own values. This is surely a different method from submitting the movement to an examination according to the criteria of the observer (whether they are presented or not as 'universal' criteria, which every 'reasonable person' surely would admit). Finally, the 'value-free' approach does not avoid comparisons (a point often not perceived by representatives of the 'anti-cult' approach). Contrary to the apologetic discourse, it tries to situate the given movement in its historical, social and religious contexts. It draws on parallels that may sometimes upset the members of the movement studied. They believe, as it is only normal, that their spiritual family is always 'unique', and its success depends on its privileged relation to the truth.

The Lectorium Rosicrucianum

I propose to give here a short overview of the LR. I will then situate it in its socio-religious context. I will also shortly ask questions (without really giving a final answer) on its sources of legitimization, and its relations with the New Age, and with post-modernity.

Movements that J. Gordon Melton attaches to the 'ancient wisdom' family[3] always have multiple references to the founding myths of the esoteric tradition, such as the 'wisdom from the East', Gnosticism, hermeticism, the Knights Templar, or the Rosicrucians. One can however identify sub-families with reference to a dominant myth. We may thus refer, among others, to a Rosicrucian sub-family, where the symbolism of the Rosy Cross predominates. Both Frances Yates and Roland Edighoffer[4] have over the last few years given reliable historical accounts of the origins of the Rosy Cross and of its influence on the birth of modern Freemasonry. The first Rosicrucian societies, in the modern sense of the word, appeared at the end of the 18th century. Rosicrucian groups punctuated the esoteric revival of the 19th century: in France around Papus (Gérard Encausse, 1865-1916) and Joséphin Péladan (1858-1918), in England with the Societas Rosicruciana in Anglia, and in the United States with the Fraternitas Rosae Crucis of Pascal Beverly Randolph (1825-1875).[5] The Rosicrucian movement continued into the 20th century, at first with Arnoldo Krumm-Heller (1876-1949),[6] whose Fraternitas Rosicruciana Antiqua spread particularly in Latin America. Max Heindel (Carl Louis von Grasshoff, 1865-1938), a Danish-born German esotericist formed in the milieu of the Theosophical Society, created the Rosicrucian Fellowship in Los Angeles in 1907. In 1915, also in the United States, Harvey Spencer Lewis (1833-1939) established the AMORC, the Ancient and Mystical Order Rosae Crucis. Whilst AMORC experienced remarkable success, it has also experienced a number of schisms and problems in more recent years.

In the 1920s Jan Leene (1896-1968) and his brother Zwier Wilhelm Leene (1892-1938) became the most important leaders of Max Heindel's Rosicrucian Fellowship in the Netherlands.[7] According to them, the birth of the present LR should be dated as 24 August 1924, a date that is held in high spiritual esteem by the movement. However the Leene brothers — who were joined in 1930 by Mrs H. Stok-

3. Melton 1996.
4. Yates 1972; Edighoffer 1994.
5. On Randolph, see Deveney 1997. On the various Rosicrucian movements, see Introvigne 1990, 184-215.
6. On Krumm-Heller, see König 1995.
7. On the origins of LR, see Lectorium Rosicrucianum 1989.

Huyser (1902-1990) — only declared their independence from the Rosicrucian Fellowship in 1935. After the premature death of the older of the two brothers in 1938, Jan Leene (using the pen-name Jan van Rijckenborgh) and Mrs Stok-Huyser (who signed as Catharose de Petri) began to put the doctrines of the movement into writing. When the Nazis entered Holland the movement was forbidden, its possessions confiscated and its temples razed. Several members, including Jewish members, found their death in the gas chambers. After the difficulties of the war the movement adopted the name LR in 1945.

Interested in Catharism, the two founders met Antonin Gadal (1871-1962) in France in 1948. Gadal was one of the key figures of the Cathar revival in our century.[8] When a branch of the LR was created in France in 1957, Gadal became its first president. The statutes were established by Richard Dupuy, a notary public who at that time was the Grand Master of the Grand Lodge, one of the rival branches of French Freemasonry. At the same time the LR began to spread, first in Germany — where the Rosicrucian myth was as important as the Cathar tragedy in Southern France — and then in a number of other countries. The most notable success of the LR came after the death of van Rijckenborgh (1968) and of Catharose de Petri (1990), who were replaced by an International Spiritual Directorate. The approximately 15,000 adherents are divided into 14,000 'pupils' and about a thousand 'members' (who, as mentioned earlier, await admission as pupils).

After a period of one or two years, the 'pupils' must engage themselves in a way of life where a 'balance of consciousness' is essential.[9] From this engagement stems a research for mental, emotional and physical purification, encouraged by vegetarianism, and abstinence from alcohol, tobacco and drugs. There is also a clear reticence with regard to 'unhealthy influences', in particular those allegedly transmitted by television[10] (a point which has already caused a lot of ink

8. See claims by Gadal 1980a, Gadal 1980b.
9. The most important textbooks of the LR are originally published in Dutch. English translations of key texts include van Rijckenborgh 1957; 1958; 1962; 1980; 1993; and de Petri 1995.
10. See, for an Italian example, Scuola Internazionale della Rosacroce d'Oro 1981. The booklet existed in various languages. Its distribution has now been discontinued.

to flow). To the outside observer, these reservations towards television continue to be seen as the most evident trait of the Lectorium. Critical observers would also focus on its belief in the unhealthy manipulation of the world of the living by the world of the dead (the 'reflective sphere') and by occult forces that are fed by erroneous thoughts and actions of both good and bad human beings.[11] In fact, we are confronted here with a process of identity claiming and boundary maintenance between pupils and non-pupils. The abstention from meat, alcohol, tobacco and television plays an important role for the LR, comparable to the 'word of wisdom' for the Mormons. Yet, the essence of the doctrine of the LR is not there.

In order to understand the LR it is crucial to refer to Gnosticism and to the Cathar tradition. The LR proposes a classical Gnostic dualism between the divine world (static) and the natural world (dialectic), of which the true God is not the creator. As Antoine Faivre has noted, it is difficult to reconcile this dualism with the Rosicrucian tradition.[12] The latter, at least in its 17th century origins, is not dualistic. The 'dialectical' world includes both the living and those dead that, in a state of dissolution, await a new incarnation. The latter can only be understood within the framework of the notion of man as a microcosm, a notion that has been largely developed by the LR. The popular theories of the reincarnation of the personal ego are refuted. The only function of the ego consciousness is in fact to sacrifice itself for the 'resurrection of the original soul', the divine spark to be found at the heart of the human microcosm. The so-called 'living', which we are, having forgotten their divine origin are imprisoned in this dualist and absurd world. Yet, they possess a 'spirit spark atom', which manifests itself in many as a remembrance or pre-remembrance and nostalgia. The path of transfiguration as proposed by the LR aims to awaken the divine spark ('the rose of the heart') and to lead humans back to their original condition.

One finds here the classical picture of all forms of Gnosticism. Yet, this Gnosticism organizes itself according to a language and models that are often taken directly from the Cathar tradition. Over and above the debate on the role of Gadal and his neo-Catharism, the dual-

11. See van Rijckenborgh 1958.
12. Faivre 1996, 246-54.

ism of the LR and that of the Cathars (which according to Anne
Brenon developed gradually)[13] is remarkably similar. The dualism of
the LR (as that of the Cathars) is not only to be found in their cosmology, but also inspires human behaviour. Actions can help to progress
towards transfiguration or, on the contrary, further imprison humans
in the dialectic field. The LR provides an esoteric interpretation of
man and his body. It also presents a vision of the future. Here, one
finds texts on the coming of a false Christ and Armageddon that may
be regarded as millennialist or apocalyptic. These labels are meaningful only if one defines clearly in what sense the terms may be used
within the frame of a Gnostic worldview. In fact, one can apply several conclusions to the LR that recent scholarship applies to the medieval Cathar movement. Even if one can find various influences at
work, essentially it represents a dualist and Gnostic Christianity.

Sources of Legitimization

Contemporary 'ancient wisdom' movements claim their legitimacy
in esoteric circles according to three different models:

a) There are those who claim a legitimacy of *origin*. They claim an
   'apostolic succession' supposedly at work without interruption
   'throughout history, starting from certain ancient initiates.
b) Others claim a legitimacy given by signs or manifestations (levita-
   tion, clairvoyance, theurgy).
c) Finally, there are those who seek their legitimization according to
   the purity of their doctrine, which can ensure contact with a spiritual current (or an eternal 'gnosis'), regarded as more important
   than any historical affiliation.

These are of course three ideal types, because many groups claim all
three types of legitimacy (although one may remain dominant). One
is struck here by the difference, within the same Rosicrucian family,
between AMORC and the LR. For AMORC the legitimacy of origin is
of capital importance. It is on the basis of a number of initiations received by its founder that AMORC claims to be the only authentic

13. Among Brenon's large production, see on this point Brenon 1996.

Rosicrucian organization. For other groups, including the Fraternitas Rosicruciana Antiqua (as evidenced by Krumm-Heller's novel *Rosa Cruz*)[14] true legitimacy stems from supernatural 'signs'. For the LR, signs of this kind — spiritualism and magic in the usual sense of these words — have no legitimacy. Yet for the LR there is also a noble and acceptable sense in the word 'magic'. Legitimate 'magic' is the use of forces supporting a process of spiritual awakening of the soul that has already begun (as opposite to the self-aggrandizement of the ego consciousness and its 'powers'). It is only in this sense that one can define the LR as a 'magical movement'. The LR forcefully rejects all occult practices. They render humans, it claims, victims of an illusion that they themselves have created. Jan van Rijckenborgh noted the importance of sexual magic in the esoteric milieu, but he severely condemned such practices. He claimed that in the context of the esoteric anatomy he had outlined, they create the greatest dangers.[15]

As every esoteric group, the LR also claims a certain legitimacy of origin — particularly through Gadal's neo-Catharism — yet this element very rarely comes to the fore. In fact the most important element for the LR is the doctrine and the contact with the eternal gnosis as a spiritual current. The gnosis is a manifestation of the radiation field of Christ, a 'Universal Brotherhood' which is not limited to its human manifestations.

Claims of legitimacy of origin normally expose esoteric movements to the danger of empirical verifications by sceptics. AMORC's credentials were strongly criticized by R. Swinburne Clymer (1878-1966) of the Fraternitas Rosae Crucis (and vice versa).[16] They are also criticized by contemporary authors such as Robert Vanloo.[17] More recently a journalist and author, Christian Bernadac, attacked the LR with the typical language of the anti-cult movement in a work devoted to Nazi neo-Cathar Otto Rahn (1904-1939), *Montségur and the Grail*.[18] The author, who does not seem to be very familiar with LR, apparently does not understand the difference between the varying legitimacy

---

14. A modern edition is Krumm-Heller 1984.
15. van Rijckenborgh 1980, 219-26.
16. See for example Clymer 1935.
17. Vanloo 1996.
18. Bernadac 1994.

claims. The legitimacy of the AMORC is promoted with a strong reference to its origin and 'apostolic succession'. The LR refers to Gadal, but it does not insist particularly on origin as its key legitimizing factor. This difference in the process of legitimization could explain certain controversies involving the AMORC and the LR. In the new 1996 edition of the presentation of the AMORC in questions and answers, the AMORC states that 'none of the (other) so-called Rosicrucian movements (…) can claim an authentic link with the true Tradition of the Rosy Cross. Today, it is the AMORC that is the inheritor of this Tradition and which perpetuates it'.[19] One can see here a typical claim centred on the legitimacy of the origin. The AMORC even reminds its readers that 'it has nothing to do with a cult. It has never been mentioned as one in any of the official reports that have been published on cults'.[20] This is a rather inelegant allusion to the rather bizarre mention of the LR in the list of 'cults' of the 1996 French parliamentary report *Les sectes en France*,[21] whose list has been widely criticized. The fact that this report gives extremely inaccurate information on the LR,[22] while the AMORC is declared explicitly innocent of any 'cultic' connection,[23] raises some very delicate questions. Should we suppose that conflicts over different claims to Rosicrucian legitimacy will be decided in the future by parliamentary commissions?

The LR, the New Age and Post-Modernity

The LR is not part of the New Age movement. It considers all that is in fashion in this milieu to be typical of the dialectical field. Nevertheless, the LR has recruited members from the New Age environment and in some countries this has not happened by chance. For example, I had a chance to watch public lectures where the LR was clearly preaching to the New Agers. This happened in 1997 at the

19. *L'ordre de la Rose-Croix AMORC en questions* 1996, 98.
20. Ibid., 17.
21. *Les sectes en France* 1996. For criticism by scholars and by the mainline churches see Introvigne and Melton 1996.
22. Ibid., 24, 54.
23. Ibid., 64.

Bodhi Tree bookstore in Hollywood, a true Mecca of the Californian
New Age movement, and at the esoteric book fair in Tours, France.
Many young LR members in Italy do not have any classical esoteric
training. Rather, they became interested in esoteric ideas by reading
New Age authors and journals (that they now criticize in view of
their new identity). One could analyse here the hypotheses of Wouter Hanegraaff on the New Age as a form of esotericism in the mirror
of secular thought. The path of some LR members seems to go back-
wards. They try to desecularize what currently passes for esotericism
among the New Agers. LR pupils are looking for esoteric models regarded as more 'pure' and closer to a genuine ancient wisdom (Gnostic or Cathar). They are seeking rather distant models since they are
clearly dissatisfied with the present-day offer of the New Age. They
may also perceive New Age's current crisis as described by J. Gordon
Melton.[24]

Yet, the theories of Hanegraaff can be somewhat applied here. We
may ask ourselves whether the personal itineraries of New Agers
who join the LR are a transformation of the identity of the New Age
rather than its rejection. For example, the LR affirms that present-day
theories on reincarnation are false, yet that the core idea of reincarnation is correct. One could also ask oneself if a backward path is really possible and if the understanding of Gnosticism and Catharism today does not itself take place in Hanegraaff's 'mirror of secular
thought'.

It may also be argued that the recent success of the LR is somewhat connected to postmodernity. It is of vital importance to distinguish between postmodernism and postmodernity. There is no society created on the basis of postmodernist theories, and sociologists of
religion are quite right in general to affirm that the ideas of postmodernist theorists have hardly had any influence in the religious field
(with some exceptions).[25] However, one can speak of postmodernity
as a fact, and of a postmodern society as a contemporary society
where there is a crisis of typically modern values and ideals, such as
rationality and science. If this society of postmodernity exists (irre-
spective of postmodernist theories), it is normal that religious forms

24. See Melton 1998.
25. See Flanagan and Jupp 1996.

that are distant from modernity will flourish. Yet these forms will not
necessarily follow the ideas of postmodernist theoreticians, and may
in fact be far removed from them. This is the case, I believe, of the LR.
It is a movement that prospers typically in the context of postmodernity, while its conception of truth and gnosis is to be found at the anti-
podes of the postmodernist theories. The LR is postmodern in the
sense that it criticizes rationalism and modernity, yet does not promote a return to premodern values nor does it regard premodernity,
as a whole, as a golden age. On the other hand, the LR is very much
remote from postmodernist theories since it affirms its gnosis as an
absolute and universal truth. In doing this the LR claims to offer a
connection with an oppositional and persecuted brand of premodernity, Catharism. Hanegraaff argued that esotericism survived into the
New Age only by somewhat accepting to be transformed and re-
shaped by secular thought. Although the LR is at times surprisingly
faithful to Catharism as reconstructed by modern scholarship, it is
unclear whether living according to an unadulterated Cathar worldview is really possible in the contemporary world. Perhaps — as
Hanegraaff's esotericism in the New Age — the LR's brand of Catharism may only survive as Catharism in the mirror of secular
thought.

Bibliography

Bernadac, C. 1994. *Montségur et le Graal. Le mystère Otto Rahn.* Paris:
  France-Empire.
Brenon, A. 1996. *Les cathares. Vie et mort d'une église chrétienne.* Paris:
  Jacques Grancher.
Clymer, R.S. 1935. *The Rosicrucian Fraternity in America. Authentic and
  Spurious Organizations.* Quakertown: The Rosicrucian Foundation.
Deveney, J.P. 1997. *Paschal Beverly Randolph. A Nineteenth-Century
  Black American Spiritualist, Rosicrucian, and Sex Magician.* Albany
  (New York): SUNY Press.
Edighoffer, R. 1994. *Les Rose-Croix* (4th edition). Paris: Presses Univer-
  sitaires de France.
Faivre, A. 1996. 'Les courants ésotériques et le rapport. Les exemples
  de la Nouvelle Acropole et de la Rose-Croix d'Or (Lectorium
  Rosicrucianum)'. In Introvigne and Melton 1996, 233-54.

Flanagan, K. and P.C. Jupp (eds.). *Postmodernity, Sociology and Religion.* London/New York: MacMillan Press – St. Martin's Press.
Gadal, A. 1980a. *De l'héritage des Cathares.* Haarlem: Rozekruis Pers.
Gadal, A. 1980b. *Montréalp de Sos: Le Château du Graal. Montréalp de Sos: La Montagne des Rois – Le Château du Graal.* Haarlem: Rozekruis Pers.
Hanegraaff, W. 1996. *New Age Religion and Western Culture. Esotericism in the Mirror of Secular Thought.* Leiden/New York/Köln: E.J. Brill.
Introvigne, M. 1990. *Il cappello del mago. I nuovi movimenti magici dallo spiritismo al satanismo.* Milan: SugarCo.
Introvigne, M. and J. G. Melton (eds.), 1996. *Pour en finir avec les sectes. Le débat sur le rapport de la commission parlementaire* (3rd edition). Paris: Dervy.
König, P.-R. 1995. *Ein Leben für die Rose (Arnoldo Krumm-Heller).* Munich: Arbeitsgemeinschaft für Religions- und Weltanschauungsfragen.
Krumm-Heller, A. 1984. *Rosa Cruz. Novela de ocultismo iniciatico.* Santa Fe/Buenos Aires: Editorial Kier.
Lectorium Rosicrucianum 1989. *La Rose-Croix Vivante. 24 août 1924-24 août 1989. Parole, lumière, vie.* Haarlem: Rozekruis Pers.
Melton, J.G. 1998. 'The Future of the New Age Movement'. In: E. Barker and M. Warburg (eds.), *New Religions and New Religiosity.* Aarhus: Aarhus University Press, 133-49.
Melton, J.G. 1996. *Encyclopedia of American Religions* (5th edition). Detroit: Gale.
L'Ordre de la Rose-Croix AMORC en questions. 1996. Le Tremblay: Diffusion Rosicrucienne.
de Petri, C. 1995. *Transfiguration* (2nd edition). Haarlem: Rosycross Press.
van Rijckenborgh, J. 1957. *The Coming New Man.* Haarlem: Rosycross Press.
van Rijckenborgh, J. 1958. *Unmasking.* Haarlem: Rosycross Press.
van Rijckenborgh, J. 1962. *Dei Gloria Intacta: The Christian Mystery of Initiation of the Holy Rosycross for the New Era.* Haarlem: Rosycross Press.
van Rijckenborgh, J. 1980. *The Gnosis in Present-Day Manifestation.* Haarlem: Rosycross Press.

van Rijckenborgh, J. 1993. *The Mystery of Life and Death* (2nd edition). Haarlem: Rosycross Press.

Scuola Internazionale della Rosacroce d'Oro 1981. *I pericoli della televisione: argomenti scientifici ed esoterici.* Caux: Lectorium Rosicrucianum.

Les sectes en France. Rapport fait au nom de la commission d'enquête sur les sectes. 1996. Paris: Les Documents d'information de l'Assemblée Nationale.

Vanloo, R. 1996. *Les rose-croix du nouveau monde. Aux sources du rosicrucianisme moderne.* Paris: Claire Vigne.

Yates, F. 1972. *The Rosicrucian Enlightenment.* London: Routledge.

CHAPTER 2

Swedenborg, Freemasonry, and Swedenborgian Freemasonry: An Overview[1]

Jan A.M. Snoek

'One thing is certain: Swedenborg himself had nothing to do with it'.[2] Thus opens the excellent paper by Robert Gilbert on our subject: Swedenborgian Freemasonry. Indeed, 'Swedenborg was not a Freemason and at no times had any connection with or gave any attention to the Society'.[3] However, among the followers and admirers of Swedenborg there were many Freemasons, and it would have been perfectly

1. This article is based on a presentation for Session 6: 'Swedenborg', of the 11th International CESNUR Congress, held from 7-9 August 1997 in Amsterdam. It has not been significantly altered since then. Only references to some new publications have been added. I wish to acknowledge the kind help which I received from H. Berg, B. Borg, M.L. Brodsky, Prof. A. Faivre, Dr. K.C.F. Feddersen, R.A. Gilbert, Dr. H.-H. Granse, Dr. W.J. Hanegraaff, P. Mollier, Dr. D. Schulte (†), and Dr. Jane Williams-Hogan.
2. Gilbert 1995.
3. Coil 1961; cf. also Gilbert 1995, 123-24. It seems that nowadays only Marsha Keith Schuchard still believes that Swedenborg was a Freemason. Cf. Schuchard, especially 1988. It is highly regrettable that someone who has read so much and has done such interesting research is arguing so strongly for preconceived ideas, thus including totally unreliable sources and applying argumentation that is replete with logical fallacies. This holds true for all of her works that I have seen so far, including — besides the above-mentioned — her 1975 and 1992 works. I shall not regress into a demonstration of the problematic quality of her publications, but neither can I admit her work as a valid argument in the debate concerning our current subject. Cf. on the quality of the work of Schuchard, Williams-Hogan 1998, 205-6, note 13.

in line with the habits of the second half of the 18th and 19th century, if they had created rituals — and even whole Rites — in which the ideas of their teacher had been incorporated. Indeed, many authors have indicated different masonic Rites as 'Swedenborgian'. Thus, the central questions in this article will be:

1. Which masonic Rites have been referred to as Swedenborgian?
2. Which of these Rites show clear Swedenborgian influences, and thus may properly be referred to as Swedenborgian Freemasonry?

Before turning to that subject, however, let me briefly describe who Swedenborg was, and what his main ideas were, and then explain a little bit about Freemasonry.

Swedenborg

Swedenborg was born in Stockholm in 1688 as Emanuel Swedberg. He studied natural sciences and worked successfully for the government, especially in the mining industry. When he was 31, his family was ennobled and adopted the name Swedenborg. Fifteen years later, his *Opera philosophica et mineralogica* established his reputation as a scientist. Soon he became a member of many academies, both in Sweden and abroad. In 1744, at the age of 56, he had several dreams in which he encountered Christ who redeemed him. This experience changed his life completely. From then on he had mystical experiences during which he talked with the spirits of deceased persons, such as Vergil, Luther and Melanchthon. These experiences began to dominate his active life. He therefore resigned from all his official functions in order to devote himself to creating his own esoteric theosophical system, which also includes cabbalistic elements, and to write his mystical works. He died while visiting London in 1772, 84 years old.

As it is impossible to do full justice here to the teachings of Swedenborg, I shall only deal with the following elements.[4]

4. On Swedenborg, see, for example, Benz 1948; Jonsson 1971; Sigstedt 1981; and Larsen 1988. For a short and concise biography, see also Williams-Hogan 1988. See also Fabry & Faivre 1996.

— Firstly, Swedenborg follows the doctrine of the two books, as found in the works of Jakob Böhme and others: God expresses himself in, and thus can be known from, two books: the Bible and Nature.

— Swedenborg also adheres to the old doctrine of correspondence: there are three levels of reality: the natural, the spiritual and the celestial. Each thing in the natural world represents at the same time something in the spiritual, and, through that, something in the celestial world.

— Life is always divine. It flows from God, manifests itself and divides itself into three streams, which flow into three realms: the celestial, the spiritual and the natural.

— The symbol of the dawn of a New Age is the New Jerusalem, as described by St. John in the Biblical book of Revelations.

— There is a special relation between God and Man. God is divine love itself, and love desires to give to another which is not himself. So God created the human race in the natural world, which was the proper domain for that 'otherness' — the world of nature was the material of man's body and was his own realm. His mind operates actively to the principles of heaven.

— Man was created to fill the heavens to eternity. Each person who chooses to be an image of God is a jewel, which is one facet of the 'Grand Man', the primeval Man, Adam Kadmon, which consists of the community of celestial beings, such as the angels.

— God is Light and Heat, and Light and Heat are divine. God is seen in the spiritual son of the spiritual world.

— And, finally, Man's greatness consists of worshipping God, by living an active and useful life.

This enumeration of the elements of Swedenborg's teachings is in no respect complete, but it suffices for my present purpose: the identification of Swedenborgian elements in masonic rituals.

Freemasonry

Let us look now at Freemasonry. This is, principally, a method of working with rituals. Most forms of Freemasonry have no doctrine, but just this method. The rituals are exercised, and since they are expressed in symbols throughout, they are open to whatever interpretation the individual members wish to read into them.

All of the more complex masonic Rites are based on a system of three degrees — Entered Apprentice, Fellow Craft, and Master Mason — collectively referred to as the Craft, symbolic, St. John's, or 'blue' degrees. There are two main pillars on which the rituals are based: First, the most important ones show the structure of an initiation ritual as found throughout the world. Briefly, this implies the symbolic death of the old person, and the symbolic rebirth or resurrection of the new one.[5]

The second important aspect of masonic rituals is the use of the allusive method, which works as follows. During the rituals, there are some texts pronounced. When hearing these texts, a naive listener might notice nothing special. But educated listeners will recognize that in these texts there are implicit quotes from books they know. The collection of all the books, from which such quotes are taken, is called the 'referential corpus'. This corpus may consist of one or more books. In most masonic rituals, the Bible forms part of the referential corpus. In other words, a listener who knows the Bible reasonably well may recognize implicit quotes from the Bible in the texts of the rituals. This, however, is just the beginning. For the text quoted will often have been selected because it has parallels, either in the same book or elsewhere, which the beholder may now be reminded of. For example, a text quoted from Isaiah in the Old Testament may well point the attention of the educated listener to another text in the New Testament.[6] In that way, the text of the ritual may gain extra meaning for those to whom these extra texts invoked are significant. In another case, a ritual text may remind the listener of a parallel text in a work

5. See Snoek 1987.
6. For example, 'l'étoile flamboyante, qui marche devant nous semblable à cette Colonne de feu qui brilla pour guider le peuple dans le désert.' ([Wolson] 1751, 43) clearly refers to Exodus 13:21-22: 'And the Lord went before them by day in a pillar of a cloud, to lead them the way; and by night in a pillar of fire, to give them light; to go by day and night: He took not away the pillar of the cloud by day, nor the pillar of fire by night, from before the people.' This again refers to Isaiah 4:5-6: 'And the Lord will create upon every dwelling place of Mount Zion, and upon her assemblies, a cloud and smoke by day, and the shining of a flaming fire by →

of one of the church fathers, which refers to a text in Revelations, which in turn invokes a parallel in Ezekiel.[7] It is this allusive method which opens the possibility to create something like a Swedenborgian ritual, by including implicit references to the ideas of Swedenborg, that pass unnoticed by those who do not recognize them (and thus are not offended by them), but give extra significance to the ritual for those who do recognize their source and attach importance to it.

Beswick's Swedenborgian Rite

Now that we have an idea about the teachings of Swedenborg, as well as about Freemasonry, let me return to my main questions: which masonic Rites have been referred to as Swedenborgian, and which of them do show clear Swedenborgian influences and thus may properly be referred to as Swedenborgian Freemasonry?

Bob Gilbert's paper deals mainly with one such Rite: the one promoted, if not created, by Samuel Beswick. The account by Gilbert being excellent, I shall only give a short summary of the subject here, just for the sake of completeness.

In 1870 Beswick published a book: *Swedenborg Rite and the Great masonic Leaders of the Eighteenth Century*. It claims that the Rite started in 1859 in New York City, but it seems doubtful that it really began much before the publication of the book. In fact, 'the first Grand Lodge of the Swedenborgian Rite had only a brief existence' (128) between 1870 and 1872 and 'we can ... be certain [only] that in the real world the Swedenborgian Rite had at least six members in the United States of America' (128), among whom Beswick himself acted as Supreme Grand Master. The 'only recorded formal act [of this Grand Lodge] was on 3 June 1872, when it issued a charter for a Supreme Grand Lodge and Temple for the Dominion of Canada'

→ night: for upon all the glory shall be a defence. And there shall be a tabernacle for a shadow in the daytime from the heat, and for a place of refuge, and for a covert from storm and from rain.' This image can be interpreted as depicting both the Lodge, and the Stable with the Star of Bethlehem (Matthew 2; Luke 2), and from there it may point even further to other texts, each enriching the meaning of the first one. For other examples, see Snoek 1999, 47-70; 1997b, 291-94.

7. This example is spelled out in Snoek 1997a, 23-29.

(128), but this Grand Lodge 'with its headquarters at Maitland, Ontario, was not finally set up until 1873' (128) with McLeod Moore as its Grand Master. The Rite continued to exist in Canada, at least on paper, until the death of McLeod Moore in 1890.

The 'one significant act that the Grand Lodge and Temple of Canada did perform' (128) was that, on 1 July 1876, it chartered John Yarker to work the Swedenborgian Rite in the United Kingdom. 'According to the warrant, Emmanuel Lodge and Temple of "The Primitive and Original Rite of Phremasonry otherwise known as the Swedenborgian Rite" was to be held at Manchester, with Yarker as Worshipful Master' (129). The Rite flourished in the UK for three decades. Other important members, besides Yarker that is, included Kenneth Mackenzie (1876), William Wynn Westcott (1876), Samuel Liddell MacGregor Mathers (1887), Henry Steele Olcott (1880), Gerard Encausse ('Papus') (1901) and Arthur Edward Waite (1902).

On 21 February 1902, Yarker issued a charter to Theodor Reuss to 'constitute "The Swedenborg Lodge of the Holy Grail No. 15 at Berlin"' (135). 'It was to be "the Mother Lodge of Germania with power to form a 'Provincial Grand Lodge and Temple' of the 'Swedenborg Rite', and to found Subordinate Lodges"' (135). However, despite this expansion, the Rite was about to die a silent death. The last information about it dates from 1908 — only six years later.

Be that as it may, we have at least one Swedenborgian Rite here, which we can be sure really existed. Bob Gilbert's paper demonstrates this beyond doubt.[8]

Pernety and the Illuminé d'Avignon

But Gilbert claims more. In a section of less than one page under the heading 'The First Rite of Swedenborg' he writes:

If any of the many 18th century manufacturers of Rites and Degrees deserves the title of creator of the 'Swedenborgian Rite' it is Dom Antoine Joseph Pernety (1716-1796). At the age of fifty Pernety left the Benedictine Order and

8. For some examples of the Swedenborgian nature of the Beswick rituals, see Appendix I.

settled at Avignon where he redirected his alchemical enthusiasm into masonic channels and allegedly created a 'Rite Hermétique' that reflected his
interests. From Avignon he moved to Berlin where he became librarian to
Frederick the Great and began to translate the works of Swedenborg into
French.

Here he met a Polish Count, Thaddeus Leszczy Grabianka (1740-1807),
who was equally enthused with Swedenborgian doctrines. When Pernety returned to Avignon in 1784 Grabianka followed ... and in 1786 they founded
the Société des Illuminés d'Avignon. ...

These bizarre activities of the Illuminés d'Avignon came to an end with
the upheavals of the French Revolution ... (123)

This is indeed the opinion on these matters, generally found in all
sources before 1974.[9] But in that year, Robert Amadou published an
article on Pernety[10] in which he is very careful:

Antoine Joseph Pernéty, was he a Freemason? I don't know, and, if he was
one, I don't know where he received the masonic Light. I know of no document whatsoever bearing on his possible masonic career. On the other hand,
many details can be found with all the authors who have attributed to him
the creation of a Rite hermétique, of the degree of Chevalier du Soleil, of the
Académie des Vrais Maçons, etc. Superfluous to point out all these errors and
legends. For it involves, beginning with Ragon and ending with Bricaud,
nothing else (1974, 993 = 1991, 919-20).

9. Meillassoux claims that Claude Mesliand was in fact the first to deny that
   Pernety was a Freemason, referring to his 'Renaissance de la franc-
   maçonnerie avignonnaise à la fin de l'Ancien Régime, 1774-1789', *Bulletin
   d'histoire économique et sociale de la Révolution française*, Paris, B.N., (1972)
   23-82 (Meillassoux – Le Cerf 1992, 156, note 15). However, this article by
   Mesliand does not appear in the particular issue of the above-named
   periodical that Meillassoux refers to, and I have not been able to trace it.
   Therefore I do not know if it was indeed published as early as 1972.
10. Amadou 1974.

In 1992, Micheline Meillassoux even goes as far as to state clearly that 'since several years, all investigations agree to affirm that Pernety has never been a Freemason. Nowhere, in any of the places where he has stayed, has one been able to find a trace of any initiation in a lodge, nor any masonic document concerning him'.[11] Pierre Mollier, however, informed me that Pernety's masonic engagement has now been proved,[12] but he at once adds that he seems not to have been very zealous. 'In his search for secret divine knowledge, the famous Benedictine seems to have preferred the Swedenborgian circles rather than the lodges'.[13]

Even if Pernety was a Freemason, however, it still seems extremely unlikely that he was the creator of any masonic Rite, degree or ritual. No doubt he was the leader, though not the creator of the group that became known as the Illuminés d'Avignon. This group started in 1778 or 1779 in Berlin with Prince Henry of Prussia (the brother of King Frederick II), Jacques Pernety (older brother of Antoine Joseph), and Claude Etienne Le Bauld de Nans.[14] Soon others joined the group, among whom (indeed) Grabianka and Antoine Joseph Pernety. Grabianka was the one who consecrated all the others.[15] Pernety was consecrated on 1 April 1779.[16] In 1783 the group moved to Avig-

11. Meillassoux 1992, 156-7.
12. Personal communication dated 8 July 1997: 'Pour ce qui est de la qualité maçonnique de Pernety, elle est maintenant établie par le *'Tableau général des frères francs-maçons qui ont été initiés aux mystères de l'ordre dans la très juste et très parfaite loge La Royal Yorck de l'Amitié à Berlin – année 5782'* (80 pages). Ce document est passé en vente au enchère et j'ai pu le voir. C'est assez drôle car concernant la ligne consacrée à Dom Pernety il y a, a peu près, les informations suivantes, *'a été initié en France'* ... *'a reçu la plupart des hauts-grades en France'* ... et surtout une formule du type *'demande qu'on ne le dérange pas'* ... ce qui montre l'intérêt tout relatif qu'il portait à la Maçonnerie à cette époque.' The auction referred to was on 11 February, 1996 in Saint-Germain-en-Laye, and the catalogue of the auction states: '272 – Tableau général des frères francs-maçons ... Notamment Antoine Pernetti dont l'appartenance maçonnique contestée, y est bien repris' (p. 7).
13. Mollier 1996, 242.
14. Meillassoux 1992, 110.
15. Idem., 115.
16. Idem., 120.

non. Pernety was 67 then. A few members stayed behind, and some others joined. All in all, only 21 persons participated for a shorter or longer period in the group.[17] In 1792, as a result of the Revolution, the group was dispersed, and in 1793 it was completely abolished.[18]

The group had rituals for the consecration of its members (which have not been published)[19], but its main activity was the practice of Alchemy. Its other characteristic trait was the consultation by its members of 'the Sacred Word' (la Sainte Parole), mediated by one of its members, viz. Brumore.[20] Meillassoux states explicitly, however, that despite the active interest of some of its members for the teachings of Swedenborg and/or Freemasonry, it was neither a Swedenborgian group, nor a masonic lodge.[21] The Illuminés d'Avignon must therefore be ruled out as a masonic Swedenborgian Rite.

17. Idem., 113.
18. Idem., 224.
19. The only description of the rituals I could find is this: '[les Illuminés d'Avignon] formaient deux classes supérieures aux grades maçonniques proprement dits: Les Novices ou Mineurs et les Illuminés qui avaient pour chef le Mage, appelé aussi Pontife ou Patriarche. Le candidat à l'initiation se confessait, entendait une messe dite par Pernéty, puis recevait une 'consécration' ou 'ordination' au cours d'une cérémonie propre à la secte. Elle avait lieu au sommet d'une colline où 'l'autel de puissance', construit en gazon, s'élevait au centre d'un 'cercle de puissance', tracé sur le sol. Pendant neuf jours le catéchumène, accompagné de ses instructeurs, montait sur la colline au lever du soleil; il brûlait de l'encens sur l'autel et prenait, par des formules solennelles, l'engagement de se vouer au service de 'son Dieu'. Quand la candidature était agréée par la divinité, l'élu apercevait l'ange qui lui servirait dorénavant de guide et qu'il pourrait 'interpeller' quand il aurait besoin d'un avis sur sa conduite dans la vie ou sur ses travaux hermétiques' (Le Forestier 1970, 877-78). Le Forestier's claim that the consecration of the Illuminés d'Avignon 'formaient deux classes supérieures aux grades maçonniques proprement dits' seems unlikely, since not only men, but also women and children were consecrated. Regrettably, Le Forestier does not indicate his source(s) for this, rather global, description. I don't understand how Alec Mellor (n.d., 299) can claim that 'Les cérémonies par lesquelles devaient passer ses adeptes ont été minutieusement décrites par des érudits tel qu'A. Viatte, [1928] et R. Le Forestier [1970]'.
20. Meillassoux 1992, 102 ff.
21. Idem. 89, 158.

Pernety and the Rite Hermétique

However, as Robert Amadou reminds us, 'The Illuminés d'Avignon is one thing, the Rite hermétique is another'.[22] Could Pernety have created that? After all, we saw that Gilbert stated that, 'At the age of fifty Pernety left the Benedictine Order and settled at Avignon where he redirected his alchemical enthusiasm into masonic channels and allegedly created a 'Rite Hermétique' that reflected his interests'. 'Allegedly', indeed. And that holds true for this whole visit to Avignon. In fact, it is most likely that he went directly from Paris to Berlin. It is known that the Hermetic degrees were worked in Avignon from 1774.[23] Pernety left Paris for Berlin in 1767 and none of his biographers believe that he returned to France before he travelled to Avignon in 1783/84. As Amadou remarks cleverly, 'Pernety could have travelled through Avignon [i.e. on his way from Paris to Berlin], though that is rather unlikely'. 'According to Ragon he came there in 1766, and according to Clavel in 1760' (ibid). But even if he did, there was no masonic activity in Avignon between 1764 and 1772, due to the activities of the Inquisition against Freemasonry during that period (ibid). The Rite Hermétique was in fact created in the lodge Saint Jean d'Ecosse in Marseille, where some members of the lodge, which was founded in 1774 in Avignon, received its degrees, and it was this lodge of Marseille that constituted the lodge Saint Jean d'Ecosse in Avignon on 31 July 1774.[24] It is clear therefore that Pernety had nothing to do with the creation of the Rite Hermétique either.

The Rite Hermétique and the Rite Ecossais philosophique

But even if Pernety was not its founder, then the Rite Hermétique could still be a Swedenborgian masonic Rite. In order to find out, let us look at it a little closer.

22. Amadou 1974, 993 = 1991, 920.
23. Amadou 1974, 994 = 1991, 920-21; Meillassoux 1992, 157.
24. Le Bihan 1998, 121.

The organization

Robert Amadou neatly summarized its complicated history, a subject which was later elaborated by Litvine, and most recently — and most reliably — by Le Bihan.[25] For the present purpose, the following suffices. After two attempts by Pierre Claude de Saint-Léger to create a new lodge in Avignon in 1772 and 1774 had failed, Charles d'Aigrefeuille succeeded in 1774 in obtaining a warrant from the Mère Loge Ecossaise de Marseille, *Saint-Jean d'Ecosse* for the lodge *Saint-Jean d'Ecosse* d'Avignon. However, Avignon was at that time still a pontifical domain. So, on 3 February 1775, the rooms of the new lodge were raided, its possessions confiscated, and the lodge dissolved. It reorganized itself on French territory, however, taking the name of *Saint-Jean d'Ecosse de la Vertu persécutée*. Early in 1776, its Orator, Laurant Jean Antoine Deleutre, was affiliated in the Parisian lodge *L'Equité* (successor of *Saint-Lazare*), which then asked *Saint-Jean d'Ecosse* d'Avignon for a constitution for its Rite Ecossais, and this was granted in April 1776. The chapter for the practice of the high degrees of this Rite was consecrated on 5 May 1776. This chapter took the name of *Chapitre Métropolitain de la Mère Loge Ecossaise de France*. At the same time, the blue lodge *Saint Lazare* asked the Grand Orient to change its name to *Saint-Jean d'Ecosse du Contrat Social*, which was accepted in May 1776. During the French Revolution, in 1792, the Mother-lodge *Contrat Social* resolved to suspend work, and in 1805 the Lodge *Saint-Alexandre d'Ecosse* became the new head or Mother-lodge.[26]

The Rite

The Rite Hermétique d'Avignon and its successor, the Rite Ecossais philosophique, like many other Rites, developed in the course of time. According to Amadou,[27] when *Saint-Jean d'Ecosse* d'Avignon was created in 1774, it had to promise its mother lodge of Marseille

25. Amadou 1974, 994 = 1991, 920-21; Litvine 1997; Le Bihan 1998 and 2000.
26. Thory 1812, 166. Often Thory is not quite reliable, though. According to Le Bihan (2000, 111), 'en juillet 1791, [Thory] signa le dernier texte, consacré alors à Saint-Jean d'Ecosse'. But he confirms that 'En 1805, [Thory] était 1er surveillant du Chapitre et vénérable de la loge' (112).
27. A third part of the article by Le Behan, dealing especially with the degrees has been announced.

that it would not work in any other degree than that of the three symbolic degrees — 1. Entered Apprentice, 2. Fellow Craft, and 3. Master
— and

4. Maître Parfait,
5. Elu,
6. Ecossais d'Ecosse ou Vrai Maître, and
7. Chevalier Maçon dit de l'Orient.

At the end of its existence, the Rite Ecossais philosophique had developed into a much more complex system. Clavel gives the following
list of degrees above the symbolic ones for 1843:

1. 2. 3.   Chevalier de l'Aigle noir ou Rose-Croix d'Hérédom de la
           Tour (divisé en trois parties),
4.   Chevalier du Phénix,
5.   Chevalier du Soleil,
6.   Chevalier de l'Iris,
7.   Vrai maçon,
8.   Chevalier des Argonautes,
9.   Chevalier de la Toison-d'Or,
10.   Grand-inspecteur parfait initié,
11.   Grand-inspecteur grand écossais,
12.   Sublime maître de l'anneau lumineux.[28]

The rituals

In order to answer our prime question as to whether the Rite Hermétique and/or the Rite Ecossais philosophique can be regarded as
Swedenborgian masonic Rites, we shall now turn to the contents of
the rituals for these degrees — as far as they are known. All manuscripts available of rituals of the Rite Ecossais philosophique are rather
late, i.e., from after 1800. However, the rituals contained in them may
be considerably older. My personal impression was that none of these
rituals shows any marked Swedenborgian influence. But, not being
an expert in Swedenborgianism myself, I asked Jane Williams-Hogan

28. For a more complete description of the development of this Rite, see
    Appendix II.

to screen them for Swedenborgian elements. She found only three instances of texts which might be interpreted as such, and none of them compelling. So, we have to conclude that, as far as the known rituals are concerned, the Rite Ecossais philosophique was not a Swedenborgian masonic Rite.

Chastanier and the Illuminés Théosophes

Harold Voorhis, like Robert Gilbert, assumes that there are at least two Swedenborgian Rites. He opens his introduction to his publication of the Beswick rituals thus:

There have been at least two systems of Freemasonry which claimed the title of *The Swedenborgian Rite*: the first is referable to London, and one Benedict Chastanier, circa 1784, based on the Order of Illuminated Theosophists, established there by him in 1767; the second is the more modern [i.e. the Beswick one].[29]

So, maybe the Chastanier Rite is Swedenborgian. Ragon gives the following information:

Rite of Bénédict Chastanier (Les Illuminés théosophes) (1767).
In 1767 Chastanier, a French Freemason, established in London a purely Christian theosophical secret society, which had the object to propagate the system of Swedenborg. Soon the secret became public. He founded the Illuminés Théosophes, and modified Pernety's Rite. He instituted the six degrees with the names:

1. Theosophic Apprentice
2. Theosophic Fellow Craft
3. Theosophic Master
4. Sublime Scottish Mason or Celestial Jerusalem (Illuminated theosophist)
5. Blue Brother
6. Red Brother[30]

29. Voorhis 1938, 17.
30. Ragon 1853, 152-53.

According to Coil and Mackey, these degrees came 'above the Craft degrees'.[31] It may be noted that the degrees of Beswick's Swedenborgian Rite were called: 4th degree: Enlightened Phremason, or Green Brother, corresponding to the Entered Apprentice; 5th degree: Sublime Phremason, or Blue Brother, corresponding to Fellow-Craft; and 6th degree: Perfect Phremason, or Red Brother, corresponding to Master Mason.[32] Apparently, Beswick was aware of the names of the degrees of Chastanier's system.

Chastanier was a member of the Illuminés d'Avignon[33] and a Freemason, member of the Grande Loge de France and Master of the lodge 'Socrate de la Parfaite Union' in Paris.[34] Frick claims that Chastanier left for England as a Protestant refugee, since the Huguenots lived under significant pressure in France until the Revolution.[35] In London, he published several translations of works of Swedenborg, some compiled by himself, some in his Journal *Novi-Jérusalémite*. Coil mentions that '[Chastanier's Rite] abandoned masonic forms and became dedicated to the promotion of Swedenborg's theories and theosophy and apparently merged with the Theosophical Society formed at London in 1784.'[36] According to Frick, it was rather the Marquis de Thomé who created the Swedenborgian Rite as a modification of the system of the Illuminés d'Avignon c. 1783, after which Chastanier brought it to England.[37] After the preceding analysis of the Illuminés d'Avignon, however, this hypothesis seems rather unlikely. The problem with this system, however, is that so far no rituals or other documents concerning this system have been found[38] which could prove its existence and the claims by Voorhis and Ragon

31. Coil 1961, 545; Mackey 1946, 196.
32. Voorhis 1938, 112-14.
33. Le Forestier 1970, 785.
34. Bord 1908, 262.
35. Frick 1975, 599.
36. Coil 1961, 545; cf. also Mackey 1946, 196, who, correctly, refers to Lenning 1822, Vol. 1, 71: 'Chastanier (Benedict), französischer Herkunft und Wundarzt, stiftete 1767 in London eine maurerische Loge, um die Grundsätze *Swedenborg's* darin zu lehren. Diese Loge artete aber bald in eine bloß theosophische Secte aus und dauerte als solche in London mehrere Jahre fort, ohne sich fernerhin der maurerischen Formen zu bedienen'.
37. Frick 1975, 600-1.
38. P. Mollier, personal communication, letter of 9 June 1997.

about its masonic character. If it existed, however, there can be little doubt, that it was Swedenborgian.

The Elus Coën

In his chapter on Swedenborg, Ragon addresses two masonic Rites: the Elus Coën[39] and the Swedish Rite.[40] With regard to the Elu Coën, we can be brief. As far as I can see, Ragon is the only one to suggest that it is Swedenborgian. I would be highly surprised if it were. It is the masonic ritual expression of the philosophy, theosophy, and occultism of its founder, the mystic Martines de Pasqually. The Rite started working in 1761 and ceased to exist in 1781 when its third Grand Sovereign, De la Casas, handed the archives over to the Philaletes. Besides Martines de Pasqually himself, its most important members were the Marquis Louis Claude de Saint-Martin (the founder of Martinism) and Jean-Baptiste Willermoz (the founder of the Rite Ecossais Rectifié). The last turned out to be the most successful of the three Rites: it absorbed both the others and it remains one of the principal Rites of Freemasonry up to the present day. All three of these men stood clearly in the line of Western Esotericism. Besides, all three were mystics as well as highly original thinkers. They had all this in common with Swedenborg. They may have known Swedenborg's works and it may even be possible to find parallels between their works and those of Swedenborg. Frick claims that 'Pasqually [was] in his teachings dependant on him',[41] but I doubt if it would be possible to prove any direct influence of Swedenborg on the works of these three men, including the masonic Rites they created,[42] especially

39. Ragon 1853, 257-58.
40. Idem. 259 ff.
41. Frick 1975, 584.
42. Antoine Faivre and Bob Gilbert confirmed my assumption: 'I have familiarized myself for many years with Martines de Pasqually's writings and system. I find it extremely unlikely that they were ever so little influenced by Swedenborg' (Faivre, personal communication, letter of 13 October 1997); and, 'Frick is quite wrong to claim that Pasqually was dependent on Swedenborg. Nothing in his system shows that, and Pasqually's and Saint-Martin's doctrine of the 'Repairer' is closer to traditional Christianity than to Swedenborg' (Gilbert, personal communication, letter of 23 August 1997).

since the French translations of Swedenborg's works were only published from 1781 onwards,[43] the year in which the Order of the Elu
Coën ceased to exist. The Latin originals had been printed, mainly
secretly, from 1745 onwards, and were very difficult to obtain during
the first decades.[44] Therefore, given this little promising prospect, I
decided not to spend any time investigating this line.

The Swedish Rite

With respect to the Swedish Rite, things are different. Ragon was not
the only one to assume that it would be Swedenborgian. A serious
historian like Gould wrote: 'It is also affirmed that the mystical teachings of Emmanuel Swedenborg are discernible in the doctrines of the
Rite'.[45] And Starcke is even more precise: '... although the Swedish
system nowhere refers to [Swedenborg] explicitly, its whole worldview is the child of his mind. The whole method of the system is Swedenborgian, and many ideas from Swedenborg's *Celestial Arcana*, his
interpretation of the Apocalypse and his presentation of the New
Jerusalem, are found in the high degrees of the Swedish Rite'.[46]

  Beswick's book, *Swedenborg Rite and the Great masonic Leaders of the
Eighteenth Century* is notorious for its mixture of facts and fiction. It is
interesting, however, to see that he uses the terms 'Swedish Rite' and
'Swedenborgian Rite' as synonyms. For example, he writes that 'the
first [Swedenborgian] Lodge was opened in Stockholm, sometime

43. The translations by Jean-Pierre Moet de Versailles and Chastanier were
    published in London between 1781 and 1787; those by Pernety in 1782
    and 1786 in Berlin; and one by Brumore (Guyton de Morveau) in 1784,
    likewise in Berlin.
44. Meillassoux 1992, 75-76.
45. Gould 1903, 383.
46. '... wenn auch das schwedische System sich nirgends unmittelbar auf
    [Swedenborg] beruft, so ist ihre ganze Grundanschauung seines Geistes
    Kind. Die ganze Methode des Systems ist Swedenborgs, und viele Vor-
    stellungen, die in Swedenborgs himmlischen Arcana, in seiner Ausle-
    gung der Apokalypse und in seiner Darstellung des Neuen Jerusalem ent-
    halten sind, kehren in den Schwedischen Hochgraden wieder'. Starcke
    1913, 98-99. Frick 1975, 302 clearly quotes this source without reference.

between the year 1750-1755 …'.[47] That corresponds rather accurately with the fact that in 1756, Eckleff founded the first St. Andrew's Lodge in Stockholm, which marked the birth of the Swedish Rite. Coil makes the same mistake when he claims that Zinnendorf based his Rite on, i.a., the Swedenborgian Rite,[48] while clearly the Swedish Rite is intended.

Are these claims correct? At first, it may seem rather obvious to suspect the Swedish Rite of Swedenborgian influences. However, on second thought it is not so obvious at all. The idea seems to be based mainly on the association of both with Sweden. But we have seen that Swedenborg himself was no Freemason, nor was he influenced by Freemasonry, as far as we know. Also, during his lifetime, his ideas were far from applauded in Sweden, and most of his works were published abroad, especially in London and Amsterdam.

In order to find out if, and to what degree, the Swedish Rite can be regarded Swedenborgian, we first need to take a brief look at the history of its development. In addition to the St. John's Lodges (working the degrees 1 to 3), Karl Friedrich Eckleff (1723-1784) founded in 1756 the first St. Andrew's Lodge for degrees 4 and 5, and in 1759 the first Chapter for degrees 6 to 9. That completed the creation of his version of the — explicitly Christian — Swedish Rite.[49] Eckleff

47. Beswick 1870, 70-1.
48. Coil 1961, 565 sub-Zinnendorf Rite.
49. Eckleff 'gründete 1756 die erste schwedische St.-Andreas-Loge und drei Jahre später ein Ordenskapitel mit den höheren Graden nach der fortan 'Schwedisches System' benanten und von ihm begründeten Lehrart' (Lennhoff & Posner 1975, 396-97). 'Am 30. November 1756 stiftete er mit sechs anderen schottischen Meistern die erste St.-Andreas-Loge 'L'Inno-cente', am 25. Dezember 1759 als Ordensmeister ein Ordenskapitel, das 'Chapitre Illuminé de Stockholm'. Damit war die höchste Abteilung des schwedischen Freimaurersystems organisiert' (idem. 397). Cf. also: Rudbeck 1931, 48 ff. When Eckleff founded his St. Andrew's Lodge L'Innocente on 30 November 1756, the seven founders only registered themselves as St. Andrew's Masters. Receptions in the Lodge were not started until 9 June 1758 (Rudbeck 1931, 53). Also, 'on Christmas Day 1759 only the foundation of the Chapter took place. Actual work started in 1760' (H. Berg, Grand Officer of the Swedish Grand Lodge, personal communication, letter of 8 August 1997).

claimed to have received the documents on which he based his system (including the necessary rituals, as well as a Charter which authorized him to do so) from abroad. The general reading in non-Swedish literature is that these documents were in French and came from Geneva. Modern Swedish sources indicate, however, that Eckleff received in fact two consignments. The first, which he received in 1756, contained seven degrees — viz. the Craft, the St. Andrew's, and two chapter degrees — in German, and came probably from Strasbourg.[50] Late 1758 or early 1759, Eckleff received additional material in French, probably from Geneva, including two more degrees. Before ever having worked the two chapter degrees, which he received in 1756, he now inserted one of the new degrees between the two old ones, and added the other new one to the system, which now had 9 degrees. Of these, only the 9th (the Xth of today) was rather incomplete.[51]

At least the Strasbourg rituals are most likely based on the Parisian material. It was in Paris that Von Hund found the material on which he was to model the System of the Strict Observance from 1751 onwards in Germany. It was in Paris itself that the Conseil des Em-

50. On a possible Strasbourg source, see Feddersen 1991, 97. Feddersen also notes that 'Am 13. Januar 1752 gründeten neun Freimaurer die ... Johannisloge "St. Jean Auxiliaire" in Stockholm' (ibid. 96). The first Master of this lodge was Count Knut Carlsson Posse, who had been made a Mason in 1746 in France and received several 'high' degrees in Strasbourg. 'Posse brachte ... Unterlagen für sieben Grade nach Stockholm' (ibid. 97). 'Der 6. Grad war "St. Johannis förtrolige bröder" (St. Johannis' Vertraute Brüder), der 7. Grad die "Utvalde bröder" (Auserwählte Brüder)' (ibid. 99).

51. H. Berg, personal communication, letter of 8 August 1997. Also: '[Eckleff] erhielt die Unterlagen für die Ausarbeitung der Rituale aus Straßburg und Genf' (Anon. 1996a, 2) and 'Neben den drei Graden der Johannismaurerei bestanden zunächst noch zwei Andreasgrade und zwei höhere Grade, also 7 Grade insgesamt. Dieses Gradsystem entsprach wohl weitgehend dem der französischen Clermontschen Hochgrade. Das Bemühen, die Templerei in die Lehrart einzuflechten, wurde Anlaß zur Einschiebung eines Templergrades zwischen den 6. und 7. Grad und die Anfügung eines 9. Grades' (Frick 1975, 293). H. Berg informs me that 'the Eckleff documents are residing in the archives of the Swedish Order of Freemasons – Grand Lodge of Sweden (in Stockholm)' (ibid.).

pereurs d'Orient et d'Occident developed its working from 1758 onwards. All these systems show remarkable similarities, which may
have been the result of a common ancestor: the Lodge Saint-Jean de
Jérusalem, founded in Paris in 1745.[52] To this must be added the Templar element, which is also characteristic of all of these ritual systems.
The first place where this element is found is the ritual of the 'Ordre
Sublime des Chevaliers Elus' from 1750.[53] This Order worked in Paris
and Quimper (Bretagne), and supposedly is at least a few years older than the date of these documents. It is now supposed that this ritual was the source of all the other systems in which the Templar element is found. Von Hund introduced Templar degrees in Germany
after 1751 from whence they were adopted by several other
systems.[54] It seems that the material Eckleff received in late 1758 or
early 1759 from Geneva, is of the same family. Be this as it may, what
is sure is that Eckleff created the first version of the complete Swedish Rite in 1759. This system was adapted in 1768-1770 by Johann
Wilhelm Ellenberger, named (Kellner) von Zinnendorf (1731-1782), to
form the rite practised since then by the Große Landesloge von
Deutschland.[55] The Swedish Rite itself, and all of its rituals, was reformed by its Grandmaster Duke Charles (1748-1818, brother of King
Gustavus III, and from 1809 on King Charles XIII) in two stages: one
in 1778-1780 and one in 1798-1801.[56]

The sources are not quite unanimous on the precise dates of these
reforms:

52. Naudon 1978, 62-66, esp. 64.
53. Kervalla & Lestienne 1997.
54. Bernheim 1998, 71 ff. Frick, following Schiffmann, traces the Templar element back to c. 1744 (Frick 1975, 298, 300).
55. Cf. Rudbeck 1931, 79 ff.
56. 'In 1777, becoming dissatisfied with the Rite, [Duke Charles] ordered all
rituals returned and from 1778 to 1780 he personally rewrote and revised
them. They can be seen today in his own handwriting' (Denslow 1957,
I.199 sub Charles XIII). In 1780 a convention, headed by Duke Charles,
approved that first revision of the rituals (Thulstrup 1898, 73). It was during this revision that the 4th degree was restyled to represent two degrees: IV/V, so that from now on the higher degrees shifted upwards one
position, giving the current system of ten degrees (Frick 1975, 293). A second revision, executed by Duke Charles himself in the period 1798-1801,
gave the whole system its current form, with the exception of the Xth.

Herzog Carl und seine Mitarbeiter ... bearbeiteten vor allen vor [i.e. von]
1798 bis 1802 die Eckleff'schen Rituale gründlich, wobei diese so perfekt ges-
taltet wurden, dass sie noch heute, mit ganz wenigen Aenderungen, gleich
zelebriert werden. Hier soll noch erwähnt werden, dass eine erste grosse Rit-
ualrevision schon im Jahre 1780 unternommen wurde, die im ganzen gese-
hen gleich bedeutungsvoll war (Borg 1993, 85);

By two major ritual revisions in 1780 and 1800 he [i.e. Duke Charles] created
a logical masonic system with ten degrees' (Anon. 1996b, 4).

Gould mentions only the second reform, which he dates in the period
1796-1800 (1903, 383).

However, in a personal letter of 8 August 1997, H. Berg wrote to me:

In March 1780 the Convention in Stockholm. Laws and rituals of all the degrees revised. Of course Duke Carl and his fellow-workers had been busy
with this work for some time, but there are no records of the progress of the
preparatory work as far as I know. In 1798-1800 a keen revision work going
on regarding all degrees. The new edition of the rituals was edited in 1800.
In 1801 there was a completion in the IV-V degree.

   In the years between 1780 and 1798, however, Duke Carl was from time
to time busy with the rituals of the Chapter degrees. He had full control of
the Chapters. So when he had decided of a ritual change in one of the Chapter degrees he could carry it through in Stockholm. And then he could order
the other Chapters to make the same change. There were Chapters in Kris-
tianstad from 1777, in Helsinki from 1778 and in Göteborg from 1788. Thus
there are a number of ritual changes in the Chapter degrees in the years
between the two major revisions.

This revision changed the Swedish Rite from a collection of degrees
into a fully integrated system. In 1818/19 the relations between the
Swedish Grand Lodge and the Große Landesloge von Deutschland,
which had been disturbed since the 1780's, were re-established. One
of the conditions, posed by the Swedish Grand Lodge was that the
Rite and Rituals of the Große Landesloge von Deutschland would be
brought into line with those of Sweden. This task was executed by
Christian Carl Friedrich Wilhelm, Freiherr von Nettelbladt, between

1826 and 1837.[57] The next revision of these rituals, was made between 1880 and 1890. The initiative for this revision came from the Grandmaster, Emperor Frederick III, who wanted a much more sober ritual. For this revision, the Eckleff files were consulted again.[58] Since then, the rituals used by the Große Landesloge von Deutschland have been revised several times. Especially since 1945, they have in fact been under constant revision.[59] The Swedish version, however, has never been reformed after 1800, with the exception of the Xth degree, which was revised on some occasions, even in the 20th century.[60]

All in all, then, we have several versions of the Swedish Rite: the Eckleff version, the Zinnendorf version, the version of Duke Charles, the Nettelbladt version, the Emperor Frederick version and the later German versions.

In all of these versions, the first group of degrees are the usual 'Craft', 'blue' or 'symbolic' degrees of Entered Apprentice, Fellow Craft and Master Mason, in the Swedish system collectively referred to as the degrees of the St. John's Lodge. Next follow, also in all these systems, the degrees of St. Andrew's Apprentice, Fellow Craft and Master,[61] together forming the St. Andrew's Lodge. The ritual of St. Andrew's Apprentice, however, always blends smoothly into that of St. Andrew's Fellow Craft. These two degrees are always granted at the same occasion in one ritual session, but counted as two degrees. In the Eckleff and Zinnendorf versions, they were even only one degree. When it was split into two, all the higher degrees were shifted

57. Cf. the anonymous biography of Nettelbladt in Von Nettelbladt 1879, IX-XII and Jaskulewicz 1976, 43 and 51. On Nettelbladt in general, see Feddersen 1994, 241-330; on his work on the rituals esp. 251-58 and 269-71.
58. Jaskulewicz, 1976 and K.C.F. Feddersen, personal communication, letter of 4 August 1997.
59. Dr. D. Schulte (†), Grand Officer of the Große Landesloge von Deutschland, personal communication, letter of 2 August 1997.
60. H. Berg, personal communication, letters of 23 and 25 July 1997. On the influence of the Swedish System on the creation of the R.E.R., see Noël 1998.
61. The names of all these degrees changed in the course of time, not only with the several versions of the Rite, but also within one and the same version. I have purposely simplified this point in my presentation.

up one position. As a result, referring to the higher degrees of the
Swedish System by their numbers is always ambiguous. In order to
avoid that ambiguity, I shall indicate the degrees of the (original)
nine-degree systems with Arabic numbers, and those of the (current)
ten-degree systems with Roman numbers (as is usual today). Finally,
there are the Chapter degrees. Around 1805-1806 Schröder published
German translations of the rituals of the Eckleff system of c. 1780,
with the exception of the 8th (i.e., the current IXth). French manuscript rituals of 1777 of the Chapter degrees of the Eckleff system also
exist, likewise omitting the 8th (IXth) degree.[62] From this material it
is clear that the first two chapter degrees were ready at that time, viz.,
Knight of the East and of Jerusalem (the current Knight of the East,
VIIth degree) and Under-Officer and Illuminated Knight of Sweden,
Knight Templar of Sweden (the current Knight of the West, VIIIth degree). The current IXth degree (Trusted Brother of St. John) seems to
have been ready in 1759 as well.[63] The ritual of the Xth degree (Elect
Brother, Confidant of St. Andrew) was not yet complete at that time.
I did not find any trace of the IXth and Xth degrees with Zinnendorf.[64] The Xth degree was completed by Duke Charles and revised
on some occasions afterwards. Both the IXth and the Xth were possibly included in the German version by Nettelbladt. At least they
form part of the system worked today in de Große Landesloge von
Deutschland.

62. Kloss Mss. VIII.C.4/5 = GON 191.C.12/13.
63. It is to be found in *Emottagnings-Capittel för Capitlets officianter, jemvael kal-
    lade Förtrogne Bröder af St Johannis Logen*, a manuscript of 1759 in Eckleff's
    readable hand-writing (H. Berg, personal communication, letter of 30 July
    1997).
64. Coil, too, mentions only two Capitular degrees in the Zinnendorf Rite.
    The problem here is, however, that the names that Coil mentions for these
    degrees are 'Favourite of St. John [and] … Elect Brother', which names
    seem to refer to the IXth and Xth degree respectively rather than to the
    VIIth and VIIIth (Coil 1961, 565 sub. Zinnendorf Rite). An article in *Der
    Signatstern* V (1809) gives as the names of the VIIth and VIIIth degrees
    (here indicated as 6th and 7th) Swedish Rite (Duke Charles version): 'Den
    Ritter in Osten oder das Noviciat (nach Zinnendorf: den Vertrauten Jo-
    hannis – der den Ritter in Osten ganz, und einen Theil des Ritters in
    Westen enthält.)' and 'Den Ritter in Westen, wirklicher Tempelherr-Unterrof
                                                                          →

Now, if any version of the Swedish Rite may legitimately be referred to as Swedenborgian, who could have been responsible for it? Based on the texts of Eckleff's masonic speeches, Rudbeck concludes that 'his worldview is healthy and serious, and he was clearly not interested in mysticism and occultism'.[65] Von Zinnendorf originally belonged to the Strict Observance, but broke with it, and became one of its strongest opponents, once he had discovered the Swedish Rite.[66] And a recent pamphlet of the Große Landesloge von Deutschland[67] suggests that Nettelbladt probably no longer believed in the descent of the Order from the Templars. Indeed, Nettelbladt seems to have been a historian, rather than a mystic.[68] And the Emperor Frederick III would, in his striving after more sober rituals, have removed rather than added Swedenborgian elements. Summarising: it does not seem likely that any of these men were much inclined to the mys-

→ ficiant; (nach Zinnendorf, … den Auserwählten – der das übrige vom Ritter in Westen nebst Zinnendorfs Zusätzen, und späterhin den Adoptatus coronatus enthält.)'. For the Swedish system two more degrees are then added: 'Den Ritter in Süden (Commendeur – Magister templi – Auserwählter – Oberofficiant, Großofficiant.)' and 'Den Vicarius Salomonis (Magister templi)' (207). Of the first of these two, it is stated that 'hier bezieht sich alles auf ein Neues Jerusalem, und zwar nach dem 21sten Kapitel der Apocalypse' (218). That applies indeed to the current IXth degree. So, despite their names, which might suggest that these two belong rather to those honorary ranks that are additional to the degrees proper, they are in fact the IXth and Xth degrees of the current system. All in all, this seems to suggest that on the occasion of the harmonization of the German and Swedish systems, not only the German one was brought in line with the Swedish one, but also vice versa, by applying the names of the two last degrees of the German system (VII and VIII) to those of the Swedish one (IX and X).

65. 'Seine Lebensanschauung ist gesund und ernst, und für Mystizismus und Okkultismus fehlte es ihm offenbar an Interesse' (Rudbeck 1931, 78).

66. Feddersen confirms 'dass sich keine Anhalte für Einflüsse Svedenborg [in Von Zinnendorf's system] nachweisen lassen, auch kaum Nachweise des Tempelherrenordens, nur allgemeine christliche Ritterideale' (personal communication, letter of 4 August 1997).

67. Deecke et al., 5-6.

68. Also: 'Bei allen seinen Forschungen und Bemühungen um die verschiedenen Lehrarten der Freimaurerei bewahrte er seine kritische Vorsicht, die ihn davor bewahrte, mystische Irrwege zu gehen' (Feddersen 1994, 268).

ticism of Swedenborg. Finally, it would be rather surprising if Swedenborgian elements had been introduced into the system after 1890.
Duke Charles, though, had not only been Grand Master of the Strict
Observance in Germany for several years, he may also have liked the
works of Swedenborg.[69] Interested as he was in all forms of esotericism,
it would be surprising if he had overlooked Swedenborg's works.
Having the connections he had,[70] it would not have been too difficult
for him to obtain copies.[71] Also, the negative attitude, which Swedenborg had encountered in Sweden during his lifetime, had been more
or less forgotten.[72] So, if any version of the Swedish Rite is influenced
by the ideas of Swedenborg, it must be Charles'. In all the rituals of
the other versions of the Rite that I have seen, I found indeed only
one sentence which might be interpreted as Swedenborgian, but not
necessarily.

Unfortunately, from a scholarly point of view, the Swedish Grand-
lodge is extremely restrictive in allowing access to the texts of its rituals, and since the Duke Charles version is essentially the one still in
use, I could not get a copy of their text.[73]

This is all the more regrettable, since the IXth degree, 'Trusted
Brother of St. John', has a strong relation to the last book of the

69. 'Er war ein Mann, der zu mystischer Schwärmerei neigte und manches in
    seine Ritualreformen hineinbrachte, was ihn bewegte und von
    hintergründiger Weisheit und Erleuchtung schien. Dazu gehörte mit Si-
    cherheit auch Svedenborg.' (K.C.F. Feddersen, personal communication,
    letter of 4 August 1997).
70. One of his personal trustees was Silverhielm, nephew and follower of
    Swedenborg (Meillassoux 1992, 66, n. 194).
71. Swedenborg used to send copies of his work to prominent and influential
    persons and institutes. I have not been able to trace an inventory of the
    library of the King, so I cannot be sure if it contained such copies, but I
    would be surprised if it did not.
72. Meillassoux 1992, 82.
73. Also with regard to the Nettelbladt version and the current German ver-
    sion, I could consult no more than the rituals of the first three degrees,
    which, as far as I can see, show no trace of any Swedenborgian influence.
    As stated before, German translations of the Eckleff rituals of c. 1780 were
    published in Schröder's *Ritualsammlung* (Vol. 13b, GON 213.B.37, St.
    John's Lodge; Vol. 13c, GON 213.B.38, St. Andrew's Lodge; and Vol.
    11a/11b/11c, GON 213.B.32/33/34, Chapter degrees) in 1805/6. The
    →

Bible.[74] In itself, that does not necessarily betray any Swedenborgian influence. All parallels to the building of the Temple of King Solomon were used as the basis for rituals of masonic degrees, especially during the second half of the 18th century. These include the building of the Ark of Noah, of the Second Temple of Zerubbabel and of the 'Third Temple', viz., the resurrection of Christ. It would thus have been rather remarkable if the New Jerusalem had been left out. One of the rituals using this theme, the Chevalier d'Orient et d'Occident, is now the 17th degree of the Ancient and Accepted Scottish Rite, the well-known system of 33 degrees. But if any of the degrees of the Swedish Rite would lend itself to a Swedenborgian revision, it would have been this IXth. So, if Duke Charles really had any Swedenborgian inclination, I would have expected the ritual he designed for this degree to show this. I have not been able to verify that, however.

Summary

The preceding may be summarized as follows.

1. At present, Beswick's Swedenborgian Rite is the only rite which, with certainty, can be confirmed as Swedenborgian.

2. With only two exceptions, all the other Rites discussed — which have in the past been referred to as Swedenborgian — have turned out to show no significant Swedenborgian influence whatsoever.

→ same collection also contains the Zinnendorf rituals of c. 1770 (Vol.?/10a, GON 213.B.21/30, St. John's Lodge; Vol. 10b, GON 213.B.31, St. Andrew's Lodge,* whereas Vol. 11c, GON 213.B.34, contains pp. 27-36 a catechism of a '7th and last' degree of c. 1774). The *G.U.V. Freimaurer-Logenbuch*, Leipzig 1836 (GON 203.G.11) contains the rituals for the St. John's Lodge; these are probably the Nettelbladt rituals, just as those in *Die enthüllten Geheimnisse der Freimaurerei*, Theil II, Altona 1877 (GON 68.C.8). The library of the Grand East of the Netherlands (GON) has also a copy of the official rituals for the first three degrees of the GLLvD of 1958 (84.E.16-21). *The Zinnendorf rituals for the St. Andrew's Lodge were also published in *Der Signatstern* III (1804) 1-139 and in [Karl Friedr. Ebers], *Sarsena* etc., [Bamberg] 1816, 166-234.

74. O. Hieber [c. 1959].

3. The two exceptions are Chastanier's Illuminés théosophes — if this Rite indeed existed — and Duke Charles' version of the Swedish Rite. These two Rites may turn out to be forms of Swedenborgian Freemasonry. But this cannot be decided before rituals of these systems can be investigated.

4. If Chastanier's Illuminés théosophes did exist, and if rituals of this system can be found and turn out to be masonic, then there can be little doubt that this was a form of Swedenborgian Freemasonry.

5. Should it turn out that Duke Charles' version of the Swedish Rite is Swedenborgian, then there would still be one Swedenborgian Rite practised today. Through the Nettelbladt reform, Swedenborgian elements present in the Swedish rituals might even have been incorporated into those of the system of the Große Landesloge von Deutschland, and, surprisingly, Beswick would have been right after all in his assumption that, in 1870, it was proper to refer to the Swedish Rite as the Swedenborgian Rite. However, several practitioners of the Swedish Rite, both in Sweden and in Germany, have assured me that they are convinced that the rituals currently in use do not contain any Swedenborgianism at all, and they may well be right.

Appendix I
Swedenborgian Elements from the different Rites

The following pages contain some examples of texts, taken from Beswick's rituals of the Swedenborgian Rite (in the right column), to which are added (in the left column):

1. The equivalent texts from the Emulation Ritual (the standard English ritual).[75]

75. The reasons why I think it makes sense to compare Beswick's text with the Emulation ritual are that (1) Beswick himself had been initiated in England with this or a comparable ritual before leaving for America; (2) in America, the lodges used both the rituals of the Antients and of the Moderns, though more often those of the Antients; and in 1813, before the Union, the Lodge of Promulgation had turned the ritual of the Moderns into one, compatible with those of the Antients; the Emulation ritual, therefore, is to some extent comparable to the rituals of the Antients, practised in America.
I have compared Morgan 1827 with both Beswick's and the Emulation ritual, and found it to be close in all respects to the Emulation Ritual and different from Beswick's. It would have been ideal if I could have used an American ritual of c. 1870, but unfortunately I had no such ritual at my disposal. I compared the Beswick texts also with Cross 1857, but that of course is not a ritual.
It should be noted that the ritual of the United Grand Lodge of England may itself not be free of Swedenborgian influences. It was composed around 1816 in London, where at that time there was an important Swedenborgian 'New Church' with a respectable history. Elements in the Emulation ritual, such as the calling of the Brethren 'from labour to refreshment, and from refreshment to labour, that profit and pleasure may be the result'*, and the long charge on charity, would also qualify. The reason that such elements — despite the fact that they would be recognized as Swedenborgian by Swedenborgians — do not recur in Beswick's rituals, is of course because he assumed that the Candidate had already passed through the rituals of the first three degrees.

*The oldest form of this element is found in *Three Distinct Knocks* (1760): 'it is our Master's Will and Pleasure, that this Lodge is called from Work to Refreshment, during Pleasure' (37).

2. Relevant quotes from the Bible (in bold face), in order to show the sources for Beswick's texts.

3. My comments in italics.

The number of examples could be multiplied *ad infinitum*, since the Beswick rituals are of this nature throughout.

Added to these are a few quotes from other rituals, presented in the same layout. However, these are *all* of the possible Swedenborgian texts which could be found in these rituals.

Emulation Ritual and Biblical quotes

The Bible is opened in all three degrees; in Continental Freemasonry it is opened always on St. John 1:1; but in Anglo-Saxon Freemasonry this is often not specified. *Three Distinct Knocks* (1760) is the first English text to mention explicit Bible-openings for each of the three degrees: II Peter, Judges 12 and I Kings 7, respectively, while *Jachin and Boaz* (1762) only mentions in the description of the first degree that 'the Bible [is] opened at the Gospel of St. John' (8). K.P. Went, *The Freemason's Own Ritual* (London, n.d.) gives II Chron. 6 for all three degrees and the illustrations in J.L. Cross, *The Masonic Text-Book* (New York 1857) suggest Psalm 133, Amos 7 and Ecclesiastes 12, respectively.

[The unusual use of Genesis may well refer to Swedenborg's 'Celestial Arcana'.]

Beswick's Swedenborgian Rite

The Bible is opened in all three degrees; in the 5th on Genesis 2 and in the 6th on Genesis 4, so I assume in the 4th degree it is opened on Genesis 1.

1st degree;
Entered Apprentice
Opening of the Lodge:

W.M. Bro. Junior Warden, your place in the Lodge?
J.W. In the South.
W.M. Why are you placed there?
J.W. To mark the sun at its meridian, to call the Brethren from

4th degree;
Enlightened Phremason
section 3: 'Officers Stations and Duties':

W.M. Bro. J.W., the pillar of your station, its name and symbolic meaning?
J.W. The pillar of Beauty. It is a symbol of the power which adorns and beautifies, also of

labour to refreshment, and from refreshment to labour, that profit and pleasure may be the result.

[*The Swedenborgian version is not only much longer — which is normal for late 19th century ritual texts — but also contains such words/expressions as: 'the Temple', 'the [three] creative power[s] in the sacred triad of all nations', 'the great circle of the Heavens', 'Providence'*(*) *and references to the astrological signs (Eagle, Man and Lion)*(**)*, the Stars, the Cherubim, and the seasons, all of which are not found in standard Masonic rituals, but which are characteristic of Swedenborgianism. Also the stressing of 'one Temple, Ritual, Altar and God' clearly refers to the anti-trinitarian doctrines of Swedenborg.*

(*) The term 'Providence' is used once in J.L. Cross, 'The Masonic Text-Book', New-York 1857: 'the beautiful border which surrounds [the Mosaic pavement is emblematical of] those manifold blessings and comforts which surround us, and which we hope to enjoy by a faithful reliance on Divine Providence ...' (43)

(**) Of course these refer also to the 'animals' of Revelation and Ezekiel.]

the third creative power in the sacred triad of all nations.

W.M. Your station in the Temple?

J.W. In the South. As the Sun is seen in the South at midday, so stands the J.W. in the South at High Meridian of the Masonic day.

W.M. The position of your station in the great circle of the Heavens?

J.W. In the sign of the Eagle, as seen from the South; it is a symbol that the event we now commemorate was under the far-seeing eye of Providence, and the shadow of its wings on account of its reference to this memorable event; the Cherubim of all nations, representing Providence, had an Eagle's head, and was covered with Eagle's wings.

W.M. Your duty in this station?

J.W. To give style, finish and beauty to the work, to call the Stars from yearly labour to partake of the ripened fruits of Autumn, superintend their midday operations during refreshment, that order may prevail during the Masonic day and year, and temperance rule supreme in the Meridian of pleasure.

W.M. Your Jewel? J.W. The Plumb.

W.M. Your duty in the South with this Jewel?

J.W. To plumb the highest attainment and conduct of the Stars, by the standard of this Jewel, which is a symbol of uprightness; it is a common standard for the whole world, because there is but one Temple, Ritual, Altar and God. (pp. 28-29)

From Section 6: Candidate Admitted:

[There is nothing equivalent to this in standard Masonic ritual practice, but it is very Swedenborgian. It may be formulated contra a text in J.L. Cross, 'The Masonic Text-Book', New-York 1857: '… from [those who are called to officiate as officers of the Lodge], our brethren who are less informed will expect an example worthy of imitation.' (23)]

W.M. The Supreme Architect of the Universe is the only true model of a Master Builder and His work, the Great Temple of Nature, is the only perfect model work worthy of our imitation. (34)

From idem.:

W.M. … In this, and all other Symbolic Temples, we put our highest trust in God, like a son of light, who has received the moral effect of this first impression, you will kneel at God's Altar and give evidence of your highest trust in Him by uniting with us in asking His aid and counsel. (Cand. led to the Altar and kneels on the left knee. …)

W.M. How does [the Candidate] hope to obtain [the] privileges [of Freemasonry]?

I.G. By the help of God, being free and of good report. …

  (The Senior Deacon places the kneeling stool in the North-East corner. … The Junior Deacon then takes the Candidate's right hand with his left and leads him to the kneeling stool). …

W.M. … I will thank you to kneel, while the blessing of Heaven is invoked on our proceedings.

  (… The Worshipful Master or Chaplain … offers the following prayer).

  Vouchsafe Thine aid, Al-

W.M. Almighty God, Creator of the visible and invisible universe. We adore Thee! We praise Thee! and we seek the aid and counsel of Thy Spirit and the Light of Thy countenance! … Let us pray!

mighty Father and Supreme Governor of the Universe, to our present convention, and grant that this Candidate for Freemasonry may so dedicate and devote his life to Thy service as to become a true and faithful Brother among us. Endue him with a competency of Thy Divine Wisdom, that, assisted by the secrets of our Masonic art, he may the better be enabled to unfold the beauties of true Godliness, to the honour and glory of Thy Holy Name. ...

W.M. In all cases of difficulty and danger, in whom do you put your trust?

Can. In God.

W.M. Right glad am I to find your faith so well founded: relying on such sure support you may safely rise and follow your leader with a firm but humble confidence, for where the name of God is invoked we trust no danger can ensue.

[Compare Revelation 22:1: '**And he shewed me a pure river of water of life, clear as crystal, proceeding out of the throne of God and of the Lamb.'**]

[*Here again, besides the fact that the Swedenborgian text is much longer, what is striking are such expressions as:*

W.M. There is one Who hath erected the great Temple of Nature, and lit up the Heavenly lamps therein; Whose sacred river of life issues from underneath His Altar and Throne, and flows there along the star-covered path; Who hath planted His Eden for you, and sitteth in judgment over its harvest fields; Who looketh down upon His Altar and answereth those who worship Him on bended knees with humility; He is the Most High and Holy One; your Sovereign. We are Thy Temple, O Grand Master! and on the Mountain of Thy Truth let our Enlightened, Sublime and Perfect edifice display its glory; look down with a flood of light and let Thine All Seeing Eye behold us, leading this son of light into Thy Temple, and presenting him at the Altar of Enlightment [sic!] for Thy acceptance. May his mind, as steps, mount Thy Holy hill, and his vision thence be as wide as Thy Truth, and as serene as the Heavens! May he obey Thy laws as faithfully as the Sun which sails along the floods of the blue firmament and may the unseen Jewels of his soul, like yonder Jewels of the sky, tell of Thy Mighty Handiwork, of Thy unknown *'son of light', 'Almighty God, Creator of the visible and invisible universe', 'the great Temple of Nature', 'the Heavenly lamps', 'Whose sacred river of life issues from underneath His Altar and Throne, and flows there along the star-covered path', 'those who worship Him on bended knees with humility', 'We are Thy Temple', 'let our Enlightened, Sublime and Perfect edifice display its glory', 'His mind / vision / deeds', 'the unseen Jewels of his soul', and a call for a 'vision ... as wide as Thy Truth'. None of these occur in standard masonic practice, whereas all are characteristic of Swedenborgianism. Also, in most Masonic rituals[*], no adoration of God is found, something which was essential to Swedenborg.*

(*) An exception is found in J.L. Cross, 'The Masonic Text-Book', New-York 1857: 'At opening the Lodge, ... we are taught to worship and adore the supreme JEHOVAH ...' (24).]

W.M. It is customary, at the erection of all stately and superb edifices, to lay the first foundation stone at the North East corner of the building. You, being newly admitted into Masonry, are placed at the North-East part of the Lodge, figuratively to represent that stone, and from the foundation, laid this evening, may you raise a superstructure perfect in its parts and honourable to the builder.

deeds, and of Thy unmeasured benevolence. ... (36)

Section 9: Enter the Sacred Land:

W.M. ... the model work of the Great Master Builder was founded in Strength and eternal durability. ... The Creator is the only true Model of a Master Builder, and His Work, the only perfect model worthy of our imitation. Our Ritual embodies it by representing the labours during the six great days of creation. This labour, on the first great day, was the creation of light, and His last

[*Some relevant Biblical texts:*

Ezekiel 47:1-6, 8-9a:
Afterward he brought me again unto the door of the house; and behold, waters issued out from under the threshold of the house eastward: for the forefront of the house stood toward the east, and the waters came down from under from the right side of the house, at the south side of the altar.

Then brought he me out of the way of the gate northward, and led me about the way without unto the utter gate by the way that looketh eastward; and, behold, there ran out waters on the right side.

And when the man that had the line in his hand went forth eastward, he measured a thousand cubits, and he brought me through the waters; the waters were to the ancles.

Again he measured a thousand, and brought me through the waters; the waters were to the knees. Again he measured a thousand and brought me through; the waters were to the loins.

Afterward he measured a thousand; and it was a river that I could not pass over: for the waters were risen, waters to swim in, a river that could not be passed over.

And he said unto me, Son of man, hast thou seen this? Then he brought me, and caused me to return to the brink of the river. ...

labour, the crowning work of Man's creation. ... You will now rise and complete the seventh labour, which is designed to remind you of the primitive introduction of man into that model land prepared by the Great Architect. ...

... You are now where the Supreme Master has placed a sacred dwelling place or enclosure; its length from West to East is three times its width from North to South; a river of life goes forth from the West towards the South, and along its three sides, North, South and East; from thence it parts into four heads which spread over the Northeastern territory, now before you, all over the country lying in the middle of the river's path; and on either side of the Southwestern course is the tree of life, called KIKI or KIIM (KI-YIM), whose leaves are for the healing of nations; you have permission to enter the sacred territory and measure the fords of the four streams running into the sacred river; you will do well to notice the depth and difficulty of crossing as the fords increase.

[the four fords are measured and reported as:] 'Up to the ankles/ knees/ loins/ neck.'

Then said he unto me, These waters issue out toward the east country, and go down into the desert, and go into the sea: which being brought forth into the sea, the waters shall be healed.

And it shall come to pass, that everything that liveth, which moveth, whithersoever the rivers shall come, shall live: ...

[*This text points to the description of the New Jerusalem in Revelation 21 & 22, where is also found the image of the high mountain.*]

Ephesians 2:20-22:

And [ye] are built upon the foundation of the apostles and prophets, Jesus Christ himself being the chief corner stone;

In whom all the building fitly framed together groweth unto an holy temple in the Lord:

In whom ye also are builded together for an habitation of God through the Spirit.]

[*The Ezekiel part of the Beswick ritual has no equivalent whatsoever in standard Masonic practices, but it has a definite Swedenborgian flavour. Also expressions such as 'the seventh labour', 'that model land', 'a sacred dwelling place', 'the tree of life ... whose leaves are for the healing of nations', and 'the necessity of giving the moral truths of your Temple' are not standard Masonic, but very Swedenborgian.*]

S.D. It is a stream that cannot be passed with safety and much too deep for fording.

W.M. These four streams spring up in the N.E. corner of the Sacred Land, descend Southwards across it, and fall into the main river, whose length is equal to the East, South and West sides of the territory, and at these fords the streams are successively higher by the human standard of measurement: ankles, knees, loins, neck. Brother Senior Deacon, conduct your charge to the source of the greater river and place him in the highest source of any river in the world. (Candidate placed in N.E. corner.) You are now in the N.E. corner of that sacred territory, where our progenitors were first placed and, for a similar reason, because it represents the highest source of human action. It was the highest source known to them, from which water can flow to fertilize the earth, and the highest solid foundation in the world known to them on which to build a Temple to the Living God. ... In this symbolic Temple you represent the chief corner stone upon which two sides of the building rest, whose upright position is determined by this first corner stone; as you are placed so are all the stones to be placed, in the sides and ground floor of the future Temple. You are hereby taught the necessity of giving the moral truths of your Temple, the highest and most lasting foundation, making sure they are laid upright and well cemented together. This is your first duty, and your next lesson in Phremasonry will teach you how to build a perfect Temple upon that sure foundation. ... (42-46)

From Section 11: Charge:

W.M. ... As an individual, let me recommend the practice of every domestic as well as public virtue: let Prudence direct you, Temperance chasten you, Fortitude support you, and Justice be the guide of all your actions. Be especially careful to maintain in their fullest splendour those truly Masonic ornaments which have already been amply illustrated, Benevolence and Charity. ...

From the very commendable attention you appear to have given to this charge, I am led to hope you will duly appreciate the value of Freemasonry, and indelibly imprint on your heart the sacred dictates of Truth, of Honour, and of Virtue.

W.M. ... The world without is only a vast and mighty symbol of the world within, and as God's laws of order rule supreme in the world without you, bringing good out of seeming evil, streaming mercies and blessings, with unmeasured profusion over the wide universe, with the seeming design of giving the greatest amount of happiness to the greatest number; so must the laws of virtue and of moral order reign supreme in the world within you; educing good out of seeming evil, that the hand of the Supreme Master may scatter His higher mercies and blessings with unmeasured profusion along your symbolic

[The above are the two sections in the corresponding charge from the Emulation ritual which come closest to the Beswick text. Clearly there is no trace in it of the relation between the worlds without and within, 'educing good out of seeming evil', or of the award which is awaiting us in the Grand Temple above. These elements are Swedenborgian.]

journey to that Grand Temple above, where virtue meets its like on points of true fellowship and the upright perfect Phremason receives his due reward. (55-56)

2nd degree; Fellow-Craft

[The phrase 'behold your brother' may well refer to St. John 1:29: **'The next day John seeth Jesus coming unto him, and saith, Behold the Lamb of God, which taketh away the sin of the world.'** and/or 19:26-27: **'When Jesus therefore saw his mother, and the disciple standing by, whom he loved, he saith unto his mother, Woman, behold thy son! Then saith he to the disciple, Behold thy mother!'**]

[In the Emulation ritual there is a charge at this place, but nowhere are the Brothers addressed as 'Sons of Light' or as 'Stars', terms which are indicating Swedenborgianism.]

[Genesis 2:8: **'And the Lord God planted a garden eastward in Eden: and there he put the man whom he had formed.'**

Genesis 13:10: **'... the plain of Jordan [was] ... as the garden of the Lord ...'**]

5th degree; Sublime Phremason
Section 8. Rite of ... Illumination:

W.M. ... Sons of Light, behold your brother! ... [follows a charge.] Stars of the East, behold your brother.

S.W. Stars of the West, behold your brother.

J.W. Stars of the South, behold your brother. (65)

Section 10. Lecture on the Symbols:
W.M. ... We have described the elementary principles of a symbolic Temple, ... which was in the garden of God, ... (74)

Isaiah 51:3: 'For the Lord shall comfort Zion ... he will make her wilderness like Eden, and her desert like the garden of the Lord ...'

Ezekiel 28:13: 'Thou hast been in Eden the garden of God ...' (also 31:8-9)]

[No equivalent statement in any standard ritual. The expression 'garden of God' is Swedenborgian.]

[Compare Isaiah 66:1: 'Thus saith the Lord, The heaven is my throne, and the earth is my footstool: where is the house that ye build unto me? and where is the place of my rest?' (also quoted in Acts 8:49)]

[No equivalent text in any standard masonic ritual. The expression 'make your earthly dwelling place a delightful Temple, in which you may worship and adore the Almighty' is Swedenborgian.]

3rd degree; Master Mason

... O Lord my God, is there no help for the widow's son? ... [Referring to Hiram Abif, the Master Builder.]

[1 Kings 7:13-14: 'And king Solomon sent and fetched Hiram out of Tyre. He was a widow's son ...']

Section 11. Charge:

W.M. ... As a Sublime Phremason, the lessons of this degree will teach you to live uprightly with God and man, and make your earthly dwelling place a delightful Temple, in which you may worship and adore the Almighty, as an All Wise, All Powerful and ever present Master, Whose Majesty is enthroned in the sunny firmament with the clear blue heavens for a throne, and the green earth for a foot-stool. (75)

6th degree; Perfect Phremason
Section 15. Hairam Raised

... O, Lord my God, is there no help for the only begotten? ... [Referring to Hairam Abi, the Master Builder.] (99)

[The indication 'the only begotten' clearly identifies the Master Builder as Christ, an interpretation which, in standard masonic rituals, is possible, but not necessary. It is logical, however, that a Swedenborgian Rite is explicitly Christian.]

Quotes from other rituals (1)
The Rite Ecossais philosophique

GON 122.B.110, (Maître-parfait &) Parfait Elu [Signé: 6-11-1812 Thory]

[Repentance and charity are themes which may be recognized easily as Swedenborgian. However, the theme of repentance is not uncommon in this degree, which dates from c. 1745. It is a common degree in many French Rites. This version in the REPh. is not very different from the usual ones.

Charity as such is even an extremely common subject in masonic rituals. It is assumed to have been so, even before 1700. However, it is from minutes rather than from ritual texts that we know this. It used to be contemplated on in addresses which had no prescribed text, and thus are not found in the rituals. The fixation of such texts in rituals appears rather late, in rituals such as the Emulation Ritual (c. 1825). Not only in England, but also in France the subject was commonplace. The ritual of the Rite Ecossais Rectifié (1782) included it even in the obligation of the first degree, as one of the first duties of a Freemason:

... La soif dont Joabert se sentit dévoré, après avoir immolé l'assassin, nous représente l'homme qui, après s'être laissé emporter par le transport d'un premier mouvement, réfléchit sur son action et voit qu'elle ne sauroit être entierement justifiée. Le repentir qu'il en eût ne peut pas être mieux figuré que par la soif ardente qu'il ressentit comme la premiere punition de sa [68] désobéissance. La Fontaine qu'il trouva et qui servit à le désalterer, doit être regardée comme le doux et flatteur espoir que le repentir fait naître dans nos coeurs. ... (67/68)

... Enfin, l'ardente Charité, que vous devez avoir pour vos Freres, vous est figurée par les coeurs enflammés qui ornent les cordons des Elus. La Charité est celle de toutes les vertus qui flatte le plus l'humanité et qui lui est la plus utile; c'est aussi celle qui plaît le plus à la divinité, puisqu'elle est la

'Moi … Je promis sur le Saint Evangile, en présence du Grand architecte de l'Univers, et m'engage sur ma parole d' honneur devant cette respectable assemblée, d'être fidele à la Sainte Réligion Chrétiene, a mon Souverain et aux Loix de l'Etât, d'être Bienfaisant envers tous les hommes lorsque je pourrai leur être utile. …']

[Here I have put those texts in italics which are relatively unusual in masonic rituals. They may be Swedenborgian. However, ALL lodges working the first three degrees are always called St. John's lodges, because the two St. Johns are traditionally the patron Saints of the Order.]

conservatrice de ses ouvrages les plus parfaits. (70)

Kloss XXV.52, GON 240.E.41, Grand Ecossais

D.   Où avés-vous été reçu Ecossais?
R.   Dans la Loge S^t. Jean.
D.   Où saint Jean a-t-il tenu Loge?
R.   Sur les bords du Jourdain où il donna le baptême au fils de Jehova.
D.   Pourquoi dites-vous la Loge de S^t. Jean?
R.   *Parceque S^t. Jean fut le premier qui tira les parallèles de l'avenue du Messie et le premier ouvrier appelé au Seigneur*
D.   Comment se peut-il qu'un homme seul ait tenu Loge?
R.   *La Trinité y présidait.* (6/7)

Kloss XXVI.3, GON 193.C.68, Académie des Vrais Maçons

[The expression 'Grand homme' is definitely very Swedenborgian. However, the 'Grand homme' referred to in this text is just Hiram Abiff, according to the masonic tradition the architect of the

… il ne me reste plus qu'à vous hâter à marcher sur les traces d'un Grand homme, dont la présence nous fut si chère et si utile et dont le souvenir nous sera à jamais précieux. (15)

Temple of Solomon. In the 3rd degree it is told how he was murdered. Several 'high' degrees elaborate on one theme or another from the Hiramic Legend, presented in the 3rd degree. The sentence concerned seems in no respect at all unusual to me (as opposed to most of this very alchemical ritual, which is highly unusual indeed).]

Quotes from other rituals (2)
The Swedish Rite (Eckleff system)

[for Christ as the New Adam, see Romans 5:14 and 1 Corinthians 15.]

*[The New Adam is mentioned in no standard masonic ritual, but it is a very Swedenborgian subject. It could, however, be derived from other sources, including the Bible, as well. Today, the formulation in Germany is: 'So legt nun von Euch ab den alten Menschen und ziehet den neuen Menschen an, der nach Gottes Bilde geschaffen ist in Unschuld, Reinheit und Gerechtigkeit.' Compare this to Colossians 3:9-10: '... **ye have put off the old man with his deeds; And have put on the new man, which is renewed in knowledge after the image of him that created him'** and Ephesians 4:24: '**And that ye put on the new man, which after God is created in righteousness and true holiness.'** In this version, the reference to Swedenborgianism has been removed.]*

Knight of the West, 7th degree in 1780, corresponding to the VIIIth degree now:

Gott der Herr entledige dich des alten Adams, und verliehe dir den neuen, der nach dem Bilde Gottes in Wahrheit und Gerechtigkeit erschaffen ist.

My conclusion would be that even if all the indicated instances of possible Swedenborgian traces in these rituals (apart from the Beswick ones) could plausibly be regarded as such, then, in general, they occur only on rare occasions in rituals which are not Swedenborgian. At least I would not suppose these few occasions enough for the whole Rite, or even some degree of it, to qualify as Swedenborgian and certainly not to the extent that the 'Vrai Maçon', for example, could be called alchemical (though, of course, it is interesting that there may be some Swedenborgianism in these rituals after all).

Appendix II:
The development of the Rite Ecossais
philosophique

In the foregoing I have given a short summary of the development of the REPh., without justifying my conclusions. I shall attempt to do so in the following.

According to Amadou, when *Saint-Jean d'Ecosse* d'Avignon was created in 1774, it had to promise its mother lodge of Marseille that it would not work in any other degree than that of the three symbolic degrees 1. Entered Apprentice, 2. Fellow Craft and 3. Master, and

4. Maître Parfait,
5. Elu,
6. Ecossais d'Ecosse ou Vrai Maître, and
7. Chevalier Maçon dit de l'Orient.

But these were not the only degrees worked in Avignon at that time. Amadou claims that 'the "three philosophical degrees", the "three colours", the Chevalier de la Toison d'Or and the Vrai Maçon ... are well attested in Avignon since 1774 or 1775, and that at that time a Rite Ecossais decorated with several philosophical degrees and perfectly hierarchized was known there'.[76]

Just before warranting its daughter lodge in Paris in 1776, however, the lodge in Avignon had changed its regulations, which now enumerated its degrees as:

Freemasons, 'being so fortunate as to be decorated with the three colours',
Rose-Croix,
Grand Ecossais,
Maitre Parfait and
Elu.

76. Amadou 1974, 995 = 1991, 921.

Amadou adds that 'this hierarchy is confirmed and specified by the *Règlements généraux des Chapitres Ecossais* where, among others, the "grands aigles noirs" appeared and, at the summit, the Vrai Maçon or "degree of the wisdom". Now, since this list gives the impression of an inversion of part of the previous one, I take it that, in the first place, the indication 'Freemasons, "being so fortunate as to be decorated with the three colours"' should be interpreted as the summit of the system and thus cannot refer to the symbolic degrees, but rather pertains to the highly alchemical degree of Vrai Maçon, the 'three colours' referring to the alchemical ones: black, white and red. Furthermore, I assume that the three symbolic degrees are implicitly supposed to be included anyway. Also, the Grand Ecossais will correspond to the Ecossais d'Ecosse ou Vrai Maître of the first list. Finally, the inversion of the order of the Maitre Parfait and the Elu seems unintended. In normalized order, we have then (above the symbolic degrees):

4. Maître Parfait,
5. Elu,
6. Grand Ecossais,
7. Rose-Croix and
8. Vrai Maçon.

This would mean that, compared to the Rite of two years before, the Chevalier de l'Orient had been replaced by two degrees: the Rose-Croix and the Vrai Maçon. The position of the mentioned 'grands aigles noirs' must have been somewhere here too, apparently lower than the Vrai Maçon. This, then, was the so-called Rite Hermétique, which was exported in 1776 from Avignon to Paris. There it took the name of Rite Ecossais philosophique.

Pierre Mollier has recently reconstructed an early form of the Rite Ecossais philosophique.[77] He concludes that the whole Rite was worked in three bodies: the lodge *du Contrat Social* worked in the three symbolic degrees: 1. Entered Apprentice, 2. Fellow Craft, and 3. Master; the *Souverain Chapitre Metropolitain Ecossais* in the degrees

---

77. Mollier 1996, 239.

4. Maître Parfait,
5. Parfait Elu, and
6. (Grand) Ecossais;

and the *Académie* in the degrees

7. Rose-Croix,
8. Chevalier du Soleil,
9. Chevalier du Phoenix,
10. Chevalier de l'Aigle Noir, and
11. Sage Vrai Maçon.

This list corresponds neatly with the previous one, placing the Chevalier de l'Aigle Noir, as expected, just below the Vrai Maçon, while still adding two degrees: 8. Chevalier du Soleil, and 9. Chevalier du Phoenix. The Chevalier du Soleil may well have been added in Paris. At least it is attested there for the first time, 18 July 1761,[78] and thus probably not a product of Avignon.

Even this list, however, does not account for the 'three philosophical degrees' and the Chevalier de la Toison d'Or of which we saw that Amadou claims that they 'are well attested in Avignon since 1774 or 1775'. On the other hand, it does regard 7. Rose-Croix and 10. Chevalier de l'Aigle Noir as different degrees. But that is not necessarily so. In the oldest ritual for the traditional Rose-Croix degree, the so-called Ritual-Strasbourg of 1760,[79] the degree is called 'Chevalier de l'Aigle, du Pelican, de Rose Croix, de St. André, ou le Parfait Maçon'. And a ritual of a degree from the Rite Ecossais philosophique itself is called 'Chevalier de l'Aigle noir, dit Rose-Croix'.[80] On the other hand, it is not impossible to have two degrees with such names in one such a system, since the two degrees just mentioned are, despite their titles, not related at all.

Things become even more complex if we take into account the lists of degrees produced by later authors. Ragon gives for the Rite Hermétique or Rite Ecossais d'Avignon the following degrees (after the symbolic ones):

78. Amadou 1974, 995 = 1991, 921.
79. GON 240.C.53 = Kloss MS. XXVIII.40.
80. GON 240.E.74 = Kloss MS. XXVIII.45.

4. Vrai Maçon,
5. Maçon de la Voie Droite,
6. Compagnon de Paracelse,
7. Maître de la Table d'Hermes,
8. Maître de la Table d'Esmeralda,
9. Maître des Secrets Hermétiques,
10. Chevalier de l'Iris,
11. Chevalier de la Toison d'Or,
12. Chevalier des Argonautes,
13. Chevalier de l'Etoile d'Or,
14. Chevalier du Nord,
15. Chevalier du Triangle,
16. Chevalier du Secret et de la Chambre du Centre,
17. Grand et Sublime Chevalier de l'Etoile Flamboyante.[81]

Even though this list includes the Chevalier de la Toison d'Or, it does not seem at all to be in accord with the evidence just presented. However, Ragon may in fact be referring here to a much later Rite Hermétique, which may have existed in his day.

For the Rite Ecossais philosophique, Thory, who was Grand Librarian since 1788, and as such had firsthand knowledge of the Rite in his own day — and could use the extended archives of the Order for information concerning the past — gives two lists, one for 1766 and one for 1815. The one for 1766 is as follows:

4. Le Vrai Maçon,
5. Le Vrai Maçon dans la Voie droite,
6. Le Chevalier de la Clef d'Or,
7. Le Chevalier d'Iris,
8. Le Chevalier des Argonautes,
9. Le Chevalier de la Toison d'Or;[82]

81. Quoted from Ligou 1991, 1038. I have not been able to trace the source for this list in the works of Ragon.
82. Quoted from Ligou 1991, 1037. I have not been able to find this list either in the works by the author which Ligou claims to quote, and the year 1766 is clearly impossible. However, Thory calls 'Vrai Maçon dans la voie droite' the '2e. grade du système hermétique de Montpellier.' (1815, 321) and dates the 'Rite de la Maçonnerie Hermétique' as 'Fondé à Avignon en
                                                                                    →

and the one for 1815 runs thus:

4. Maître Parfait,
5. Chevalier Elu Philosophe (ou Chevalier Philosophique),
6. Grand Ecossais, (3)
7. Chevalier du Soleil,
8. Chevalier de l'Anneau Lumineux,
9. Chevalier de l'Aigle Blanc et Noir, (6)
10. Grand Inspecteur Commandeur.[83]

And we can even add the list, provided by Clavel for 1843:

1-2-3. Chevalier de l'Aigle noir ou Rose-Croix d'Hérédom de la Tour (divisé en trois parties),
4. Chevalier du Phénix,
5. Chevalier du Soleil,
6. Chevalier de l'Iris,
7. Vrai maçon,
8. Chevalier des Argonautes,
9. Chevalier de la Toison-d'Or,
10. Grand-inspecteur parfait initié,
11. Grand-inspecteur grand écossais,
12. Sublime maître de l'anneau lumineux.[84]

Ragon gives the same list as Clavel.[85] Both explicitly start numbering again from 1 after the symbolic degrees. Were it not that in the Kloss

→   1770, et transporté à Montpellier en 1778' (ibid. 317). Ligou numbers this list from 1 to 6.

83. Quoted from Ligou 1991, 1037. Neither have I been able to find this list in the works of the author which Ligou claims to quote, but it is confirmed by Coil (1961, 555), who mentions that the 6th degree would be omitted. Thory, however, refers to the 'Grand Ecossais' as the third, and to the 'Chevalier de l'Aigle Blanc et Noir' as the sixth of the Rite (1815, 306-7 and 291 respectively). Ligou numbers the list from 1 to 7.

84. Clavel 1843, 64; the list is still the same in the third edition of 1844.

85. According to Ligou, adding after the fifth degree the 'Sublime Philosophe', thus providing a system of 13 degrees, but in fact this is not the case for the list in Ragon (1853, 169). Coil (1961, 555) quotes this list from Clavel correctly.

library there are two manuscripts with the titles: 'Huitième degré: Chevalier des Argonautes' (Kloss MS. XXVI.4; GON 63.F.69) and 'Neuvième et dernier degré: Chevalier de la Toison d'Or' (Kloss MS. XXVI.5; GON 63.F.70), these lists by Clavel and Ragon could be discarded, based on the generally supported assumption that the Rite Ecossais philosophique died out shortly before the death of Thory in 1827.[86] The two Kloss library manuscripts correspond exactly and only with the 8th and 9th degrees of the first list ascribed to Thory and the list of Clavel. That this manuscript of the 9th degree also claims this degree to be the last of its Rite, would at least suggest that the 'Grand Inspecteur' degrees — present in Clavel's list but absent yet in the first one ascribed to Thory — did not originally belong to this system, but were later adopted from elsewhere, i.e., from the Rite Ecossais Ancien et Accepté. Also the threefold degree of Chevalier de l'Aigle Noir ou Rose-Croix is represented in the Kloss collection: 'Chevalier de l'Aigle noir, dit Rose-Croix; Premier Grade du Rit. Ecossais philosophique' (Kloss MS. XXVIII.45; GON 240.E.74), 'Le Commandeur de l'Aigle noir, dit Rose-Croix; Second Grade du Rit Ecossais philosophique' (Kloss MS. XXVIII.46; GON 240.E.75), and 'Le Grand Prieur du Chevalier de l'Aigle noir, dit Rose-Croix; 3me grade du Rit Ecossais philosophique' (Kloss MS. XXVIII.47; GON 240.E.76). In other words, the Rite, described by Clavel, did exist once. And it probably existed several decades after Thory died. Clavel's claim that the Rite was still active in 1843 could well be correct, since it is not in conflict with Coil's claim that 'after the expiration of the Rite, most [of the 2000 volumes of its library] found their way into the hands of the Grand Lodge of Scotland by way of gift in 1849'.[87] The Rite would have expired then between 1844 (3rd edition of Clavel) and 1849.

As to the new degrees that popped up in the post-Thory period, we should remember that the Rite Hermétique d'Avignon was also exported to Montpelier by d'Aigrefeuille, and that new degrees had been added to it there. Mollier[88] believes that these included the Chevalier des Argonautes and the Chevalier de la Toison d'Or, and that

86. E.g. Coil 1961, 555.
87. Coil 1961, 555.
88. Personal communication, letter of 8 July 1997.

does not seem unlikely to me. In that case, Ragon's list for the Rite Hermétique or Rite Ecossais d'Avignon (cf. supra) would in fact reflect the Rite Hermétique de Montpelier, and it is not at all impossible that in the post-Thory period, the new degrees from Montpelier were brought to Paris and added to the system of the Rite Ecossais philosophique.[89] Thory's list for 1766 would then, in all respects, have to be discarded.

To summarize, the Rite in question probably developed from (a) the list which St. Jean d'Ecosse d'Avignon agreed upon with its mother lodge of Marseille in 1774, to (b) the list in its new regulations of 1776, to (c) the early list, reconstructed by Mollier for Paris ≥1776, to (d) the list of Thory for 1815, to (e) the list of Clavel for 1843.

89. Idem.

72   Jan A.M. Snoek

Bibliography

A[madou], R. 1974. 'Pernety'. In: D. Ligou (ed.), *Dictionnaire universel de la franc-maçonnerie*. 2 vols. [Paris?], 990-95; and idem in idem *Dictionnaire de la franc-maçonnerie*. Paris 1987, 3rd ed. 1991, 917-22.

Anon. 1996a. *Der Schwedische Freimaurer Orden; Große Landesloge von Schweden; Geschichtlicher Hintergrund und heutige Organisation.* Stockholm.

Anon. 1996b. *Facts on the Swedish Order of Freemasons, Grand Lodge of Sweden.* Stockholm: Swedish Order of Freemasons.

Benz, E. 1948. *Emanuel Swedenborg; Naturforscher und Seher.* München: Rinn.

Bernheim, A. 1998. 'La Stricte Observance'. *Acta Macionica* 8 (1998), 67-97.

Beswick, S. 1870. *Swedenborg Rite and the Great masonic Leaders of the Eighteenth Century.* Edition used: New York 1912: Macoy.

Bord, G. 1908. *La Franc-Maçonnerie en France des Origines à 1815.* Paris: Nouvelle Librairie Nationale.

Borg, B. 1993. 'Ueber das Schwedische Freimaurer-System'. *Alpina*, vol. 3, 85-88.

Clavel, F.-T.B. 1843. *Histoire pittoresque de la Franc-maçonnerie.* Paris. Pagnerre.

Coil, H.W. 1961. *Coil's masonic Encyclopaedia.* New York: Macoy.

Cross, J.L. 1857. *The masonic Text-Book.* New York.

Deecke, E., et al. (n.d.) *Leitfaden durch die Kapitelgrade der Großen Landesloge der Freimaurer von Deutschland; Der Grad des Ritters von Westen; Nach alten Unterlagen der BBr. Ernst Deecke, Adolf Widmann, Otto Hieber, Hermann Gloede, Gerhard Kück, Wilhelm Stuckenberg u.a. neu bearbeitet von Br. Heinz G. Klusmann, Lübeck und Br. Gerd Pickrun, Dortmund.* [No publisher].

Denslow, W.R. 1957. *10,000 Famous Freemasons.* Richmond, VA: Macoy.

Fabry, J. and A. Faivre, 1996. 'Emanuel Swedenborg (1688-1772), savant naturaliste et connaisseur du monde invisible'. *ARIES*, vol. 20, 5-31.

Feddersen, K.C.F. 1991. 'Ueber die Anfänge der Freimaurerei in Schweden'. *Quellenkundliche Arbeit*, vol. 7. Schriften der freimaurerischen Forschungsvereinigung Frederik der Großen Landesloge der Freimaurer von Deutschland, Flensburg, 81-108.

Feddersen, K.C.F. 1994. 'Christian Carl Friedrich Wilhelm Freiherr van Nettelbladt', *Quellenkundliche Arbeit*, vol. 11. Schriften der freimaurerischen Forschungsvereinigung Frederik der Großen Landesloge der Freimaurer von Deutschland, Flensburg, 241-330.

Frick, K.R.H. 1975. *Die Erleuchteten*. Graz: Akademische Druck und Verlagsanstalt.

Gilbert, R.A. 1995. 'Chaos out of Order: The Rise and Fall of the Swedenborgian Rite'. *Ars Quatuor Coronatorum*, vol. 108, 122-49.

Gould, R.F. 1903. *A Concise History of Freemasonry*. London: Gale & Polden.

Hieber, O. [c. 1959]. *Leitfaden durch die Ordenslehre der Großen Landesloge der Freimaurer von Deutschland; Der Grad des Vertrauten der Johannisloge*, durchgesehen und bearbeitet von W. Stukenberg und G. Kück. Bad Harzburg: Sasse.

Jaskulewicz, W. 1976. 'Wie die schwedische Lehrart nach Hamburg kam und sich von dort verbreitete'. *Quatuor Coronati Jahrbuch*, vol. 13, 41-55.

Jonsson, I. 1971. *Emanuel Swedenborg*. New York: Twayne.

Kervalla, A. and Ph. Lestienne 1997. 'Un haut-grade templier dans les milieux jacobites en 1750: l'Ordre Sublime des Chevaliers Elus aux sources de la Stricte Observance'. *Renaissance Traditionnelle*, 112, 229-66.

Larsen, R. (ed.) 1988. *Emanuel Swedenborg: A Continuing Vision*. New York: Swedenborg Foundation.

Le Bihan, A. 1998. 'Le Souverain Chapitre Métropolitain de la Respectable Mère Loge Ecossaise Saint Jean d'Ecosse du Contrat Social'. *Ordo ab Chao* (Bulletin of the Suprème Conseil de France), vol. 37, 117-31.

Le Bihan, A. 2000. 'Le Souverain Chapitre Métropolitain de la Respectable Mère Loge Écossaise Saint-Jean d'Écosse du Contrat Social (II)'. *Ordo ab Chao* (Bulletin of the Suprème Conseil de France), vol. 42, 79-119.

Le Forestier, R. 1970. *La Franc-Maçonnerie Templière et occultiste aux XVIIIe et XIXe Siècles*. Publié par A. Faivre. Paris: Aubier-Montaigne.

Lennhoff, E., and O. Posner, 1975. *Internationales Freimaurerlexicon*. Unchanged reprint of 1932 edition. Wien/München: Amalthea.

Lenning, C. 1822. *Encyclopädie der Freimaurerei*. Leipzig: F.A. Brockhaus.

Ligou, D. (ed.) 1991. *Dictionnaire de la Franc-Maçonnerie*, 3rd ed. Paris: PUF [Presses Universitaires de France].

Litvine, J. 1997. 'Le Rite Ecossais philosophique'. *Acta Macionica*, vol. 7, 135-77.

Mackey, A.G. 1946. *Encyclopedia of Freemasonry*. Chicago: The Masonic History Company.

Meillassoux – Le Cerf, M. 1992. *Dom Pernety et les Illuminés d'Avignon*. Milano: Arche.

Mellor, A. (n.d.) *Dictionnaire de la Franc-Maçonnerie et des Francs-Maçons*. Paris: Pierre Belfond.

Mollier, P. 1996. 'Contribution à l'étude du grade de Chevalier du Soleil'. *Renaissance Traditionnelle*, vol. 107-8, 231-42.

Morgan, W. 1827 (= 1826). *Illustrations of Masonry*. Batavia N.Y.; facsimile edition in Harry Carr (ed.) 1981, *Three Distinct Knocks and Jachin and Boaz*. Bloomington, Ill.: The masonic Book Club.

Naudon, P. 1978. *Histoire, Rituels et Tuileur des Hauts Grades Maçonniques; Le Rite Ecossais Ancien et Accepté*. 3rd ed. Paris: Dervy.

Noël, P. 1998. 'De Stockholm à Lyon. D'un rituel suédois et de l'usage qu'en fit J.B. Willermoz'. In: *Ars Macionica 8*, 99-150.

Ragon, J.-M. 1853. *Orthodoxie maçonnique*. Paris: E. Dentu.

Rudbeck, J. 1931. *Karl Friedrich Eckleff, der Begründer des schwedischen Freimaurersystems*. Uebersetzung aus dem Schwedischen. Berlin: Mittler.

Schuchard, M.K. 1975. *Freemasonry, Secret Societies, and the Continuity of the Occult Tradition in English Literature*. (PhD Dissertation). Austin: University of Texas.

Schuchard, M.K. 1988. 'Swedenborg, Jacobitism, and Freemasonry'. In: E.J. Brock (ed.), *Swedenborg and his Influence*. Bryn Athun, PA: The Academy of the New Church, 359-79.

Schuchard, M.K. 1992. 'The Secret History of Blake's Swedenborg Society'. *Blake: An Illustrated Quarterly*, vol. 26, 40-51.

Sigstedt, C.O. 1981. *The Swedenborg Epic; The Life and Works of Emmanuel Swedenborg*. New York: AMS Press.

Snoek, J.A.M. 1987. *Initiations; A Methodological Approach to the Application of Classification and Definition Theory in the Study of Rituals*. Pijnacker: Dutch Efficiency Bureau.

Snoek, J.A.M. 1997a. 'A propos de l'origine de 3 éléments fondamentaux du degré de l'Arche Royale'. In: (anon. ed.) *Grand Chapitre de la Sainte Arche Royale de Belgique, Réunion Annuelle, 19 avril 1997.* [Bruxelles], 23-33.

Snoek, J.A.M. 1997b. 'Le développement des rituels maçonniques aux Pays-Bas de 1734 à nos jours'. *Acta Macionica,* vol. 7, 283-94.

Snoek, J.A.M. 1999. 'De allusieve methode / The Allusive Method / La méthode allusive'. *Acta Macionica,* vol. 9, 47-70.

Starcke, C.N. [1913]. *Die Freimaurerei, ihre geschichte Entwicklung und kulturelle Bedeutung bei den verschiedenen Völkern.* Hamburg: F.W. Rademacher.

[Thory, C.-A.] 1812. *Histoire de la Fondation du Grand Orient de France.* Paris: P. Dufart.

Thory, C.-A. 1815. *Acta Latomorum.* Paris: P. Dufart.

Thulstrup, C.L.H. 1898. *Anteckningar till svenska frimureriets historia II,* Stockholm: Beckmans.

Viatte, A. 1928. *Les sources occultes du romantisme.* Paris: Champion. (New Edition 1965).

Von Nettelbladt, C.C.F.W. 1879. *Geschichte Freimaurerischer Systeme in England, Frankreich und Deutschland.* Berlin: Ernst Siegfried Mittler.

[Voorhis, H.V.B. (ed.)], 1938. 'The Primitive and Original Rite of Symbolic Phremasonry'. *Collectanea,* vol. 1, 17-116.

Williams-Hogan, J.K. 1988. 'Swedenborg: A Biography'. In: E.J. Brock (ed.), *Swedenborg and his Influence.* Bryn Athyn, PA: The Academy of the New Church, 3-27.

Williams-Hogan, J.K. 1998. 'The Place of Emanuel Swedenborg in Modern Western Esotericism'. In: A. Faivre & W.J. Hanegraaff (eds.), *Western Esotericism and the Study of Religion; Selected Papers presented at the 17th Congress of the International Association for the History of Religions, Mexico City 1995.* Leuven: Peters, 201-52.

Wolson, T. 1751. *Le maçon démasqué.* London [Paris?]: Owen Temple Bar.

CHAPTER 3

How Traditional are the Traditionalists? The Case of the Guénonian Sufis.[1]

Mark Sedgwick

In many cities in Europe and the United States, groups exist which describe themselves as 'Centres' or 'Foundations' for 'Traditional [sometimes, 'Metaphysical'] Studies.' Normally, these groups derive from a French 'metaphysician', René Guénon (1886-1951); often they are the public face of a Sufi tariqa, or occasionally of a Masonic lodge. There are also political Traditionalists, normally deriving more from the Italian writer Julius Evola, but often also acknowledging Guénon; the most important of these is perhaps the Moscow Center for Special Metastrategic Studies — a serious organization despite its fanciful name, or at least an organization which has to be taken seriously, to judge by the weekly print-run — 50,000 copies — of its in-house journal, *Elementy*.[2]

My purpose in this article is not, however, to survey the vast and growing influence of René Guénon, but rather to ask how traditional Traditionalists really are, concentrating on Sufi Guénonians. My choice of Sufism is based on two grounds: firstly, that it is arguably the mainstream of Guénonianism, since Sufism was the path which Guénon himself chose. My second ground is more pragmatic: Sufism in the Muslim world is my own principal field. A second limitation is that in this article I am asking how traditional Traditionalists are, not

---

1. This article is a shortened version of the original paper, and has been cut especially in its earlier sections. A full version of the original text may be found in *ARIES* 22 (1998).
2. Paillard 1993.

how traditional Traditionalism is. The 'perennial philosophy' of course
sees itself as anything but new, but for various reasons I have no intention of approaching here the question of whether it is modern or
perennial.[3] Instead, I will look at practice, associating non-traditional
or 'new' with organizations such as Encausse's *Ordre martiniste*, where
Guénon's career started, and 'traditional' with tariqas such as the
Hamdiyya Shādhiliyya, the almost entirely traditional Egyptian
tariqa[4] where Guénon's career ended.

In order to situate my subject, I will start with a classification of
Sufism in the West. Western Sufism can in general be divided into
four groups: immigrants' tariqas, standard tariqas, novel tariqas, and
non-Islamic groups.[5] The two extremes are the easiest to describe. An
immigrants' tariqa is a transplant: Senegalese Mourides in Italy or
Egyptian Burhāmīs in Denmark, tariqas taken with immigrants to
their new countries, following shaykhs who are also followed in the
immigrants' home countries. Non-Islamic groups are usually self-
identified as such — the 'Sufi Movement' of Idries Shah, for example,
which argues that Sufism is separate from Islam, many of whose
members are not and would never describe themselves as Muslim.

Non-Islamic Sufi groups are, clearly, not traditional — they are
new. Though there have been occasional cases of Sufi shaykhs in the
Muslim world having non-Muslim followers, and occasional cases of
Sufi tariqas which stray outside Islam,[6] it is axiomatic for a scholar of
Sufism, or indeed for 99.9% of Sufis in the Muslim world, that Sufism
is a path within Islam. Equally, immigrants' tariqas are clearly traditional: although the new environment within which they exist inevitably has consequences and leads to changes, this is part of the

3. For a fuller consideration of questions of this type, see *ARIES* 11, 12 and
    13; and Quinn 1997.
4. Gilsenan 1973 of course argues that the Hamdiyya Shādhiliyya was, in
    Islamic terms, novel. Whilst not wanting to enter this dispute here, I
    would merely observe that the Hamdiyya Shādhiliyya is sufficiently well
    within the Egyptian Islamic mainstream for its novel features not to be of
    concern to us.
5. I find this more useful than the binary definition adopted by Hermansen
    1997.
6. One of the most interesting of these is the 'Ahl-i Ḥaqq' — see Mir-Hossei-
    ni 1994.

normal rhythm of Sufism; Sufi tariqas have been moving into new environments since first there were tariqas.

My two remaining classifications are less easily described. A standard tariqa is easiest to define by example: that of the Naqshbandiyya of Muḥammad Nazim al-Ḥaqqanī (1922-), a Turkish shaykh who has many followers in Turkey, Syria and Malaysia. Al-Ḥaqqanī is a standard shaykh in terms of Islamic studies, but was educated in Cyprus under the British and so happens to speak English — and also has numerous English, German, American and other converts amongst his followers.[7] His English Naqshbandiyya is not an immigrants' tariqa, since even though there are many immigrants amongst al-Ḥaqqanī's followers in London they did not take the Naqshbandiyya with them to England; there are also many non-immigrants amongst his followers. I would argue that this 'standard' tariqa is traditional (rather than new) in three senses. First, al-Ḥaqqanī is a shaykh on the classic Islamic pattern, taking his *silsila* or spiritual descent from a universally accepted source, and recognized and followed by born Muslims in the Muslim world. Secondly, his tariqa is — in mainstream Islamic terms — orthodox: although not every follower of his conforms to the Islamic Sharia in every respect, al-Ḥaqqanī does his best to hold his followers to the Sharia, and is in most cases successful. Finally, this tariqa is standard and traditional because its spread conforms to an established pattern: for a charismatic shaykh such as al-Ḥaqqanī to spread Islam in non-Muslim lands is something which has been happening for centuries, notably in Africa, but also in various parts of Asia — and now in Europe and America.

The remaining classification, then, is of 'novel' tariqa, into which I would put any tariqa which does not fit into one of my three other categories. It is into this category that Sufi Guénonians, or Traditionalist Sufis, fall. A 'novel' tariqa may be traditional, or may be new.

---

7. Almost the only published study of this tariqa, Habibis 1990, is somewhat disappointing. My information is drawn from my own fieldwork and from Holdijk 1997.

Guénon and Aguéli

Ivan Aguéli (1860-71), from whom Guénon took his first tariqa, and Guénon himself both made their débuts in Paris, in existing non-Christian spiritual and esoteric organizations. Aguéli, a painter, left his native Sweden for Paris at the age of 21, and, as well as painting and taking an interest in anarchism, joined the Theosophical Society in 1891. Guénon arrived in Paris from his native Blois a few years later in 1904, and interested himself in various esoteric groups,[8] initially those established by Gérard Encausse, 'Papus' (1865-1916). Encausse had also been a co-founder of the Theosophical Society in France (though he later opposed the Theosophists).[9] The Theosophical Society thus features in Guénon's early years as well as Aguéli's.

Aguéli took the Shādhiliyya ʿArabiyya tariqa in Egypt in 1907, from ʿAbd al-Raḥman ibn Muḥammad ʿIllīsh,[10] and received an *ijāza* [authorization] to give the tariqa himself.[11] ʿIllīsh in fact gave so many *ijāzas* 'to anyone applying for them' that Fred De Jong concludes that 'he does not seem to have taken the requirements of [his] position seriously.'[12]

Guénon, meanwhile, had taken part in the Spiritualist and Masonic Congress in Paris in 1908,[13] and in the same year had founded his own *Ordre du temple rénové*, in which elements of Theosophy and of the Hermetic Brotherhood of Luxor can be distinguished.[14] As a result of the establishment of the *Ordre du temple*, Guénon and his followers were expelled from the *Ordre martiniste* by Encausse. In 1909, Guénon joined the Gnostic Church of Fabre des Essarts ('the Patriarch Synésius'), and edited until 1912 the periodical *La Gnose*, described as 'the official organ of the Universal Gnostic Church.'[15]

8. Chacornac 1958, 25-27, 31-33 and 42-43.
9. Waterfield 1987, 33.
10. Chacornac 1958, 45.
11. Rawlinson 1997.
12. De Jong 1978, 173-74.
13. Chacornac 1958, 31-33. One of the Masonic orders followed the *Rite national espagnol*, and the other the *Rite primitif et originel swédenborgien*.
14. Godwin 1996. The Hindu terms for symbolic metaphysics can be traced to the Theosophists, and the conception of cyclic periods to the HB of L.
15. He was consecrated a bishop (Chacornac 1958, 33-39); there was no lower rank than this (Rawlinson 1997).

From 1910-11, Guénon published in *La Gnose* a series of articles on Hinduism which were later to form the basis of two of his most important works, the *Introduction générale à l'étude des doctrines hindoues* and *L'homme et son devenir selon le Védânta*.[16] It is unclear from whence Guénon drew his knowledge of Hinduism on which these articles and his later books were based.[17] Chacornac states that both books were approved of by 'the orthodox pundits' of Benares,[18] and they have met with approval from sections of the Indian public in recent years.[19] French orientalists however considered Guénon's work second-hand and his method unscholarly.[20] The *Introduction générale* was rejected by Professor Sylvain Lévi of the Sorbonne, where Guénon submitted it as a thesis, 'because it was so thoroughly opposed to any form of historicity'.[21] The same might of course be said of many works originating from within a religion rather than from scholars outside a religion. In general, partisans of Guénon commend his understanding of Hinduism, and opponents criticize it.[22] I am not aware of any study so far carried out by an independent scholar, and am myself unqualified to perform one.

It was through *La Gnose* that Guénon met Aguéli, and also Albert Puyon, Comte de Pouvourville, a prominent Gnostic who had been initiated into a Chinese Taoist secret society a few years before; his

16. Guénon 1921a and Guénon 1925.
17. Chacornac points out this problem and is unable to suggest a solution (Chacornac 1958, 39-42). Martin Lings suggests that the Hindus in question must have been of the Advaita Vedanta school (Lings 1995, 21-22), since Guénon's views on Buddhism were uncharacteristic of other Hindu schools (Lings 1996).
18. Chacornac 1958, 72. It is unclear in what language these works were available in Benares.
19. The *Introduction générale*'s English translation was published in New Delhi in 1992 (Munshiram Manoharlal), as was *L'homme et son devenir*'s English translation in 1981.
20. Borella 1992, 335.
21. Rawlinson 1997.
22. A one-time follower of Guénon, for example, later wrote: 'Vedanta is not the heartless, aloof and repellent body that it seems to have become in the hands of Mr. Guénon, [who] seems often to aim more at promoting his peculiar theory of the oneness of spiritual tradition than at laying bare the truth itself' (Levy 1951, 98, quoted in Rawlinson 1997).

Taoist name was Matigoï. Both Aguéli and Guénon took Taoist initi-ations from Pouvourville; the three all wrote in *La Gnose* on various aspects of Eastern religion.[23] Aguéli, for example, wrote on the doc-trinal identity of Islam and Taoism.[24] In 1912, Guénon became Mus-lim, taking the Shādhilī tariqa from Aguéli; he took the name of ʿAbd al-Wāhid.

Guénon and Islam

Guénon's conversion to Islam was followed by an unequivocal repu-diation of his earliest connections and interests, testified to by two books in which he attacked and exposed Theosophy and spiritualism in general and, in particular, a number of organizations ranging from Aleister Crowley's Golden Dawn to the Hermetic Brotherhood of Luxor.[25] He retained however a conviction of the efficacy of magic, as we will see, as well as an interest in Masonry, which he considered to contain the vestiges of 'valid' Western 'initiatic traditions'.[26] Lings suggests that Guénon's secluded lifestyle in Cairo — extending to a refusal to give his actual address even to regular correspondents — was the result of a fear of attack by magic by certain Europeans;[27] these were, according to a slightly dubious source, Téder and Charles Debré, enemies of his from the days of the *Ordre du temple*.[28] In a let-ter to Evola in 1948, Guénon wrote that an 'attack of rheumatism' in 1939 had been caused by 'une influence maléfique,' and disagreed

23. See Rawlinson1993 for Aguéli; for Guénon, Lings 1996. See also Rawlin-son 1997.
24. Rawlinson, 1993.
25. Guénon 1921b and Guénon 1923. See Chacornac 1958, 61-62, 65-66.
26. He published articles to this effect in 1913-14 (Chacornac 1958, 51-53).
27. Lings 1995, 31-32. Guénon advised Lings never to have anything to do with magic, since a person who did thereby made himself more vulner-able to magic (Lings 1996).
28. This is said to be from letters written by Guénon in 1932, referring to 'the blood of black animals', which Robin glosses as 'Sethian magic' (Robin 1986, 261, 266-67). I describe this source as 'somewhat dubious' since, amongst other things, Robin describes Aleister Crowley as 'a notorious spy, working simultaneously for France and Britain' (Robin 1986, 272). Whilst I know little of Crowley, this sounds like the fruit of an over-heat-ed imagination.

with Evola, who had evidently said that such things could not hurt those who have spiritual stature. Guénon pointed out that the Prophet himself was made ill by sorcerers.[29] Most Guénonian biographers tend to gloss over Guénon's concern with magic, sometimes referring to attacks of persecution mania when Guénon was ill, but in one sense such apologies are unnecessary: a belief in the efficacy of magic is not un-Islamic, as Guénon's own reference to the Prophet reminds us. Such a belief was (and is) widespread in Egypt amongst all types and classes of person,[30] and so may be described as traditional within Islam.

Guénon also retained his interest in non-Islamic religions; indeed, Oldmeadow argues that he had not abandoned Catholicism, but his evidence is far from conclusive.[31] Guénon's writings certainly continued to emphasize Hinduism; it has been suggested that this was because Westerners who might reject Islam as 'another religion' ('we have had enough of religion') might more easily accept 'truths' which came from something 'on the surface very different,' and possibly be-

29. Robin 1986, 265-66.
30. That Guénon might have earned the enmity of European practitioners of magic is also likely.
31. He bases his argument (Oldmeadow 1982, 24-25) largely on Guénon's 1912 marriage to a Catholic wife, and his continuing social and intellectual contacts with Catholics, and on the view of Olivier de Fremond, a friend of Guénon's at this time. Rawlinson, similarly, points out that Guénon married according to the Catholic rite despite his 'initiation' (Rawlinson 1993). I am unsure of the value of the views of Fremond, but social and intellectual contacts with Catholics seem to me to prove little, since Guénon maintained such contacts with believers in a variety of religions (including Catholic Christianity) until the end of his life. Oldmeadow, himself a Catholic Guénonian, may be tempted to read more into them than they bear. Both Guénon's conversion to Islam and his marriage happened in the same year, 1912. I am unsure which happened first, but if Guénon did marry in a Catholic ceremony whilst a Muslim, this is not inexplicable. His (French) wife's relatives would presumably have been less than delighted at the idea of a Muslim ceremony, even supposing that one were possible in France at that time; and so long as steps were taken to ensure that the legal requirements of marriage under the Sharia (*mahr* etc) were also met at some point, it would not be hard to make a case for the acceptability of *participation in* (as opposed to *belief in the elements of*) a Christian ceremony.

cause Hinduism is an Aryan religion, and Westerners have an Aryan heritage.[32] In similar vein, Pallis writes: 'Guénon felt that a knowledge of the Eastern tradition, notably the Hindu and the Taoist, might be a means of spurring Christians into rediscovering the deeper meaning which the teachings of the Church harbour implicitly and this, for Guénon, was the only remaining hope for the West'.[33] Hinduism was certainly the tradition which most interested the Western reading public at that time.

Despite this continued interest in Hinduism and other religions, however, Guénon's own practice was (as far as we know) purely Islamic. He is not known ever to have recommended anyone to become a Hindu,[34] whereas (as we will see) he introduced many to Islam.

As well as the two important works on Hinduism already mentioned, Guénon also published in 1927 his *La crise du monde moderne*; these three works, expanded by his most important later work, *La règne de la quantité et les signes des temps* (1945), contain the heart of Guénonianism. Guénon is perhaps best described as an influential commentator on modernity, which — he argues — is the Last Age (*kali yuga*). His method is not to analyse modernity sociologically or to argue against it on the grounds of modernity's own characteristics: this sets him apart from other critics of the age, from Marx to Spengler or Baudrillard. He instead expounds the Traditions (principally, the Hindu tradition), and leaves the reader in this light to judge the modernity the reader himself has experienced. Guénon is also the great exponent of Tradition in a second sense, in the sense of the need to adhere to one of the great orthodox religious traditions which embody 'perennial' Truth. This concept of the Transcendent Unity of Religions is one of Guénon's most important and problematic legacies; its compatibility with Islam is considered below.

Early Guénonians

The years after Guénon's conversion to Islam were devoted mostly to writing; Guénon wrote more than half of his books, and all save one

---

32. Lings 1995, 24 and 29.
33. Pallis 1978, 183-34.
34. Lings 1995, 29.

of his most important works, in the 1920s. In 1914, excused military service on health grounds, he had began a series of periods of employment as a high-school philosophy teacher which lasted until 1927, all either in Paris or his native Blois (save for the year 1917-18, spent at a school in Sétif, Algeria). In 1927, however, a new period in Guénon's life began. His wife died, and the niece they had been bringing up (having had no children themselves) was taken back by her mother in 1928. In 1930 Guénon went to Egypt to collect texts for an esoteric publishing house,[35] but remained in Cairo until his death in 1951, marrying an Egyptian in 1934. In Cairo, Guénon dressed in a *jallābiya* and spoke fluent Arabic;[36] although he shunned the company of most Europeans,[37] he continued to write books and articles for publication in France, and he also continued his involvement in Muslim and non-Muslim religious circles, in Egypt and abroad.[38] He referred many of the Europeans he encountered in this period to Frithjof Schuon (1907-).[39]

Schuon, the son of a German musician resident in Switzerland, had left school at sixteen and later moved to Paris,[40] where an interest in religions[41] led him to read extensively on Hinduism and Buddhism, and finally led him to the works of Guénon. In the early 1930s, Schuon wrote from Paris to Guénon in Cairo, asking him to recom-

35. Chacornac 1958, 55-56, 67, 83-84 and 91-92.
36. Chacornac 1958, 92-105. Arabic was the language he used to communicate with his wife (Lings 1995, 32).
37. Guénon used a post-office box for many years, and finally had people write to him c/o Martin Lings (Lings 1996).
38. In Egypt, he was a follower of the Ḥamdiyya Shādhiliyya and was also involved in discussions with non-Muslim foreigners. Guénon continued a sizeable correspondence with various figures in Europe, as well as occasionally receiving visitors (Lings 1996).
39. Lings 1996. One estimate has about 100 persons being referred in this way before 1939 (Rawlinson 1997).
40. He was born in Basel, Switzerland, of a German father and a (French) Alsatian mother. See Nasr 1991, 2-3.
41. This interest seems to have been a family interest. Schuon's father, originally a Protestant, on his deathbed requested his two sons to become Catholics. Schuon's brother later became a Trappist monk (Lings 1996).

mend a 'master.' Guénon replied that he should go to Aḥmad ibn Muṣṭafā al-ʿAlawī (1869-1934), then at Mustaghanim (Algeria).[42]

It is strange that Guénon sent Schuon to an ʿAlawī shaykh in Algeria rather than to his own shaykh in Cairo, who was by then Salāma ibn Ḥasan Salāma (1867-1939), the founder of the Ḥamdiyya Shādhiliyya, later to become one of the largest tariqas in Egypt.[43] In the same way, it is strange that he subsequently sent European visitors to Schuon (whom he had met in 1938 and 1939)[44] rather than to an Arab shaykh. Had Guénon sent his European visitors to his own shaykh, Guénonian Sufis today would most likely be followers of the Ḥamdiyya Shādhiliyya, and there would be few or no 'novel' Guénonian tariqas for this article to examine. It is interesting that, towards the end of his life, Guénon seems to have decided that sending people to Schuon had been a mistake.

The most likely explanation of his sending Schuon to al-ʿAlawī is that there are obvious reasons for sending a European aspirant to a shaykh who speaks his language and understands his culture, and Guénon may have considered al-ʿAlawī an especially suitable person to whom to send a European: although he was reluctant to speak French he understood it well, and in 1926 had led the prayer for the inauguration of the Paris mosque; many Frenchmen, from his doctor in Algeria to Jacques Berque, were clearly very impressed by him.[45] After al-ʿAlawī's death, Guénon may have considered his successor a

---

42. Lings 1996.
43. Guénon's first shaykh, ʿAbd al-Raḥman ʿIllīsh, had died soon after his arrival in Cairo. Rawlinson gives the date of ʿIllīsh's death as 1929 (Rawlinson1993), but Guénon clearly met him, since Vâlsan reports Guénon saying that ʿIllīsh had explained the esoteric meaning of the letters of the name Allah to him, and it was to ʿIllish that Guénon dedicated his *Symbolisme de la Croix* in 1931 (Vâlsan 1984, 30-31).
44. Nasr 1991, 4.
45. See Lings 1961, 14 *et passim*, and 79-82 and 116. Although Guénon never met Aḥmad al-ʿAlawī (Lings 1996), it is not surprising that he knew of such a famous shaykh: in 1923, al-ʿAlawī had as many as 100,000 followers, mostly in North Africa but also in Damascus, Palestine, and Aden (Lings 1961, 116). He had *zāwiyas* in Marseilles and Cardiff, but his followers in these places were mostly Algerian and Yemeni, respectively.

less suitable person;[46] he may, alternatively, have considered Schuon a more suitable person, for reasons which will be explored below.

In the event, Schuon had moved from Paris to Marseilles before Guénon's reply arrived, but in Marseilles he met some Algerians who belonged to an ʿAlawī *zāwiya* there. These ʿAlawīs not only insisted that Schuon visit their shaykh, but even raised the money to buy him a ticket on a boat to Oran. In 1932, Schuon travelled to Mustaghanim, where he stayed four months, taking the ʿAlawī tariqa.[47] He took the Muslim name of Nūr al-Dīn ʿĪsā.

Probably before leaving Mustaghanim, Schuon received from al-ʿAlawī's *nāʾib* [deputy], ʿAdda ibn Tunis, an undated document which has been described by later followers of Schuon's as a 'Diplôme de Moqaddem.' This is a curious document, in which Ibn Tunis gives Schuon permission to spread the message of Islam (*qad adhantu fī nashr al-daʿwa al-islamiyya*), accept people into Islam (*talqīn kalimat al-tawḥīd 'la illaha ila Allāh'*) and teach them their basic religious practices (*al-wājibat al-dīniyya*).[48] Since no mention is made anywhere of representing or of giving the ʿAlawiyya, this can hardly be considered an appointment as *muqaddam* [representative] in any normal sense; indeed, all the things 'permitted' to Schuon are things for which no permission is needed, and which are actually incumbent upon any Muslim anyhow. The 'diplôme' thus has the *form* of an appointment without any substance.[49] It is hard to think of any reason for Ibn Tunis to produce such an empty document, save perhaps to respond tactfully to a request for an *ijāza* with which he was unwilling to comply.

Schuon began writing on his return to France, publishing his first articles in *Le Voile d'Isis* in 1933;[50] these articles are Islamic, but not un-

46. According to Caspar 1974 and 1975, the tariqa went into decline after Al-ʿAlawī's death.
47. Lings 1996. Schuon found Guénon's letter on his return to France.
48. Quoted from a photocopy lent me by 'Maryami'. The photocopy was accompanied by an accurate typewritten translation into French on another sheet; the title of 'Diplôme de Moqaddem' had been added at the top of the translation in an unknown hand.
49. It is notable that Ibn Tunis uses *idhn* rather than *ijāza*.
50. After Guénon's departure from Paris, *Le Voile d'Isis* was edited by Marcelle Clavelle, who was in correspondence with Guénon (Lings 1996).

surprisingly also reflect the wider esoteric interests of the periodical in which they were published and of Schuon himself.[51] In 1934, following the death of Aḥmad al-ʿAlawī, Schuon established *zāwiya*s of his own in Basel and Paris.[52] He had no independent fortune, and continued working as a textile designer in France, living just over the border from Switzerland, making weekly visits to his *zāwiya* on the banks of the Rhine in Basel, reached down a winding staircase from the Münstergasse.[53] His *locum tenens* in Basel was Titus (Ibrāhīm) Burckhardt (1908-84).[54] Burckhardt, who was born in Florence into an established Swiss artistic family, had known Schuon since their schooldays together;[55] in the 1930s, he spent some years in Morocco, during which time he had learned Arabic[56] and encountered Sufism.[57] It is unclear at what point he became Muslim. In Paris, Schuon's *muqaddam* was Michel (Muṣṭafā) Vâlsan (1907-74), a Romanian diplomat who took the ʿAlawī tariqa from Schuon in 1938.[58]

Schuon is the second European Guénonian Muslim to act as shaykh. Aguéli, the first, had received his *ijāza* from an Egyptian shaykh who may not have taken his position seriously; Aguéli is not known to have used his *ijāza* to give his tariqa to anyone save

51. The first was 'L'aspect ternaire de la Tradition monothéiste' (June 1933), followed by 'Shahādah et Fatihah' (July 1933); in February 1934, he published 'Réflexions sur le symbolisme de la pyramide.' See Bibliography in Nasr & Stoddart 1991.

52. Rawlinson 1993 states that the first Swiss *zāwiya* was in Lausanne, but according to Lings (1996) it was in Basel, moving with Schuon to Lausanne during the Second World War.

53. Lings 1996.

54. So it would seem, since it was Burckhardt who, in Schuon's absence, was called to the *zāwiya* to meet the young Martin Lings.

55. Stoddart 1987, 3-5. His father, Carl, was a sculptor; his most famous relation was his great uncle, Jakob Burckhardt (1818-97), whose *Geschichte der Renaissance in Italien*, written in the 1870s, remains a standard work. Carl Burckhardt fills six pages in the catalogue of the British Library. Titus Burckhardt was evidently not related to Johann Ludwig Burckhardt, the explorer of Nubia, Egypt, etc.

56. Sufficiently well later to translate the *Fuṣūṣ al-Ḥikam* of Ibn ʿArabī and Jīlī's *Al-insān al-kāmil* (Stoddart 1987, 9).

57. Stoddart 1987, 8-9.

58. James 1981, 335-36.

Guénon.[59] Schuon, on the other hand, gave his tariqa to hundreds or more; he seems to have received his *ijāza* from al-ʿAlawī after al-ʿAlawī's death, in a dream. That this dream included the Buddha Amitabha did not augur well for the future Islamic orthodoxy of his tariqa.[60] It was not widely known that this had been the nature of Schuon's *ijāza*.

Later followers of Schuon make a distinction between the ability and the authority to pass on a tariqa, arguing that any 'initiate' has the *power* to initiate others even in the absence of *authorization* to do so, and that what came to Schuon in his dream was the 'title of shaykh,' i.e. authorization, not the power to initiate, and that he had already been appointed *muqaddam*.[61] While it is true that the meaning of *ijāza* is 'authorization,' this is not a distinction normally made in Sufism, and (as we have seen) Schuon's appointment as *muqaddam* was not one which had any real meaning in the context of the ʿAlawī tariqa.

In 1937, Schuon received, in a vision, 'Six Themes of Meditation' from God; these themes were introduced into the ʿAlawī practice of his *zāwiya*.[62] The receipt of some special practice, often in a vision, frequently heralds the creation of a new tariqa; receipt from God directly, without any intermediary, is highly unusual, if not otherwise unheard of.

New Traditionalist Groups

In 1951, Guénonianism entered a new phase. This year saw a breach between Schuon and Guénon, and Guénon's death; by this time his

59. Rawlinson 1997.
60. 'I had in dream seen all the prophets, and their voices were sometimes like rushing water; the Buddha Amitabha also arose, golden, before my inward eye. Sidi 'Addah ben Tunes, sitting beside the tomb of Shaykh Ahmad, gave me the Shaykh's instructions. I was then appointed *muqaddam*.' (Schuon NDa, 127-28, quoted in Rawlinson 1997). The context makes it possible that ʿAdda appointed Schuon *muqaddam* in response to a dream, but it seems much more likely that ʿAdda formed part of the dream.
61. Maryami 1997.
62. Rawlinson 1997.

fame had become sufficient for his death to be reported on the French radio.[63] The immediate grounds of the breach between Schuon and Guénon were the ever-problematic question of the Transcendent Unity of Religions.[64] Schuon went further than Guénon on this point, holding that Christian initiation retained 'virtual' validity, and needed only to be somehow 'activated.' Whilst Guénon agreed with Schuon in accepting the validity of Masonic initiation, he held that Christian baptism had ceased to have any esoteric value at the end of the Middle Ages.[65] Schuon held that it was impossible for the Christian baptism to lose all validity, since this would be a betrayal by the Holy Ghost.[66] The implications of this dispute in terms of Islam will be considered later. Guénon was also concerned about the laxity of religious practice at Schuon's *zāwiya* in Lausanne; this point will also be considered later.

Lings took Schuon's side in this dispute, even though he was Guénon's close associate, and Vâlsan took Guénon's side, even though he was Schuon's *muqaddam* in Paris.[67] As a result of this dispute the first non-Schuonian Guénonian tariqa arose, since Schuon

---

63. Chacornac 1958, 10.
64. Rawlinson 1997 mentions other grounds: that followers of Schuon felt that Guénon should become Schuon's *muqaddam*, likening the role of ʿAbd al-Wāhid Yahyā Guénon in relation to Nūr al-Dīn ʿĪsā Schuon to that of a more famous Yahyā [John] and ʿĪsā [Jesus].
65. This, of course, is not the view of Islam, which is more concerned with the Prophet Muhammad than the end of the Middle Ages.
66. Lings 1996.
67. Lings describes himself in those years as 'young and tactless'. Relations between him and Guénon deteriorated further because Guénon became concerned that Lings was not merely transmitting his letters, but also opening them. This suspicion is voiced in a letter of Guénon's dated 18 September 1950, excerpted in Devie 1996. It is likely that Guénon's letters had indeed been opened, but by the Egyptian censorship: Lings had been on one occasion summoned by the police to explain apparently coded writing (in fact, Masonic symbols) in one letter addressed to Guénon c/o Lings. Although Lings's wife continued to visit Guénon's wife, relations between Lings and Guénon were interrupted: Lings only saw Guénon once again, when he took a doctor to see him shortly before his death.

instructed Vâlsan to establish his own separate *zāwiya* in Paris, and to receive into it whoever he wanted.[68]

Following on this dispute, on Guénon's death, and on the Revolution in Egypt, the history of Guénonianism can be divided into three streams: Schuonian, non-Schuonian Muslim, and non-Muslim. Of these, the most important is the Schuonian stream: Schuon already had a large following before Guénon's death, and if anyone can be said to have inherited Guénon's position as the leading Traditionalist, it is Schuon. The non-Muslim stream falls outside the scope of this article; the other two streams are clearly 'novel' in the sense established above.

Taking my earlier criteria in reverse: their spreading is not so different from the established Islamic pattern, and on these grounds they might be classified as 'standard.' However, leaving aside for the moment the question of orthodoxy (which, as we will see, is central to the question of how traditional these groups are) groups in both streams must be classified as 'novel' if only because the shaykhs in question are not on the classic Islamic pattern. Schuon, for example, does not take his *silsila* from a universally-accepted source — while the source may be accepted, the taking is problematic. Schuon has later attracted a following among born Muslims in the Muslim world, but those non-Schuonian Guénonians who have a more normal *silsila* have not. Thus, although some Traditionalist Sufis may fulfil one of the two conditions established here, none fulfil both. We will now take Schuon's tariqa, later known as the Maryāmiyya, as one case study, and a non-Schuonian tariqa, that of ʿAbd al-Wāḥid Pallavicini in Milan, as another.

The Maryāmiyya

Schuon moved to the US in 1981,[69] settling outside Bloomington, Indiana, where a Schuonian community had come into existence under the leadership of a professor of comparative religion at Indiana University who had been using Schuon's books in his courses; one of these followers of Schuon had established a *zāwiya* near Blooming-

68. Lings 1996.
69. Nasr 1991, 5.

ton, and offered Schuon adjoining land.[70] The reason normally given
for Schuon's move is his interest in Native American religion,[71] to
which we will return.

I have not visited Bloomington,[72] and the Maryāmiyya is a more
secretive organization than is normal amongst Sufi tariqas (though
no more than is normal amongst Western esoteric organizations). My
conclusions must therefore be tentative, and may be excessively
negative, since criticism sometimes spreads faster than other varieties
of fame. The later Maryāmiyya, for example, is widely criticized for
having 'left Islam' — an accusation normally based on the presence
of non-Muslim followers of Schuon's, and on Maryāmī failure to observe the Islamic Sharia.

In having Christian (and Buddhist) followers,[73] Schuon is not
alone. The US Khalwatiyya-Jarahiyya of the Turkish shaykh Muzaf-
fer Özak, a non-Guénonian tariqa which might be classified as
'standard,' allows non-Muslims to be *muḥibb* of the shaykh, though
only Muslims may be *murīd*.[74] The Naqshbandiyya of al-Ḥaqqanī
also accepts non-Muslims as visiting participants in the tariqa's
activities, and many of these take the Naqshbandiyya *before* becoming
Muslim, though in most cases Islam follows within a few days; it is
not possible for a non-Muslim to follow the practice of the tariqa, and
though there may be a few cases of non-Muslim Naqshbandī followers,
these are anomalous; it is suggested that these individuals may be
Muslim without acknowledging it.[75] Özak and al-Ḥaqqanī thus both

70. Schuon 1993. Catherine Schuon does not give the name of the professor,
    and there is no obvious choice from the IU faculty in 1997. Catherine
    Schuon does not say that there was a 'zāwiya,' but since she talks of 'a
    house where friends could come to pray' a *zāwiya* must be meant, despite
    her later denial that there was any 'community' in Bloomington.
71. This is the explanation, for example, given by Nasr.
72. One senior Maryāmī told me that it was unlikely that Schuon would
    agree to meet me.
73. Various reports.
74. Hermansen 1997, 153. Nasr is evidently on good terms with the Khal-
    watiyya-Jarahiyya, since he wrote the foreword to an English translation
    of the works of their shaykh (Stenberg, e-mail to the author, November
    1996).
75. Observation and various interviews.

make pragmatic concessions; in contrast to Schuon, neither is known to consider Christian sacraments in any way 'valid'- Schuon sees the Christian sacraments as 'initiatory' and Christians as thus able to follow a Master while remaining Christian.[76] Although Schuonians point to great shaykhs of the classical Islamic period who had Christian followers,[77] none of these had non-Muslim followers on the scale that Schuon does. Pragmatic concessions such as those made by Özak and al-Ḥaqqanī are well within Sufi tradition; Schuon's stance is not, and so can hardly be described as traditional.

Similarly, Schuon's tariqa is probably not alone in having (reportedly) relaxed the Sharia somewhat for its adherents, at least in principle: according to Hermansen, all Sufi orders in the US allow for some laxity in the practice of the Sharia, especially for new Muslims,[78] and this is also true of al-Ḥaqqanī's Naqshbandiyya in Europe. Pragmatic concessions in this area, though in some ways dangerous, are understandable. The question is one of degree and duration: while al-Ḥaqqanī may permit new Muslims to pray three times a day rather than five, the clear understanding is that five times a day is the norm, and that this norm should be reached as soon as practicable. There is some indication that Schuon's concessions go further: although I do not know to what extent this represents Schuon's own position, other Schuonians have argued, for example, that it is permissible to delay the dawn prayer in an age of electric light, or to miss Friday prayers and conceal one's Islam in the hostile environment of the contemporary United States. This is an approach different in kind from al-Ḥaqqanī's, and — again — seems to go beyond the tradition of pragmatic concession to verge on modification of the Sharia.

One especially problematic relaxation of the Sharia is Schuon's own. In the late 1940s, for example, he kept in his room a statue of the Virgin Mary. Of this, he wrote later 'I was always strict in matters of sacred law, yet on the other hand I took my stand above all on the

---

76. Pallavicini 1996. Guénon, on the other hand, saw medieval European Christianity as retaining esoteric validity. That he saw any 'validity' in Christian esotericism even after the revelation of Islam is difficult, though not impossible, to reconcile with Islamic teachings.

77. This point was made both by Maryami 1997 and by Nasr 1996.

78. Hermansen 1997, 153.

Religio Perennis and never allowed myself to become imprisoned in forms which for myself could have no validity'.[79] This seems a clear following of Traditionalism in preference to the Sharia. We will return to this question of priorities.

The place of the Virgin Mary in Schuon's tariqa has also caused concern. In 1965, Schuon had a vision of the Virgin (*Maryām* in Arabic), as a result of which he changed the name of his tariqa to 'Maryāmiyya';[80] shortly afterwards, rumours of unorthodoxy were circulating, notably of the display of pictures of the Virgin in the Lausanne *zāwiya*. Such pictures, referred to as 'icons,' were used (at least by the 1980s) as a focus for meditation in the practice of the tariqa.[81] Maryāmīs stress that these icons are not used 'in the *zāwiya*',[82] but this is a distinction which would mean little to most Muslims. In 1985, in a further vision of the Virgin, Schuon received the unusual *wird* 'Ya Maryām ʿaleyka al-salām ya rahman ya rahīm'.[83]

Most problematic of all, however, is Schuon's interest in Native American religion. In 1959 he and his wife were 'adopted officially by the Lakota tribe' of Crow Indians, whom they had first met in Paris on 1958,[84] and in 1963 Schuon and his wife 'were received as members of the Sioux tribe' during the second of their two early visits to the United States to see the Sioux and Crow Indians of South Dakota and Montana.[85] By the 1980s, Schuon was holding events variously known as 'Primordial Gatherings', 'Pow Wows' or 'Indian Days', at which ceremonies such as the 'Rite of the Sacred Pipe' and the Sun Dance were held. Schuon presided over such occasions, sometimes wearing a Native American feather headdress with two horns, and carrying a feathered staff.[86] Maryāmīs stress that Muslim 'initiates' of Schuon were forbidden to *participate* in Native American religious

79. Schuon NDa, 264, quoted in Rawlinson 1997.
80. Rawlinson 1997.
81. Rawlinson 1997 and Sardar 1993, 35.
82. Maryami 1997.
83. Sardar 1993, 35.
84. Schuon 1993.
85. Nasr 1991, 5.
86. Sardar 1993, 35, and Rawlinson 1997. Photographs of one such Gathering were given to the author by Rawlinson.

rites, though not in dances which were not 'rites'.[87] This distinction, like that between an icon of the Virgin in different places, indicates a Schuonian concern to avoid syncretism, but again would satisfy few if any non-Guénonian Muslims; it is in no way a traditional distinction.

A further non-Islamic element in Schuon's practice is nakedness. Following his 1965 vision of the Virgin, Schuon (in his own words) had 'the almost irresistible urge to be naked like her little child; from this event onwards I went naked as often as possible;'[88] in at least the 1985 vision, the Virgin herself was naked.[89] Both Schuon and the Virgin appear naked in certain 'Tantric icons' produced by Schuon and one of his wives, Sharlyn Romaine (Badriyah),[90] and at Primordial Gatherings 'women w[ore] what amount[ed] to American Indianized bikinis' or, at the 'Rite of the Sacred Pipe,' (usually attended only by 50 or 60 followers in the 'inner circle') loin-cloths.[91] Schuon maintains that sacred nakedness is compatible with Islam,[92] a highly unusual position, again far from traditional.

Another non-Islamic element in at least Schuon's own personal life is the application to marriage of a distinction unknown to the *fiqh* or the Sharia, that between the 'vertical,' which reaches to God, and the 'horizontal,' which is of earth, which is frequently made in other contexts by Schuonians.[93] In 1965, Schuon (first married in 1949) 'married' Barbara Perry (Hamidah), in a 'vertical' marriage. That this was a 'vertical' marriage is important: Mrs Perry was still married (in a 'horizontal' marriage) to her husband, Whithall Perry, at the time.[94]

There is thus little room to argue that the practice of the contem-

---

87. Maryami 1997. The same distinction between 'rites' and 'dances' was made by Catherine Schuon in a marginal comment on a draft sent her by Devie (reproduced in Devie 1994, 10-11).
88. Schuon NDb, quoted in Rawlinson 1997.
89. Sardar 1993, 35.
90. Rawlinson 1997. Rawlinson has provided the author with a photograph of such a painting.
91. Sardar 1993, 35, and Rawlinson 1997. Rawlinson's photograph of a Gathering shows bikinis.
92. Rawlinson 1997.
93. For example, Nasr — see Stenberg 1996. The distinction may derive from Guénon's *Symbolisme de la croix*.
94. Rawlinson 1997.

porary Maryāmiyya is traditional. Though it undoubtedly contains
traditional elements, and although Schuon's published works may
often be compatible with Islamic tradition, the totality of his followers' practice contains sufficient non-Islamic elements to be described
as 'new'.

The Aḥmadiyya

In about 1949, ʿAbd-al Wāḥid Pallavicini (1926-), a wealthy young
Italian who had read Guénon's *Crise du monde moderne*, visited its Italian translator, Evola. Evola told Pallavicini that his own interests
were more in temporal than spiritual power, and referred him instead
to Burckhardt, at whose hands Pallavicini in 1951 became Muslim
and took the ʿAlawī tariqa, and the name of ʿAbd al-Wāḥid Yaḥyā.[95]
Having earlier broken with Schuon over the vexed question of the
validity of Christian initiation, Pallavicini visited (in 1971) the *zāwiya*
in Singapore of the Aḥmadī shaykh ʿAbd al-Rashīd ibn Muḥammad
Said (1918-92), an Azharī *ʿālim* as well as an important shaykh.[96]

The Aḥmadī *zāwiya* and the *dhikr* very much impressed Pallavicini, who took the Aḥmadī tariqa. During the six months he spent with
his new shaykh, Pallavicini learned the Aḥmadī *awrād*;[97] although he
could only understand ʿAbd al-Rashīd through an interpreter, he also
had numerous conversations with Ali Salim, later ʿAbd al-Rashīd's
khalīfa.[98] On one occasion, ʿAbd al-Rashīd suggested that they should
pray for the conversion to Islam of Pallavicini's parents. Pallavicini
demurred, saying that they were all right as they were, as People of

95. Pallavicini 1996. Burckhardt was no sympathizer of Evola's: when
    Pallavicini passed on a question of Evola's to Burckhardt — why was
    Burckhardt no longer publishing his articles — Burckhardt replied in sur-
    prise: 'Does Monsieur Evola not remember that he trained the SS?' The
    question of a link through Guénon and Evola to the occultist elements of
    the NSDAP is a fascinating one, which lies far beyond the scope of this
    article.
96. For details, see Sedgwick 1998.
97. Pallavicini 1996.
98. Ali Salim, 1994 & 1996. Some of these conversations took place while
    Pallavicini was playing his piano, and are remembered by Ali Salim as
    amongst the more bizarre episodes of his life.

the Book, and could expect to go to Heaven as non-Muslims — a Guénonian view more than an Islamic one. In order to resolve their disagreement, the two wrote to the Azhar for a fatwa — which, unsurprisingly, supported ʿAbd al-Rashīd.[99] Either before or despite this dispute, Pallavicini was given an *ijāza* by ʿAbd al-Rashīd.[100] Given that the two earlier *ijāzas* — which we know were received by Guénonians — were somewhat unusual, it is interesting to see how Pallavicini came to receive his. ʿAbd al-Rashīd is only known to have given four other *ijāzas*, and of these only one went to someone who was not a long-established Aḥmadī, the Director of Dakwah in Brunei, already an important Muslim dignitary. Pallavicini was a very different case, and seems to have been a departure from ʿAbd al-Rashīd's normal practice. It is impossible to say why ʿAbd al-Rashīd decided to give Pallavicini an *ijāza*,[101] but shaykhs in any tariqa do sometimes give *ijāzas* for their recipients to 'grow into'. Another partial explanation is that ʿAbd al-Rashīd was perhaps reverting to an earlier Aḥmadī practice, evidently followed at some times by his father, of distributing *ijāzas* almost wholesale. At any rate, Pallavicini's *ijāza*, unlike Schuon's, seems to have been entirely regular; on this basis his tariqa might almost be classified as 'standard'.

On returning to Italy, Pallavicini went first to Rome; he had at that time no particular intention of doing anything with his *ijāza*.[102] It was not until the end of the 1970s that a fortuitous combination of circumstances led to the establishment of an Aḥmadiyya in Europe: Pallavicini became involved in Muslim-Christian dialogue and so became famous, and used his fame to spread the Guénonian message. One of the high points of Pallavicini's involvement with this dialogue was the Day of Prayer held by Pope John Paul in Assisi on 27 October 1986, at which representatives of twelve religions met together to pray for peace.[103] Ten delegations represented Islam; Pallavicini went

99. Ali Salim 1994.
100. Pallavicini 1996.
101. He is said by his son to have later been 'very angry' with Pallavicini, though again it is not clear exactly why (Muhammad Zabid 1996).
102. Pallavicini 1996.
103. The twelve were: African and Amerindian animists, Baha'is, Buddhists, Christians, Jains, Jews, Hindus, Muslims, Shintoists, Sikhs and Zoroastrians (*New York Times* 28 October 1986, p. A3).

with the CICI, the main Islamic organization in Rome, made a speech to a 'round table of the representatives of religions' and issued a press release.[104] Pallavicini became a popular interviewee for the Italian newspapers,[105] reflecting the role he had played at Assisi, because a much-interviewed person becomes newsworthy anyhow, and because at this time the position of Islam in Italy was changing significantly. By 1990, Pallavicini had become the most-interviewed Muslim in Catholic papers, a sort of Muslim 'de confiance'[106] and was even being described by the major newspaper *Corriere della Sera* as shaykh 'of one of the most important *Sufi* brotherhoods'.[107]

During his Muslim-Christian dialogue, Pallavicini did not try to proselytize for Islam, but found that many of those persons with whom he was trying to carry out an inter-religious dialogue became Muslim (and Aḥmadī), so that in the end the 'dialogue with Christians' became a 'monologue of Muslims'.[108] By 1996, three buildings in Milan housed Pallavicini's Milan home, the *Centro Studi Metafisici 'René Guénon'*,[109] the *zāwiya* of the Aḥmadiyya in Italy, the *Associazione Italiana per l'Informazione sull'Islam* (AIII),[110] and *Sintesi* (a small publishing house).[111]

Pallavicini's followers see themselves more as members of the *Centro Studi Metafisici* than as Aḥmadīs. During their monthly meeting in January 1996, time was divided more or less equally between considering their next step in a new round of the old controversy over the validity of Christian initiation (being held with a Greek-Orthodox Guénonian in the pages of the Guénonian publication *Vers la tradi-*

---

104. Numerous verbal reports confirm his attendance.
105. Allievi & Dassetto 1993, 195.
106. Allievi 1996.
107. Trabucchi 1990.
108. Pallavicini 1996.
109. Later called simply the 'Metaphysical Studies Centre *of Milan*', after objections from Guénon's family (Yahyā Pallavicini, interview, January 1996).
110. In non-Italian contexts, the meaning of the first 'I' in AIII is usually changed from *Italiano* to *Internazionale*.
111. Where no other source is given, information such as this derives from my fieldtrip to the Milan Aḥmadiyya in January 1996.

tion),[112] and such recognizably Sufi activities as prayer, *dhikr*, and communal living in the *zāwiya*. This dual identity — as Aḥmadī Muslims and as Guénonians — persists at other times: various Aḥmadīs spend much time attending almost every conceivable possible forum to spread the Guénonian view, but also perform the normal Muslim duties and the Aḥmadī *awrād*.

The strong identity of Milan Aḥmadīs as Guénonians combines, in many cases, with a somewhat weak identity as Muslims. Milan Aḥmadīs are separated from most other Muslims not only by disputes, but by geography and language. This is not true of Pallavicini himself or of his son Yaḥyā, both of whom have contacts with the Islamic world and with various sections of the Aḥmadiyya, but it is true of almost everyone else. It is less true, in contrast, for the Western followers of al-Ḥaqqanī, who are inevitably in contact with the significant numbers of immigrants among his followers in the West, and who may also from time to time visit their shaykh in the Muslim world, as well as seeing him on his regular visits to the West.

Were it not for the dual identity of its followers, Pallavicini's Aḥmadiyya could be described not only as a standard tariqa, but also as traditional. The Milan Aḥmadīs are all Muslim, and no significant variations of the Sharia are known; their practice is orthodox and their *silsila* recognized. The spread of the Aḥmadiyya from Singapore to Milan differs little from the spread of the Aḥmadiyya from Singapore to Brunei or the Naqshbandiyya to Germany. Pallavicini himself was evidently accepted as an Aḥmadī shaykh by Aḥmad ibn Idrīs al-Idrīsī (a descendant of Aḥmad ibn Idrīs, fount of the Aḥmadiyya) when they met in Dubai, since Aḥmad ibn Idrīs al-Idrīsī instructed

---

112. Nikos Vardhikas had reviewed Pallavicini's *L'Islam intérieur* in *Vers la tradition* 61 (Sept. 1995), 55-57. The review had been generally sympathetic and complimentary, but raised questions over Pallavicini's rejection of Christian baptism as a valid rite of initiation. The following edition 62 (Dec. 1995), 49-51, carried a reply signed by the *Centro Studi Metafisici* objecting principally to Vardhikas's views on initiation, as well as a one-page reply to this by Vardhikas (p. 51). A five-page draft was discussed on at least three occasions over the weekend, for a total of several hours. The controversy was obscure to a non-Guénonian; in mainstream Islamic terms it was also incomprehensible, if not entirely meaningless.

Pallavicini to give the Aḥmadiyya to his son Yaḥyā, then aged fif-teen.[113] The dual identity, however, produces conflicts in the area of Transcendent Unity, both in doctrine (Pallavicini's recognition of the validity of Christianity, if not of Christian initiation) and in practice (a tendency to urge Italians to return to Catholicism rather than to be-come Muslim).

The Milan Aḥmadiyya came to be on very bad terms with most of the rest of the Islamic community in Italy, largely for this reason. Pallavicini's high exposure in the press, his unorthodox views on Transcendent Unity — the belief that revelations preceding Islam still remain valid for '[their] believers... not only because they believe in them, but also because [they] are indeed true relative to the commu-nity for which [they] are destined'[114] — and his emphasis on 'Sayyidunâ 'Isâ (on whom be Peace), the Christ, 'the Seal of Sanc-tity'[115] could hardly be expected to pass unremarked, and they did not. He has been criticized for his views on the transcendent unity of religions, for ignorance of the Arabic language, for 'fill[ing] the de-ficiencies [of his knowledge of Islamic] doctrine with his own person-al theories, the enunciation of which is a clear form of *kufr*', and for actually discouraging Christians from becoming Muslim.[116] Relations at one point became so bad that many non-Aḥmadī Muslims refused to return Pallavicini's *salamāt* (which is *ḥarām* unless the greeting comes from a non-Muslim). A demonstration against him was on one occasion organized outside a bookshop in Rome where he was speak-ing, and on another occasion he was physically ejected from the CICI in Rome; the Aḥmadiyya had to change the mosque in which they

113. Pallavicini 1996.
114. Pallavicini 1990.
115. See, for example, Pallavicini 1992. The description of Jesus as *rasūl* [the title reserved for the Prophet Muḥammad] (Pallavicini 1985) is presum-ably a slip of the pen.
116. Letters printed in *Il Messagero dell'Islam* from Abdu-l-Rahim Yahya (5:3, 15 Dec. 1986), Ali Schutz (5:5, Feb./March 1987) and Abdu-l-Hadi Ibn Yahya (5:16, 15 Apr. 1987). Schutz 1996 stated that his name had been borrowed by the then editor of *Il Messagero*, ʿAbd al-Raḥman (Danilo Rosario) Pasquini, who may also have been the author of the other two letters.

prayed on Fridays, and finally retreated to their own *zāwiya*.[117] This state of affairs did not last, and by 1995 Pallavicini had to some extent been 'rehabilitated'.

Sections of the Muslim community in Italy, then, clearly rejected Pallavicini's Aḥmadiyya as being (in our terms) other than traditional, but this rejection took place within a particular context. At about the same time as it attacked Pallavicini, however, *Il Messagero dell'Islam* also ran a full-page article with the title: 'Sufism is not Islam!'[118] This view is itself also far from traditional: it is characteristic of the Salafi reformers and their descendants, and while it may now have become part of a strong current within the Islamic mainstream, rejection of Pallavicini on the grounds that he is a Sufi is inconclusive. Some of the further grounds for Pallavicini's opponents' rejection of him, however, are indicative: his views on the status of Christianity, for example, are Guénonian rather than Islamic.[119]

Conclusion

Whilst immigrants' tariqas in the West are as traditional as those in non-Western countries with significant Muslim minorities or as those in the Muslim world itself, only those Western Sufi tariqas which can be classified as 'standard' can safely be assumed to be traditional. Whilst non-Muslim groups are clearly 'new' in the sense of 'New Religious Movement', the intermediate category of 'novel' tariqas, and especially the Traditionalist or Guénonian tariqas, may sometimes be significantly 'new' like the Maryāmiyya; they may also be broadly traditional, within certain limits, like the Milan Aḥmadiyya.

This conclusion is open to dispute, above all by those who see religion as a cultural construct. For those who stress the differences between Moroccan and Indonesian Islam, and who would even dispute that there *is* 'one' Islam, the implication that the Singapore Aḥmadiyya and the Milan Aḥmadiyya are the same thing might appear

---

117. Schutz 1996 and Allievi 1996, confirmed in part by Pallavicini 1996.
118. *Il Messagero dell'Islam* 5:17 (15 May 1987), 5.
119. While Guénonians may argue that this view *should* be the proper Islamic view, it is undeniable that, in general, it is not the mainstream Islamic view.

little short of preposterous. It is implicit in this article that I do not share this view. Though it is clear that not all Muslims at all times and in all places have believed exactly the same things and behaved in exactly the same way, there is a central core of beliefs and practices which all Sunni Muslims have always shared, and these — in my view — constitute 'one' Islam. Secondly, as has been pointed out by other scholars,[120] horizontal distinctions may matter more than vertical ones. The son of the Shaykh ʿAbd al-Rashīd of Singapore, from whom Pallavicini took the Aḥmadiyya, holds a PhD from a French university and teaches at a Malaysian university, and has probably more in common with Pallavicini himself, than either he or Pallavincini have with an illiterate Aḥmadī peasant from the remote northern Malay state of Kelantan.

This conclusion is also open to more serious dispute on grounds of motivation. The dual identity of the Milan Aḥmadiyya, as Guénonians and as Muslims, gives rise to the suspicion that an Aḥmadī may be Muslim *because* he is Guénonian, rather than be Muslim *and* Guénonian. In the case of Schuon and many of his followers, this Guénonian motivation towards Islam is clear: it is implicit in Schuon's reasoning over his statue of the Virgin in the 1940s, and almost explicit in what some Maryāmīs say in private conversation. Being Muslim and Guénonian potentially gives rise to the same difficulties as does being Muslim and, say, Marxist: to what extent can a Muslim legitimately defer to an authority which derives its bases from outside Islam? Being Muslim *because* one is Guénonian is even more difficult: who comes first, the Prophet Muḥammad or Guénon? That Pallavicini, for example, parted with Schuon because Schuon disagreed with *Guénon* — not with the Prophet or with Islam — would make most Muslims uncomfortable, as would Pallavicini's habit of taking Guénon (rather than God or the Prophet) as his standard authority in his speeches and articles. This question of motivation may be the final irreducible difference between Guénonian Sufis and all others. While it is not really within the realm of practice, to which I limited myself at the beginning of this article, it results in an almost tangible difference of orientation between followers of al-Ḥaqqanī — who have become Muslim because the truth of Islam and the *baraka*

120. See, for example, Abaza 1993.

of their shaykh burst upon them as a blinding light — and the Sufi inhabitants of Traditional Study Centres.

Bibliography

Abaza, Mona 1993. *Changing Images of Three Generations of Azharites in Indonesia.* Singapore: Institute of South East Asian Studies.
Ali Salim 1994. Interview in Dandara, Egypt, August.
Ali Salim 1996. Various interviews in Singapore, March.
Allievi, Stefano 1996. Interview in Milan, January.
Allievi, Stefano and Felice Dassetto 1993. *Il rittorno dell'Islam: i musulmani in Italia.* Rome: Edizioni Lavoro.
Borella, Jean 1992. 'René Guénon and the Traditionalist School'. In: Antoine Faivre and Jakob Needleman (eds.), *Modern Esoteric Spirituality.* New York: Crossroads, 330-58.
Caspar, Robert 1974 and 1975. 'Mystique Musulmane. Bilan d'une décennie [1963-1973]', *Institut de Belles Lettres Arabes* [Tunis] vol. 133, 69-101; and vol. 135, 39-111.
Chacornac, Paul 1958. *La vie simple de Rene Guenon.* Paris: Ed. traditionelles.
De Jong, Fred 1978. *Turuq and Turuq-linked Institutions in Nineteenth Century Egypt: A Historical Study in Organizational Dimensions of Islamic Mysticism.* Leiden: E.J. Brill.
Dermenghem, Emile 1923. *Joseph de Maistre mystique.* Paris: La Colombe, 1946.
Devie, Dominique 1994. *Dossier 'Affaire Schuon' ou les tribulations d'une idôle déchue.* Paris: Privately printed.
Devie, Dominique 1996. 'Lettres de René Guénon'. In: *The File on the Schuon Case: The History of a Psuedo-Guénonian Cult,* http://www.mygale.org/00/cret/ltguenon.htm, accessed 13 Dec.
Gilsenan, Michael 1973. *Saint and Sufi in Modern Egypt: An Essay in the Sociology of Religion.* Oxford: Oxford University Press.
Godwin, Joscelyn 1996. 'L'entrée des philosophes orientales dans l'ésoterisme occidentale'. Paper presented at a conference on 'Symboles et mythes dans les mouvements initiatiques et ésotériques' at the Sorbonne Nouvelle, 11-12 October.

Guénon, René 1921a. *Introduction générale à l'étude des doctrines hindoues*. Paris: M. Rivière.

Guénon, René 1921b. *Le théosophisme, histoire d'une pseudo-religion.* Paris.

Guénon, René 1923. *L'erreur spirite*. Paris.

Guénon, René 1925. *L'homme et son devenir selon le Vedanta*. Paris: Bossard.

Habibis, Daphne 1990. 'Mahdism in a Branch of a Contemporary Naqshbandī Order in Lebanon'. In: Marc Gaborieau, Alexandre Popovic and Thierry Zarcone (eds.), *Naqshbandis: cheminements et situation actuelle d'un ordre mystique musulman*. Istanbul: Isis, 603-19.

Hermansen, Marcia K. 1998. 'In the Garden of American Sufi Movements: Hybrids and Perennials'. In: Peter B. Clarke (ed.), *New Islamic Movements: New Trends and Developments in the World of Islam*. London: Oriental Press, 155-79.

Hermansen, Marcia K. 2000. 'Hybrid Identity Formations in Muslim America: The Case of American Sufi Movements'. *Muslim World*, spring 2000 (9, 1 & 2): 158-97.

Holdijk, Lammert 1997. 'The Spread of the Naqshbandī Sufi Order within the Mediterranean and Beyond'. Paper presented at a conference on Cross-cultural Encounters in the Mediterranean, American University in Cairo, 13-15 May.

James, Marie-France 1981. *Esotérisme, Ocultisme, Franc-Maçonnerie et Christianisme aux XIXe et XXe siècles. Explorations bio-bibliographiques*. Paris.

Levy, John 1951. *Immediate Knowledge and Happiness: Hindu Doctrine of Vedanta*. London.

Lings, Martin 1961. *A Sufi Saint of the Twentieth Century: Shaikh Aḥmad al-ʿAlawī*. London: George Allen & Unwin.

Lings, Martin 1995. 'René Guénon', *Sophia* vol. 1, 21-37.

Lings, Martin 1996. Interview in Surrey, England, September.

Maryāmī 1997. Interview with a senior long-term Maryāmī who wished to remain anonymous.

Mir-Hosseini, Ziba 1994. 'Inner Truth and Outer History: The Two Worlds of the Ahl-i Ḥaqq of Kurdistan', *International Journal of Middle East Studies*, vol. 26, 267-85.

Muhammad Zabid 1996. Interview in Kuala Lumpur, April.

Nasr, Seyyed Hossein 1991. 'Biography of Frithjof Schuon'. In: Nasr and Stoddart 1991, 1-6.

Nasr, Seyyed Hossein 1996. Interview in Washington DC, May.

Nasr, Seyyed Hossein and William Stoddart (eds.) 1991. *Religion of the Heart: Essays Presented to Frithjof Schuon on his Eightieth Birthday.* Washington: Foundation for Traditional Studies.

Oldmeadow, Kenneth S. 1982. *Frithjof Schuon, the Perennial Philosophy and the Meaning of Tradition: A Study of Traditionalism.* MA thesis, University of Sydney.

Paillard, Denis 1993. 'Encouragée par des activistes occidentaux: L'inquiétante renaissance de l'extrême droite'. *Le Monde diplomatique,* January.

Pallavicini, Abdul Wāhid 1985. 'Death and Immortality'. Lecture given at the Catholic University of Rome, and reprinted in Pallavicini 1995, 123-31.

Pallavicini, Abdul Wāhid 1990. 'At the Full Price'. Speech delivered at the Institute of San Carlo of Modena, printed in *Sacro e Profano,* vol. 4 (1990), and reprinted in Pallavicini 1995, 147-52.

Pallavicini, Abdul Wāhid 1992. 'On the Immanent Unity of Orthodox Religions'. Speech delivered at the Pontifical Institute for Foreign Missions, and reprinted in Pallavicini 1995, 163-71.

Pallavicini, Abdul Wāhid 1995. *L'islam intérieur: La spiritualité universelle dans la religion islamique.* Paris: Christian de Bartillat.

Pallavicini, Abdul Wāhid 1996. Various interviews in Milan, January.

Pallis, Marco 1978. 'A Fateful Meeting of Minds: AK Coomaraswamy and R Guénon', *Studies in Comparative Religion,* vol. 12, 176-88.

Quinn, William W. 1997. *The Only Tradition.* Albany: SUNY Press.

Rawlinson, Andrew 1993. 'A History of Western Sufism', *Diskus,* vol. 1(1), 45-83.

Rawlinson, Andrew 1997. *The Book of Enlightened Masters: Western Teachers in Eastern Traditions.* Chicago: Open Court Press.[121]

Robin, Jean 1986. *René Guénon: témoin de la tradition.* Paris: Guy Trédaniel.

---

121. References to this work are to a manuscript version containing some information not included in the shorter, published version. For this reason, no page references are given.

Sardar, Ziauddun 1993. 'A Man for All Seasons', *Impact International*, December, 33-36.

Schuon, Catherine 1993. Letter to Dominique Devie, 2 April 1993, reproduced in Devie 1994, 54.

Schuon, Frithjof (n.d.). Autobiography. MS, privately circulated.

Schuon, Frithjof (n.d.) 'Sacred Nudity'. MS, privately circulated.

Schutz, Ali 1996. Interview in Milan.[122]

Sedgwick, Mark J.R. 1998. *The Transmission of Tradition: The Spread and Normalization of the Ahmadiyya, 1799-1996.* Doctor Philos. thesis, University of Bergen.

Stenberg, Leif 1996. *The Islamization of Science: Four Muslim Positions Developing an Islamic Modernity.* Lund: Religionshistoriska avdelningen, Lunds Universitet.

Stoddart, William 1987. 'Titus Burckhardt: An Outline of his Life and Works'. In: Titus Burckhardt, *Mirror of the Intellect: Essays on traditional Science and Sacred Art.* Cambridge: Quinta Essentia, 3-9.

Trabucchi, Stefania 1990. '"Un centro per capire l'Islam": Lo 'shaikh' Pallavicini e l'incontro tra Allah e Roma', *Corriere della Sera* [Rome edition], 30 July, 18.

Vâlsan, Michel 1984. *L'islam et la fonction de René Guénon: recueil posthume.* Paris: Ed. de l'Oeuvre.

Waterfield, Robin 1987. *René Guénon and the Future of the West: The Life and Writings of a 20th-century Metaphysician.* UK: Crucible Press.

---

122. Ali Schutz is the Secretary of the UCOII, a major Italian Islamic organization.

CHAPTER 4

Tantric Influences in Western Esotericism

Albertina Nugteren

Edward Said's book *Orientalism* often functions as a starting point, or point of reference, in the discussion of the 'imagined' Orient versus the Orient of real people and real Earth.[1] Southern Asia (i.e., India before Independence, especially including Sri Lanka, Tibet, and Burma) certainly was the object of a vast share of images and imaginings,[2] often functioning as a projection screen on which the West projected its wishful thinking or the reverse images of its own deficiencies and preoccupations. As imagination and wishful thinking — such as par-allellism — are especially fertile in esotericism, my paper is bound to tone down some previous statements about the extent to which Tantrism swept the West.[3]

Tantrism came into existence in India, both in Hinduism and in Buddhism, between the sixth and the seventh century AD. It was a kind of esoteric reaction against established religion. It developed many philosophical, theological, and especially cosmological and liturgical aspects of its own, although in the West Tantrism is usually associated with sex: Tantric massage, Tantric sexuality, and Tantric love techniques[4]. Others, somewhat better informed, know to asso-

1. Said 1979.
2. For Tibet as a projection screen, see Bishop 1989 and 1992. For Hinduism, see Inden 1990; Breckenridge and van der Veer (eds.) 1993; Wezler 1993, 305-29.
3. For a useful introduction to the phenomenon of parallellism see Restivo 1978, 143-81.
4. Popular books among the Western public are: Anand 1989 and 1995; Mumford 1988.

ciate the word Tantrism with cakras, kundalini, and yoga.[5] Since anything in Western esotericism even vaguely connected with sacred
sexuality or with kundalini practice is being attributed to Tantrism
nowadays, I will try to put a few things straight, and reestablish their
historical proportions.

This paper is about the Western reception, incorporation and adap-
tation of this one particular aspect of Indian religion, Tantrism. First
I will make a few remarks on the influence of South Asian religions
on the West in general. In the second section, I concentrate on certain
'Tantra-like' ideas and practices in Western esotericism. In the third
section, I elaborate on the actual contents of Western Tantrism. Finally, in the fourth section, I make a few tentative remarks about Tantrism towards the new millennium.

The Influence of South Asian Religions

The influence of South Asian religions on Western thought and practice can be seen as having taken place in three waves. The *first* wave,
in the second half of the eighteenth century, is almost purely literary:
some of the main texts, having become known through the colonial
presence in India, were translated into Western languages, and could
thus exert their influence on small circles of enthusiasts, like those in
the Transcendentalist Movement and in New Thought. On the tail of
this wave, we meet the founders of the Theosophical Movement,
Madame Blavatsky and General Olcott, who actually went to India in
1879 and established their International Headquarters in Adyar,
South India. This started the gradual shift of interest in ancient Egypt
to interest in an imagined India and Tibet as sources of esoteric
thought. From the very beginning this shift met with opposition from
proponents of the Western esoteric tradition.

The *second* wave started at the end of the nineteenth century and
the beginning of the twentieth century. Most historical studies of this
process tend to over-emphasize the activities at the Western side of
the market, thus playing down the role of what enabled the actual ex-

---

5. For some popular books among Western readers see: King 1986; Swami
    Sivananda Radha 1978; Mumford 1973; Mookerjee 1982; Swami Satya-
    nanda Saraswati 1985.

change. The 1893 'World Parliament of Religions' played a vital role in this exchange by inviting representatives of Asian denominations to Chicago. But the contribution of those Indian spokesmen was a result of developments that had taken place prior to this in South Asia itself. These developments included the emergence of reform movements, such as the Brahmo Samaj, and the start of the so-called Hindu and Buddhist Renaissance.[6]

Those developments gave the Indian representatives their position, their prestige, their programme, as well as their rhetoric, and set the pattern for the following decades. On the esoteric side of the exchange, there was a noticeable tendency to promote the Indian subcontinent in the reconstruction and revitalization of the Ancient Mysteries. Even more so, the Indo-Tibetan realm was made prominent due to the myths of the Great White Brotherhood, the Himalayan Masters, and the Akasha Chronicle, as well as those of Shambhala and Shangrila. There are very few esoteric societies which remained immune to this tendency. When we study the publications of these societies, we notice the influx of general ideas as avatara, reincarnation, karma, dharma, avidya, and samsara, as well as specific notions such as kundalini, and ritual practices such as meditation and visualization. Some of the nineteenth-century Western secret societies established an inner or esoteric section for those who wanted to further explore the practice, but it was only around the turn of the century that serious adherents started to make some form of yoga into a daily discipline, and actually saw the necessity of prolonged and regular practice.[7]

American authors tend to hold that the *third* wave began with the lowering of the immigration barriers in 1965. In general, one could say that this was merely one of the factors involved. Asian teachers could more easily settle in America, establish their organizations, and

6. Good overviews are to be found in Schwab 1984; Kopf 1969; and Godwin 1994.
7. Now that the first overviews of Hindu and Buddhist presence in the Western world are being written, it is often Henry David Thoreau who is identified as the first American actually practising 'Orientalism'. This might be true in a general sense, but since he had no meditation method to rely on other than his own, I hesitate to label his musings and rêverie, however sincere, as yoga.

attract Western devotees on a far larger scale than before. Yet it should be emphasized that the post-war cross- cultural mobility and general dissatisfaction with established Western values were the main factors in the surge of all things 'Eastern'. A new wave of Indian gurus came to establish their societies all over the world, as did Zen Buddhist monks and Tibetan lamas.

What was significantly different from the previous period was the growing number of scholarly translations and monographs, as well as an avalanche of devotional and sectarian literature from masters, disciples, and disciples' disciples, both Asian and Western. Although there was a renewed interest in things occult and esoteric at the end of the 1950s, it was only with the emergence of the so-called New Age-Movement that we can speak of a continued Western esoteric tradition in a broader sense. Along with the existing traditional secret societies we notice the more open Human Potential Movement and New Age market, of which Asian religions form one of the ingredients.

Tantra-like Ideas and Practices

At this point, we shift the focus to Tantrism. As a result, we have to return to the middle and the end of the nineteenth century. Hardly anyone in the Western world knew what Tantrism was at that time, and Indian pandits only reluctantly admitted there was such a thing as a Tantric tradition or Tantric literature.[8] Tantrism can be seen as an

8. One of the earliest sources for 'Orientalist' ideas is, of course, the series of publications by the Asiatick Society of Bengal, the *Asiatick Researches*, starting in 1788. Copies were sent to Europe and America, and they created a sensation. Although the main interest was in law, language and literature, some remarks about 'Hindoo sects' seem to have made lasting impressions on Western esotericists of the nineteenth century. The actual translation of the Tantras was started by Sir John Woodroffe, alias Arthur Avalon, who made some main Tantras available from 1910 onwards. There is a rumour that he became interested in Tantras when some Tantric master had been idling and muttering mantras beneath his window in the Court Room in Calcutta. Since those mantras seemed to remedy his sleepiness and lack of concentration, he went after the fellow to hear more.

esoteric reaction to the mainstream of Hindu and Buddhist religious practice, which was dominated by caste-conscious priests (in Hinduism) and celibate scholar-monks (in Buddhism). But one could also say that it was a democratic revitalization of liturgical and ritualistic practices. Tantrism is partly drawing on Vedic ritualism, classical Yoga sources, epic cosmology, and the ancient goddess tradition. It is also partly rebellious and new, in the sense that it constructed a system and a worldview that was unconventional. In any case, it was not clerical; one qualified not by birth, like the brahmin, nor by one's status in the order of monks, like the bhikkhu, but by the state of one's inner realization. In the texts, called Tantras, philosophically and theologically the universe is seen as oscillating between two poles, often called Shiva and Shakti, or the passive male energy and the active female energy. Its most apparent characteristic is the abundance of practical methods. Mystically and esoterically it aims at the total transformation of human existence. Its most elaborate practices are ritual worship, meditation, visualization and sacred sexuality.[9]

In the nineteenth century, Tantrism was not well known and it was rarely practised outside small circles in India itself. The Victorian impact on India was such that its very existence was often denied, especially in the light of puritanical reformations then taking place. Yet some Western esotericists, experimenting with meditation, visualization, breathing exercises, and sacred sexuality (such as Paschal Beverly Randolph and the leaders of the Hermetic Order of the Golden Dawn) had certain techniques resembling those of both left- and righthanded Tantrism in India and Tibet.[10] This is why they were

9. Worth reading is Agehananda Bharati 1975, as well as his autobiography from 1970. For Buddhist Tantrism, see Guenther 1972. A thorough and scholarly exposition is Goudriaan and Gupta 1981.

10. One of the acknowledged sources of the so-called 'Tattwa' visualization at the end of the nineteenth century, is a booklet called *Nature's Finer Forces*. In the translation the author's name is given as Rama Prasada, and the subtitle as *The science of breath and the philosophy of the tattvas*. The book was published by the Theosophical Society in London and New York in 1894. I regret not having been able to trace the Indian source yet. The same goes for some references in Randolph's privately circulated writings, for instance when he speaks about the 'Tibetan method, siyalam'.

referred to, by some later authors, as 'Tantrists', 'Tantrists-avant-la-lettre', 'quasi-Tantrists', and so forth. Research in both the history of translated Tantras, and in the Western esotericism of the last two centuries, shows that there was no direct influence from Tantric texts prior to the beginning of this century. Randolph comes very close to certain aspects of Tantrism, for instance, in his prescriptions concerning the preparation for ritual sex, or his allusion to the magical use of the intense concentration of orgasm for directing the will.[11] But those techniques can only be called Tantra-like, never Tantra-derived or Tantric. The only verified way in which the scant information about Tantrism has trickled through before the twentieth century is by indirect references and in travellers' accounts from Arabia, Tibet, and India.

Some proponents of the practice of yoga around the turn of the century hinted at the subtle physiology now often connected with Tantrism. However, in some Upanishads, especially the so-called Yoga Upanishads, we already find references to the subtle body, in terms of nadis, cakras, ida, pingala, sushumna, and kundalini.[12] These Upanishads did not have the odium characteristic of the Tantras and were far better known all over India. They seem to form one of the main sources of Tantrism, but it would be an anachronism to call any allusion to this terminology 'Tantric'. Instead, it is just 'yogic'.

It is only as a result of the availability of Tantras in translation, the reports of Western travellers actually initiated into a Tantric sect in South India (such as David Curwen, a friend of Alister Crowley), or in Bengal (such as Karl Kellner, also connected with Crowley through Theodor Reuss and the O.T.O.), and the presence of Indian and Tibetan masters giving higher initiations into Tantric practice, that we can

---

11. Randolph's books that were meant for a broader public have been kept in print, but his privately printed material has become extremely rare. Of his key work, *Magia Sexualis*, only copies of the French translation (1969) are said to exist. On sexual magic, see Culling1971 — reprint 1988. A practical manual is Anand 1995.

12. See, for instance, Weiss 1986; and Varenne 1989.

speak of an actual presence of Tantrism on the margins of Western eso-tericism.[13]

Despite the growing acknowledgement of the existence of Tan-trism, some of the Indian masters were not willing or knowledgeable enough to call their higher initiations Tantric. They were from those regions where Tantrism had gradually seeped into practically all the traditional and popular forms of religion for centuries. As a result, there might have been more covert Tantrist practice (of the right-hand variety) in the first quarter of the twentieth century than we are able to prove with written documents.[14]

In general we should say that Tantrism then wasn't an acknow-ledged or accepted phenomenon outside the circle of a few eccentrics (such as that of Kellner, Reuss, Crowley, Sellon and Curwen), and that even those knew very little about it[15]. It was only when Tantras became more widely known and understood outside Asia, as a result of the pioneering efforts of Sir John Woodroffe, Alexandra David-Neel, Giuseppe Tucci, Lama Anagarika Govinda, Herbert Guenther and Agehananda Bharati, that some idea of this comprehensive system could be formed by a select audience. Still, one has to carefully dis-tinguish here between the sacred sexuality and sexual magic that had

13. For our investigation it is important to know that the German Ordo Templi Orientis, a fraternity initiating into higher grades of so-called Western Tantrism, has its obscure origins partly in Randolph's writings, partly in the Rosicrucian and Swedenborgian traditions, and partly in the Oriental travels of Karl Kellner, a wealthy German iron-founder and high-grade freemason, who claimed to have learned sexual magic from two Sufi adepts and a Bengali Tantric.

14. It is extremely difficult to avoid the pitfalls of a Western myopic preoccu-pation with scriptural tradition and yet do justice to a clear historically demarcated definition of Tantrism in the West. It could well be that with the advance of the academic study of the Western esoteric tradition that methods will be developed to do justice to some of the peculiarities of eso-teric knowledge, such as eclecticism, parallellism and the oral or initia-tory transmission of a tradition.

15. David Curwen, a friend of Crowley's, was a member of the IXth degree of the O.T.O., as well as having been initiated into a South Indian Kaula tradition. Edward Sellon, who had lived in South India for some time, wrote about the sacred writings of the Hindus, illustrating their Priapic Rites and Phallic Principles [new edition 1902].

been part of the Western esoteric tradition for much longer, and the totality of the Tantric tradition, of which the explicit sexual practice was only a minor aspect. Practices like tattva visualization and kundalini meditation were known and experimented with in several esoteric sections of theosophical and hermetic orders at the end of the nineteenth century. Studying the sources from which Madame Blavatsky had her information about things Indian or Tibetan, we could identify some of the historical Indian citizens she associated with, their libraries of Sanskrit and Tibetan texts, and the living traditions she claimed to have been in contact with. One could well say that most of her writings could have been written on the basis of books available in Western Europe at that time, and that a small but perhaps significant segment of her knowledge could only be the result of her Asian connections, whether paranormal or not[16]. In short, she might have picked up some scattered knowledge of Tantrism, but hardly endeavoured or encouraged to incorporate it. Rather, she was openly disdainful about the 'priapic element'.[17]

Most of what is called Tantric nowadays is an eclectic mixture of many ingredients, adapted to the taste of free-floating religious seekers in the West. Perhaps only those societies which have a strong commitment to the tradition by way of an acknowledged guruparampara or line of lamas, can lay claim to authenticity. But as traditional or textual authenticity was never much of a criterion in esoteric groups, it so happens that the designation 'Tantric' nowadays often

16. Many efforts have been made to trace her knowledge back to libraries, borrowed copies, personal contacts and hearsay. Even ghostwriting has been suggested. Yet, from an Indologist's point of view, it remains a fact that she mirrored many of the mistakes and errors of judgement of her Western contemporaries. Her Indian acquaintances, on the wave of the Oriental Renaissance, seem to have echoed this compulsive parallellism and monism rather than inspired her with fresh and authentic ideas.
17. It is interesting to note that the Theosophical Society had to go to great efforts to keep its record clear in this regard. Although there had always been rumours about Blavatsky's wild years, or about her relationship with Olcott, real trouble started with Leadbeater's sexual preferences. Krishnamurti, destined to remain celibate — but madly attractive to all those Western women and girls around him — also had to walk a razor's edge.

stands for accepted and celebrated sensuality and wholeness: the sexual experience as a source of higher energies and even enlightenment, and the techniques of meditation and visualization as passports into inner wonderworlds.

Actual Contents of Western Tantrism

We will now address the so-called Western Tantrism in its own right. This means that we will study the phenomenon without the criteria of textual authenticity, traditional lineage or a full-fledged worldview, but as a development of its own.

What has been intriguing about Tantrism ever since an inkling of knowledge became accessible to a few inquisitive Westerners is its life-affirming yet transformational spirituality. This universe is said to oscillate between the two poles of male and female, and this polarity is imprinted on everything in an endless repetition of that principle, like a hologram. Especially the human body carries that imprint, as the microcosmic image-carrier of the macrocosmic whole, or the enfolded potentiality of the explicit whole. Kundalini yoga aims at the gradual energization of the magnetic currents between the two poles, situated at the base of the spine and between the eyebrows. Long lines of yogis and Tantric masters had meditatively explored the map of the subtle body, and had produced what could be called a sacred cartography, a pilgrim's map of man's subtle physiology.

Asian spirituality is also very practical and methodical. It offers a wide variety of ethical guidelines for daily behaviour, and an enormous number of tools and techniques for realizing in oneself what one knows merely theoretically. Some Victorian Westerners understandably emphasized (and often mixed up with some vague knowledge of Kamasutra and Anangaranga) its explicit sexuality. Others, more esoterically inclined, were attracted by the colourful symbolism and tables of esoteric correspondences, and made use of the Tantric yoga techniques of meditation and visualization. For still others, it was ritual worship, its liturgy and iconography, which helped to manifest a sacred universe.

When Indian terminology began to enter the vocabulary of the secret societies at the end of the nineteenth century, there was considerable opposition. But there is no denying that the phenomenon of the influx of Asian religious texts in the nineteenth century, and the presence of Asian religious teachers in the twentieth century has left a significant mark. Tantrism in general has caught on as a life-affirming spirituality with a vast array of practical paths to personally experience this colourful and meaningful life. And that is how one detects traces of Tantrism in occult groups, in therapeutic circles, in alternative medicine, in art, in ritual renewal, in the eco-feminist movement, in the discussion of the paradigmatic shift, etc. Although most of the adherents have never had the tenacity or thoroughness to read a Tantra from beginning to end, the word Tantrism has become to denote something colourful, meaningful, sacred, and significantly playful as well. It specifically seems to cater to a modern need of resacralization, integration, and synthesis.

Towards the New Millennium

The fact that Tantrism addressed a modern need might well be why it will prove to be more than a fad. The epoch of Baghwan Shree Rajnees/Osho might be more or less a thing of the past; Rajneeshism has popularized and democratized Western Tantrism to a considerable extent, as did the famous Californian psychological schools. This will continue to bear on the free therapeutic use of its concepts and practices. At the same time, when the number of serious converts to some of the Indian and Tibetan traditions gradually increases here, and when the scholarly study of Tantric texts and sects continues to yield important insights about Tantrism in theory and practice, it may be expected that this archaic but strangely modern variety of the religious life makes a substantial contribution to the worldview of the new millennium.

Conclusion

When we search for the route Tantrism has taken from Southern Asia to Western Europe and Northern America, we discover three sources of information. First, the translation activities, second, the travellers' reports about South Asian customs, and third, the accounts of the first Westerners being initiated into Indian or Tibetan Tantric rites.

Analysing the contents of what was actually adopted or adapted by a developing Western Tantrism, three categories emerge: First, the use of Tantric ways of meditation and visualization (of which kundalini meditation became the best known), second, the ritual and magical use of the supposed energy current between the two universal poles (of which sacred sexuality is an overemphasized aspect), and third, the incorporation of Tantric symbol systems into tables of correspondences already extant in Western esotericism.

Many of the so-called Tantric ideas and practices prior to the beginning of the twentieth century could be called Tantra-like, but they are definitely not Tantric in a historically accepted sense.

Parallellism clearly has its pitfalls. Although in general, scholars have learned to be sceptical about all-too-easy parallels, it is rather difficult to deal harshly with parallellism in esotericism. As it is one of the main characteristics of esotericism to believe in an intricate order of correspondences, it seems natural that there are striking parallels to be found between, for instance, the writings of Randolph and Tantrism. The researcher should be wary of anachronisms here. That is why I have coined the word 'Tantra-like' for all supposed influence of Tantrism on Western esotericism prior to the twentieth century.

Although severe doubts can be raised about the 'Tantra-alloy' of twentieth-century Western Tantrism, I have taken it seriously as a development of its own, predicting that it will expand considerably in the next decades, well into the new millennium.

Bibliography

Anand, Margo 1989. *Tantra. The Art of Sexual Ecstasy.* Los Angeles: Jeremy P. Tarcher.

Anand, Margo 1995.*The Art of Sexual Magic.* Los Angeles: Jeremy P. Tarcher.

Bharati, Agehananda 1975. *The Tantric Tradition.* New York: Samuel Weiser.

Bharati, Agehananda 1970. *The Ochre Robe.* Garden City: Doubleday.

Bishop, Peter 1989. *The Myth of Shangri-La: Tibet, Travel-Writing and the Western Creation of Sacred Landscape.* London: Athlone Press.

Bishop, Peter 1992. *Dreams of Power. Tibetan Buddhism and the Western Imagination.* London: Athlone Press.

Breckenridge, Carol A. and Peter van der Veer (eds.) 1993. *Orientalism and the Postcolonial Predicament.* Philadelphia: University of Philadelphia Press.

Culling, Louis T. 1971 (1988). *Sex magick.* St.Paul, MN: Llewellyn.

Godwin, Joscelyn 1994. *The Theosophical Enlightenment.* Albany: State University of New York Press.

Goudriaan, T. and S. Gupta 1981. 'Hindu Tantric and Shakta Literature'. *History of Indian Literature, 2.* Wiesbaden: Harrassowitz.

Guenther, Herbert V. 1972. *The Tantric View of Life.* Boston/London: Shambhala.

Inden, Ronald 1990. *Imagining India.* Oxford: Basil Blackwell.

King, Francis 1986. *Tantra for Westerners. A Practical Guide to the Way of Action.* Wellingborough: Aquarian Press.

Kopf, David 1969. *British Orientalism and the Bengal Renaissance.* Berkeley: University of California Press.

Mookerjee, Ajit 1982. *Kundalini.* London: Thames and Hudson.

Mumford, John 1973. *A Chakra and Kundalini Workbook.* London: Thames and Hudson.

Mumford, John 1988. *Tantric Sexuality.* St.Paul, MN: Llewellyn.

Randolph, Paschal Beverly 1969. *Magia Sexualis,* (French translated version). Paris: Guy le Prat.

Restivo, Sal 1978. 'Parallels and Paradoxes in Modern Physics and Eastern Mysticism'. In: *Social Studies of Science* 8, 143-81.

Rama Prasada, 1894. *Nature's Finer Forces: The science of breath and the philosohpy of the tattvas.* London and New York: Theosophical Society.

Said, Edward W. 1979. *Orientalism: Western Conceptions of the Orient.* Vintage Press, New York.

Satyananda Saraswati (Swami) 1985. *Kundalini Tantra.* Monghyr: Bihar School of Yoga.

Schwab, Raymond 1984. *The Oriental Renaissance: Europe's Discovery of India and the East, 1680-1880.* Translated by Gene Patterson-Black and Victor Reinking. New York: Columbia University Press.

Sellon, Edward 1902. *Annotations on the Sacred Writings of the Hindus (Illustrating their Priapic Rites and Phallic Principles).* (New edition, privately published). London.

Sivananda Radha (Swami) 1978. *Kundalini Yoga for the West*. Spokane, WA: Timeless Books.

Varenne, Jean 1989. *Yoga and the Hindu Tradition*. Translated from the French by Derek Coltman. Delhi: Motilal Banarsidass.

Weiss, Hartmut 1986. *Quellen des Yoga*. Bern: O.W. Barth Verlag.

Wezler, Albrecht 1993. 'Towards a Reconstruction of Indian Cultural History: Observations and Reflections on 18th and 19th Century Indology'. In: *Studien zur Indologie ind Iranistiek* 18, 305-29.

Part II:

Millennialism and Eschatology

CHAPTER 5

Millennial Catastrophism in Popular Baha'i Lore

David Piff and Margit Warburg[1]

Millennialism refers to a belief in a new world order established by supernatural agency, generally through a process that involves violent overthrow or disruption of the present order. Movements founded on such beliefs have been described in a wide variety of historical, geographic and cultural settings. The Baha'i religion arose in the millennial context of 19th century Iran, and its scriptures proclaim it to be a religion of universal messianic fulfillment.[2] Baha'is believe that Mirza Husayn 'Ali Nuri (1817-1892), known as Baha'u'llah ('Glory of God'), who founded the religion, was not only 'Christ returned in the Glory of the Father',[3] but the 'Promised One of all ages',[4] whose teachings provide the basis for a future golden age of world peace and civilization. Baha'is are generally optimistic about the long-term prospects for humanity; however, they also believe that Baha'u'llah's advent has set in motion a revolutionary process by which the present-day order is being 'rolled up' and a new order 'spread out in its stead'.[5]

The present study, though touching briefly on official Baha'i texts, is mainly focused on unpublished, unofficial information circulated within the Baha'i community. 'Unofficial information' refers to the in-

1. David Piff is a member of the Baha'i religion, Margit Warburg is not.
2. For discussions of millenarian motifs in Baha'i see Smith 1982 and Collins 1995.
3. Shoghi Effendi 1965, 94.
4. Shoghi Effendi 1980b, 52.
5. Baha'u'llah 1976, 7.

formal discourse of members of the community, a broad realm which incorporates rumours, anecdotes, opinions and speculations shared orally or in written form and circulated without official sanction. It arises, in part, in response to ambiguities in official information and to observed discrepancies between the official line and happenings in the world at large. In turning to such lore, we are less concerned with a sociological analysis of formal Baha'i doctrine than with the psychosocial impact of these doctrines on members of the community. The present paper undertakes an analysis of the content and function of popular Baha'i lore regarding an expected, near-term world catastrophe. Discourse regarding such a convulsion is widespread among North American and — to a lesser extent — European Baha'i communities.

The writings of Baha'u'llah contain warnings of a future cataclysmic event, and pronouncements and writings by subsequent Baha'i leaders have elaborated this theme. This event, popularly referred to as 'the calamity', is understood to be a necessary part of God's plan to bring about the political unification of humanity and an era of universal peace.[6] The most detailed speculations regarding the calamity have been developed in unofficial texts, through the medium of 'pilgrim's notes'[7] and through the informal discourse of Baha'is.[8] Popular Baha'i discourse includes conjectures about the nature and timing of the calamity, where it will strike hardest, and what one might do to protect oneself and loved ones from its effects. As they address community fears, such speculations simultaneously reinforce Baha'is' collective self-image as members of a vitally important, if little known, religious group — privileged knowers of an enormous secret.

The present paper can be viewed as an ethnographic study of an

6. Shoghi Effendi 1980a, 126-27.
7. A Baha'i pilgrim is an individual who visits specific holy sites associated with the religion for the purpose of worship. At the present time, only sites located at the Baha'i World Centre in Israel are available for such visitation. Pilgrim's notes are written notes taken by Baha'i pilgrims; the reported comments of Baha'i leaders are an important part of such notes.
8. The present article is based on research into rumours, anecdotes and other informal lore in the Baha'i community, conducted by David Piff, 1986-96, and written in his Ph.D. dissertation, Piff 1996.

aspect of Baha'i community life and an analysis of millennial themes in popular Baha'i beliefs. The discourse of a social group contributes to the establishment and maintenance of its worldview, and the present paper instances this process. It can also be usefully viewed in relation to studies of millennial disconfirmation, in that Baha'i discourse has developed variant explanations to account for the fact that the expected calamity has failed to appear.[9]

Scriptural Sources for Catastrophic Lore

An important theme in Baha'i scriptures[10] is an ongoing condemnation of materialism. Materialism not only draws people away from spiritual and ethical values, it represents a significant source of danger to human survival. In his classic study, *The Pursuit of the Millennium*, Norman Cohn characterized the millennial worldview as including the perception of a world 'dominated by an evil, tyrannous power of boundless destructiveness — a power... which is imagined not as simply human but as demonic'.[11] Though seen as arising from human attitudes and actions rather than from superhuman forces, materialism is portrayed in the Baha'i writings as such a pernicious, multifaceted power. From the influence of this power, the present world is seen to be gravely ill, the organizing principles of its constituent nations and communities impotent and incapable of restoring it to health. Baha'is are engaged in a struggle against this power, though not in the sense of an armed revolution. Instead, Baha'is are exhorted to arise, 'detach themselves from all things', and spread the 'healing message' of Baha'u'llah across the planet. Baha'is believe that their efforts to establish and consolidate Baha'i communities throughout the world are laying the pattern for a future world order. The 'afflictive torments' through which the world must pass are seen as necessary components of the processes destined to usher in both a near-term 'lesser peace', a political arrangement between nations to

---

9. For representative studies see Festinger, Riecken and Schachter 1956; Schmalz 1994; and Balch, Farnsworth and Wilkins 1983.
10. Baha'i scriptures include the writings of Baha'u'llah and 'Abdu'l-Baha (1844-1921), Baha'u'llah's eldest son and successor.
11. Cohn 1970, 21.

outlaw war, and a more glorious future period, referred to as the 'most great peace'.

Baha'u'llah's son and successor 'Abdu'l-Baha predicted that the 'permanent peace of the world' (the lesser peace) will be 'universal in the twentieth century', that 'all nations will be forced into it'.[12] Since the 'convulsion' is to precede the lesser peace, Baha'is have expected the calamity to occur before the end of the year 2000.

The writings of Shoghi Effendi (1897-1957), successor to `Abdu'l-Baha, have been crucial in forming contemporary Baha'i attitudes towards the calamity.[13] In a letter written in July 1954 and published under the title *American Baha'is in the Time of World Peril*,[14] Shoghi Effendi discussed trends of modern life which he perceived as leading to disastrous consequences. Writing of the 'cancerous materialism' denounced by Baha'u'llah, Shoghi Effendi predicted 'dire ordeals and world-shaking crises that must necessarily involve the burning of cities and the spread of terror and consternation in the hearts of men'.[15] He further called attention to the 'multiplication, the diversity and the increasing destructive power of armaments' and spoke of the 'deterioration of a situation which, if not remedied, is bound to involve the American nation in a catastrophe of undreamed-of dimensions'.[16] Not only this, but the 'stress and strain imposed on the fabric of American society' by the persistent condition of white racism, would, if not remedied, in the words of 'Abdu'l-Baha,

cause the streets of American cities to run with blood, aggravating thereby the havoc which the fearful weapons of destruction, raining from the air, and amassed by a ruthless, a vigilant a powerful and inveterate enemy, will wreak upon those same cities.[17]

12. 'Abdu'l-Baha 1987, 21; 1978, 32.
13. 'Abdu'l-Baha appointed Shoghi Effendi, his eldest grandson, as 'guardian' of the Baha'i religion. Shoghi Effendi's ministry began in 1921 and continued until his death. His writings, though considered authoritative, are not part of the Baha'i scriptures.
14. Shoghi Effendi 1980a, 122-32.
15. Ibid., 125.
16. Ibid., 125-26.
17. Ibid. It is worth noting that the 'remedy' was to occur through a 'revolutionary change in the concept and attitude of the average white American toward his Negro fellow citizen...'

It is not surprising that this letter, coupled with predictions in the Baha'i scriptures and the Cold War tensions prevalent in the latter half of the 20th century, led American Baha'is to expect a third world war, to be fought with atomic missiles.

The disastrous events predicted in Baha'i sacred writings and Shoghi Effendi's letters do not end the story. Shoghi Effendi assured his readers that the large scale catastrophes looming in the future of America would have a beneficial result,

for... [t]hese ... fiery tribulations... [would] through their cleansing effect, purge [the American nation] thoroughly of the accumulated dross ... which [had] pre-vented her thus far from assuming the role of world spiritual leadership forecast by `Abdu'l-Baha's unerring pen...[18]

Catastrophic Pilgrim's Notes

In addition to published Baha'i writings, pilgrim's notes from the time of Shoghi Effendi reported his comments regarding the future. Such notes were often circulated in typewritten form through informal community channels. In considering them, we mark a transition between official and unofficial information; from the formal texts to the discourse of popular Baha'i. Pilgrim's notes reinforced themes Shoghi Effendi set out in his formal writings, and added appalling details. Though downplayed by Baha'i leaders as unreliable, these notes were an important stimulant to community speculations regarding the calamity.

During the 1950s, a number of Western Baha'i pilgrims reported alarming comments of Shoghi Effendi regarding an approaching catastrophe.[19] The situation appeared hopeless. It was 'too late' to save the world, which, having 'rejected' Baha'u'llah's proclamation must suffer divine chastisement until it turned towards its 'lord'. The calamity might be nuclear war, or something even worse. As the most materialistic country on earth, the United States would suffer more than any other nation. The American Baha'is were not immune from the disaster and should disperse from the large cities. The catastrophe

18. Ibid., 126-27.
19. This paragraph summarizes themes found in Moffet 1954; Brown 1954; Edge 1954; Sabri 1957; and Dudley 1957. All from collection of David Piff.

would be sudden and unexpected, but was to happen before the lesser peace. It would be unprecedented in its destructive force. World War II, terrible as it had been, was only 'the beginning'. In the catastrophe, entire cities would 'evaporate', and as many as two- thirds of humanity perish. A positive aspect of this destruction was the 'cleansing' of the world, sometimes referred to as ridding it of 'bad blood'.

One pilgrim reported, 'it is quite possible that the two-thirds of the earth's population spoken of in the Bible will be annihilated ... The world is over-populated, and the blood of the people is impure'.[20] During the same pilgrimage, it was reported that Shoghi Effendi had told the Iranian pilgrims that 'yes', the hydrogen bomb 'would be used'.[21]

The tone of pilgrim's notes was often strident. A pilgrim, for example, wrote, as though quoting Shoghi Effendi,

The situation is very grave and *I wish the friends to realize it*. They calculate too much, there is not enough self-sacrifice... While they are calculating the BLOW WILL BE STRUCK. They, themselves, WILL EVAPORATE (go up in smoke), YES THEY WILL!!! ...THE CITIES ARE DOOMED... THERE ARE VERY, VERY DARK DAYS AHEAD... America is the most disturbed nation on the earth. This is reflected in the Baha'is of the west, in their activities. THEY ARE LIVING IN A FOOL'S PARADISE.[22]

Community Speculation about the Calamity

Hearing or reading reports of this kind from pilgrims returning from the Baha'i World Centre, and with corroborative passages from the Baha'i writings in mind, it would not be surprising for Baha'is to find themselves distressed regarding the near term future.

The situation was one ripe for the development of rumour. In rumour creation,

persons deprived of authoritative news speculate about what is happening.

20. Sabri 1957, 4. The biblical reference appears to be Zechariah (13,8 and 13,9).
21. Ibid.
22. Edge 1954, 4-6. Underlining and capitalization as in the original.

They piece together what information they have. Observations are inter-preted in the light of what is taken for granted, and the definition that even-tually prevails is the one that appears most plausible.[23]

Additionally, students of rumour state that 'the amount of rumor in circulation' will increase in accordance with the 'importance of the subject to the individuals concerned' and with the 'ambiguity of the evidence pertaining to the topic at issue'.[24] In the present instance, of course, Baha'is are speculating not only about what is happening but also about what is going to happen. World events are interpreted ac-cording to the Baha'i understanding that a world calamity is inevit-able. There is no question that the prospect of such a catastrophe in the next few years is an important topic, and, while the evidence that it is to occur appears to be authoritative, there are critical ambiguities in that the nature, time and place of its manifestation are not speci-fied. Community discourse addresses these ambiguities and also affords a medium for continuous reinterpretation of the calamity in the light of its non-appearance.

Nature and effects of the calamity
In regard to the nature of the calamity, a wide range of scenarios have been circulated, addressing virtually every possible kind of disaster: war; geological cataclysm; collision between the earth and an aster-oid, meteor or comet; economic collapse; epidemic disease; techno-logical breakdown, or dire combinations of these happenings. In most instances the scenarios correspond to expectations generally abroad in the West and are not unique to Baha'is.

The notion that two thirds of humanity will perish is conspicuous among community expectations. One variation on this theme, from the Iranian Baha'i community, notes that the word for 'mankind' in Persian is *ba<u>sh</u>ar* comprised of three letters, b, <u>sh</u> and r. During the calamity (World War III), two-thirds of humanity, the 'sh' and the 'r' ('<u>shar</u>', meaning ungodly or sinful) would be wiped out, and only the 'b' (that is, the Baha'is) remain.[25] The informant reported this to be a

23. Shibutani 1968, 578.
24. Shibutani 1966, 57.

frequently heard speculation among Iranian Baha'is. It is noteworthy for its forthright expression of an us/them dichotomy, with Baha'is as the chosen people to be brought safely through the flames.

Regardless of its disastrous effects, the results of the calamity were to be positive for the Baha'i religion. The sweeping away of old order would herald an enormous increase in its influence. In fact, the 'entire world' would soon turn to the Baha'i religion 'because nothing else will have survived'.[26]

When will it be?

Guesses as to when the terrible event will strike generally harmonize with the idea that the calamity must precede the lesser peace which must be established in the twentieth century. References in the Baha'i writings to a period of 'respite'[27] and a statement in a book of Shoghi Effendi that 'for a whole century God has respited mankind',[28] coupled with a community tendency to view events in the world at large as connected to the progress of the Baha'i religion, have prompted members of the community to set dates for the calamity to coincide with 100 year anniversaries of various events in Baha'i history. However, these anniversaries passed without witnessing the expected global convulsion. Community explanations for these confirmations were, for example, that the calamity did not strike in 1992, and did not vaporize New York City in that year, because that would have prevented the Second Baha'i International Congress scheduled for that place and time.[29]

Where will it strike?

Community lore regarding where the catastrophe will strike hardest has generally harmonized with statements in pilgrim's notes that the large cities of the West (especially of the United States) are most at

25. Piff 1996, 214.
26. Ibid., 600.
27. Baha'u'llah 1983, 170, quotes a passage from the Qur'an (16:61): 'If God should chastise men for their perverse doings, He would not leave upon the earth a moving thing. But to an appointed time doth He respite them.'
28. Shoghi Effendi 1980b, 4. The passage was written in 1941.
29. Piff 1996, 220.

risk. Predictions of destruction of major cities intermingle with Baha'i discourse which is generally critical of cities as strongholds of materialism.[30] However, as many Americans and other Westerners (including Baha'is) actively enjoy life in modern urban centres and are unwilling to abandon their accustomed lifestyles, a communal sense of guilt may also play a role in this discourse: 'If we were really good Baha'is, we would be foreign pioneers.[31] Surely God will smite us for enjoying lives of convenience, comfort, and pleasure'. This psychological factor would seem to contribute to a conviction that the calamity is inevitable, because it has been earned.[32]

What can one do to prepare?

Knowing that terrible events are on the way, Baha'is have naturally been interested in learning what steps they might take to remain safe. The official answer is to resist speculating and worrying about fearful future prospects and concentrate on Baha'i work. Some Baha'is thought that they should, in fact, cease any activity not directly associated with promoting the Baha'i religion. Similar responses to im-

30. As noted by an American geographer, Arthur Hampson, who studied the expansion and diffusion of the Baha'i community, the negative attitudes of American Baha'is toward large cities is a reflection of official Baha'i views (Hampson 1980, 310).
31. 'Pioneer', in Baha'i parlance, refers to one who leaves his native land and travels to another country to proselytize the Baha'i religion.
32. David Piff's field notes, 8 November 1996. Richard Fenn, of Princeton Theological Seminary, has advanced an intriguing hypothesis along these lines (1991). Fenn suggests that in contemporary American society 'there is a slowly increasing demand — at the level of individuals if not of organized religious or political movements — for a final test of wills: a day of reckoning' (p. 53). Incorporating psychoanalytic concepts, he argues that 'societies live on borrowed psychic and emotional capital' (p. 54) and accumulate a significant debt which individuals internalize. The expected final reckoning is to settle accounts — both what one owes others or society as a whole, and what is due. 'What results is equivalent, in macro-social terms, to a transference neurosis that keeps the individual in debt to a society from which extraordinary benefits are expected. Fearing that such hopes will not be realized before payment of these debts is demanded, individuals turn to religion to provide symbolic satisfactions and to make partial payments to the larger society' (pp. 71-72).

pending millennial events have been noted in Christian movements.[33] An informant mentioned a Baha'i family, living in a Pacific
island community, who 'made no plans for investing for their children to go to college because of their conviction that all the colleges
would be destroyed by the time they were old enough to go. Their
only investment was to buy gold'.[34]

One of the most important ways of escaping the calamity was for
North Americans to leave their homes as Baha'i pioneers; calcula-
tions of where one might be relatively safe from the effects of future
disasters appear to have played some role in helping Baha'is deter-
mine where to relocate. Self-preservation as a motivation for pioneering receives no official support, and the degree to which it actually
plays a role in stimulating Baha'is to leave their homes for foreign
shores is unclear. One diarist noted, 'the Catastrophe is what jet-
propelled me, and it seems, most other pioneers, into pioneering',[35]
and several informants offered corroborating statements.[36]

Reinterpretation of the event

As the years have rolled by without the expected catastrophe, another tendency has become more prominent in the discourse of the

33. The conviction that adherents must lay aside their normal occupations
    and concentrate on proselytizing and other activities to promote their re-
    ligious views is, of course, not unique to Baha'is, and has been part of the
    official rhetoric of other millennial movements. The Millerites, for exam-
    ple, at a conference in 1842, a year before the expected return of Christ,
    formally resolved to 'do their utmost to lay before the world as extensive-
    ly as possible' their views. A period of intensive proselytization followed
    (O'Leary 1994, 104). Jehovah's Witnesses undertook similar measures in
    the years preceding 1914, the date set by founder Charles Taze Russel for
    the arrival of the millennium. Again, in advance of 1975, another year of
    serious millennial expectation in the movement, 'In addition to proclaim-
    ing this belief to a largely incredulous world, some Jehovah's Witnesses
    sold their possessions, postponed surgery or cashed in their insurance
    policies to prepare for Christ's millennial reign' (Schmalz 1994, 298).
34. Piff 1996, 216.
35. Ruhe-Schoen 1984, 98. Capitalization as in original.
36. One informant stated that a member of one of the senior Baha'i institu-
    tions had, in the 1980s, urged him to remain as a Baha'i pioneer in the
    Pacific, in order to avoid the calamitous destruction certain to be visited
    on the United States (Piff 1994, 224).

Baha'i community, one which reinterprets the notion of the calamity as other than a single cataclysmic event. One example is the notion that the calamity is an historical process, 'like the fall of the Roman Empire'.[37] A variant is the idea that calamities are constantly manifesting themselves throughout the world, disastrously afflicting various nations. 'The Cambodians have suffered their calamity', said an informant in March, 1994, 'Somalia and Bosnia are suffering theirs'.[38] In some instances, comments of Shoghi Effendi as reported in pilgrim's notes are given a new reading. For example, what Shoghi Effendi really meant by his supposed references to 'evaporating cities' was a revolution in the fortunes of the Baha'i community, and to a radical change of attitude on the part of people in Western societies, in which old points of view would vanish like dissipating vapors.[39] It is possible that such trends in Baha'i discourse are laying the groundwork for a major shift in community expectations, one which is simultaneously positive — because it means Baha'is can abandon their dire expectations of mass nuclear death — and challenging, because it may also mean that statements of `Abdu'l-Baha and Shoghi Effendi must be reevaluated.[40]

Conclusions

Though derived, in part, from authoritative sources, the calamity is not emphasized in official Baha'i doctrine. It is a topic more prominent in the unofficial lore of the movement, and is not much referred to in Baha'i proselytizing.

The Baha'i writings encourage believers to put the possibility of future calamitous events in perspective, and to maintain positive attitudes. Officially, the best response to the world situation is to align

37. Ibid., 222.
38. Ibid.
39. Ibid., 222-23.
40. That this matter possibility is potentially challenging to at least some members of the community was evidenced by remarks made by an Iranian informant, who resisted any suggestion that there might not be a third world war, and admitted wanting such a war to occur because it would 'prove' the accuracy of Shoghi Effendi's predictions (field note July 1992 recorded by David Piff).

one's actions with God's plan: to engage in Baha'i work, preferably in the international pioneering field. But the psychological effects of calamitous expectation remain with the community. Critical details of the events are missing in the formal Baha'i texts. The proliferation of speculations as to what the great catastrophe will be, and where, and when it will strike, illustrate a communal effort to resolve uncomfortable ambiguities. Implicit in this discourse is the idea that one's lifestyle, social situation, relationships and actual survival are subject to instant evaporation. Communal guilt, which acknowledges that North American Baha'is have been 'living soft' for most of this century, and not fulfilling the high hopes invested in them by the Baha'i leadership, may well play a role in these expectations, at least in America. The wide-ranging lore around this subject appears to function as a medium for managing the community's anxieties.

At the same time, such discourse strengthens Baha'i self-perception as members of an elite community: they who have recognized God's new messenger, whose advent has brought about revolutionary changes in the organization of the planet, enjoy favored insights into the future course of world events. The calamity represents divine chastisement for the world's rejection of Baha'u'llah. Its advent will, in dramatic fashion, prove Baha'u'llah's mission by fulfilling prophecies in Baha'i scriptures, and, by spreading material destruction across the planet and destroying the cities and their ungodly inhabitants, actually assist God to inaugurate His day. As the calamity is part of God's plan, Baha'is are actually its beneficiaries, and expressions of Baha'i triumphalism are woven into community lore regarding it.

Opposed to the theme of calamitous expectation is a line of discourse which, while acknowledging the present suffering and disintegration of world political and economic systems, suggests that there will be no single cataclysmic convulsion. Rather, one can expect the continuation of a gradual process, a series of smaller disasters, such as those which have been occurring since the end of the Second World War. As the expected world convulsion has failed to manifest itself, the community has entered a process of reinterpretation, creating through its discourse new formulations of calamity lore that, in various ways, account for the disconfirmation apparently looming ahead.

The idea of millennial catastrophism has been a common theme in religious thinking since the times of the Old Testament prophets, and Baha'i speculations on an impending calamity with evaporating cities echo prophecies through three millennia. Baha'i discourse on catastrophism is rich and can provide empirical material for the study of the sociology of rumours and other popular lore. Expectations as to the time and nature of the calamity have repeatedly been disproved, a fact Baha'is are coming to realize. However, we doubt that this will present a serious challenge to the adherents, thanks to the status of the idea of the calamity as close to, but not within, official doctrine.

Bibliography

'Abdu'l-Baha 1978. *Selections from the Writings of Abdu'l-Baha*. Haifa: Baha'i World Centre.

'Abdu'l-Baha 1987. `*Abdu'l-Baha in Canada*. Thornhill,Ontario: Baha'i Publications Canada.

Baha'u'llah 1983. *Kitab-I-Iqan*. Wilmette: Baha'i Publishing Trust.

Baha'u'llah 1976. *Gleanings from the Writings of Baha'u'llah*. Wilmette: Baha'i Publishing Trust.

Balch, Robert W., G. Farnsworth, and S. Wilkins 1983. 'When the Bombs Drop: Reactions to Disconfirmed Prophecy in a Millennial Sect'. *Sociological Analysis*, vol. 26(2), 137-58.

Brown, Ramona A. 1954. Unpublished pilgrim's notes, May 2, 1954.

Cohn, Norman 1970. *The Pursuit of the Millennium: Revolutionary Messianism in Medieval and Reformation Europe and Its Bearing on Modern Totalitarian Movements*. New York: Oxford University Press.

Collins, William P. 1995. 'The Millerites and Time Prophecy'. Unpublished Master's thesis, Syracuse University.

Dudley, Alice 1957. 'Notes on Pilgrimage to Haifa — April 15 to 23, 1957'. Unpublished pilgrim's notes.

Edge, Clara A. 1954 'Haifa Notes, May 16 to 25, 1954'. Unpublished pilgrim's notes.

Fenn, Richard 1991. 'The Secularization of Dread and Despair: Demand for a Day of Reckoning'. *Religion and Social Order*, vol. 1, 53-72. Greenwich, CT.: JAI Press, Inc.

Festinger, Leon, H.W. Riecken, and S. Schachter 1956. *When Prophecy Fails*. New York: Harper & Row.

Hampson, Arthur 1980. *The Growth and Spread of the Baha'i Faith*. PhD dissertation, University of Hawaii.

Moffet, Ruhaniyyih Ruth 1954. 'Visiting the Baha'i World Center' [May 17-June 1, 1954]. Unpublished pilgrim's notes.

O'Leary, Stephen D. 1994. *Arguing the Apocalypse: A Theory of Millennial Rhetoric*. New York: Oxford University Press.

Piff, David 1996. *The Book of Hearsay: Unofficial Lore in the Baha'i Community*. PhD dissertation, University of Copenhagen.

Piff, David 1986-96. Field Notes. Unpublished.

Ruhe-Schoen, Janet 1984. 'No Shade'. Unpublished typescript. Baha'i World Centre Library, (call number BP395.R83 R8).

Sabri, Isobel 1957. 'Pilgrim's Notes recorded after the nightly dinner-table talks of the beloved Guardian, Shoghi Effendi, 19th to 28th April, 1957'. Unpublished pilgrim's notes.

Schmalz, Mathew N. 1994. 'When Festinger Fails: Prophecy and the Watch Tower'. *Religion*, vol. 24(4), 293-308.

Shibutani, Tamotsu 1968. 'Rumor'. In: David L. Sills (ed.), *International Encyclopedia of the Social Sciences*, vol. 13. New York: Macmillan/TheFree Press, 476-80.

Shibutani, Tamotsu 1966. *Improvised News: A Sociological Study of Rumor*. New York: The Bobbs-Merril Company.

Shoghi Effendi 1965. *God Passes By*. Wilmette: Baha'i Publishing Trust.

Shoghi Effendi 1980a. *Citadel of Faith*. Wilmette: Baha'i Publishing Trust.

Shoghi Effendi 1980b. *The Promised Day is Come*. Wilmette: Baha'i Publishing Trust.

Smith, Peter 1982. 'Millenarianism in the Babi and Baha'i Religions'. In: Roy Wallis (ed.), *Millennialism and Charisma*. Belfast: The Queen's University, 231-38.

CHAPTER 6

Hindu Eschatology Within Modern Western Religiosity

Reender Kranenborg

Introduction

Every great world religion has its own eschatology. Within Hinduism, for example, we encounter the idea of the kali yuga ('iron age/age of darkness') with its notion that ultimately Kalkin will arrive, which will herald the beginning of a new cycle. Within Christianity we often find a strong apocalyptic view of the future, including a final battle and ending with the return of Jesus Christ, after which the eternal kingdom will begin. In addition, the many different new religious movements and the groups have their own eschatology. Groups deriving from Hinduism, such as the Hare Krishna movement, contain the above-mentioned idea of kali yuga, and evangelical groups produce their own version of Christian eschatology.

With esoteric and New Age groups derived from the Western religious tradition the situation is more complex. There, as a rule, we see an eschatology that deviates from the Christian one and various other forms of eschatology existing alongside one another. We sometimes see an anticipation that is strongly apocalyptic, as in the Ramala movement, in the channelled materials of Ramtha and in the somewhat earlier visionary Edgar Cayce, which emphasizes the occurrence of several catastrophes, through which the new era will begin; strictly speaking, this apocalyptic aspect is rooted in the Christian tradition but is coloured differently with respect to content. Sometimes the eschatology is determined by astrological motifs and it is expected that the new era will come by itself, as it were, because the time is ripe. Sometimes we also see people within the world of esotericism and New Age who wish to orientate themselves by the Hindu eschatology and speak of kali yuga, kalpas and the coming of the Golden Age.

It is this last form of esoteric eschatology that I wish to analyze more closely.

The fact that the idea of kali yuga arises within the modern spirituality of New Age is a particularly interesting fact and warrants further study. Various questions arise:

— How did this idea come to be adopted?

— When was this idea accepted within Western alternative religiosity?

— How was this idea assimilated? Do we encounter the complete eschatological system of Hinduism within certain New Age circles or have some things changed?

By way of illustration with regard to the last question, I will present the following. Hindu ideas are frequently taken into the esotericism of the West. Here one thinks of concepts such as karma and chakra, and these words were accompanied by an entire complex of other ideas. Whoever spoke about karma also accepted reincarnation, and whoever spoke of chakra also spoke of kundalini and yoga. In this way complexes of ideas were appropriated from Hinduism. But whoever subsequently analyzes the place and content of these complexes — as they were further developed in the West — must also observe that, in this appropriation and especially in the continuing use of these complexes, much has changed. The complex of karma and reincarnation, for example, has been strongly transformed and became a new whole, which in itself no longer resembles its counterpart in Hinduism. Something similar can be said of chakra and yoga: within Western esotericism this complex has become a psychological whole, within which the specifically spiritual aspect (such as that which functioned within Tantrism) has all but disappeared. In modern Western esotericism we rarely encounter the original Hindu view and manner of dealing with kundalini and chakra. The question now is whether a similar development or change is also to be found in the concept kali yuga and in the complex of ideas and views that accompany this concept. In other words, is the idea of kali yuga as it appears within certain traditions of modern esotericism and New Age still the same as that within Hinduism?

Kali Yuga Within Hinduism

For the record, it is important to sketch the complex of ideas of kali yuga. We should begin with commenting that these views are characteristic for Hinduism, although they do not occur universally and can also be worked out in various ways. The representative ideas are to be found specifically, with the exception of the Mahabharata, in the Vishnu Purana. In addition, one may note that these ideas exist and are elaborated on in Vaishnava circles in particular.

The idea of Kali[1] yuga fits into a larger whole. There are four yugas or ages: Krita yuga (or Satya yuga), Treta yuga, Dvapara yuga and Kali yuga. These ages vary in nature and length. The Krita yuga lasts for approximately 1,728,000 years, the Treta yuga for 1,296,000 years, the Dvapara yuga for 864,000 years and the Kali yuga 432,000 years; this reckoning includes beginning and ending phases. After the end of the Kali-yuga the new Krita-yuga begins immediately.[2] Together the four ages form a so-called mahayuga, which lasts for 4,320,000 years. A thousand of these mahayugas, which would therefore be 4,320,000,000 years, are called 'one day of Brahma'. The 'one night of Brahma', which follows the day of Brahma, is just as long. After this night a new day of Brahma begins, which is just as long then as the previous day. One 'day of Brahma' together with one 'night of Brahma' is referred to by the term kalpa (which is therefore 8,640,000,000 years). The system goes even further, but we need not elaborate.

1. One must note that the word 'kali' in kali yuga has nothing to do with the black goddess Kali (in this name the 'a' and 'i' are long). 'Kali', along with the names of the other yugas, belongs to the game of dice and refers to the losing die marked by one spot.
2. According to some groups the cycle of the yugas is different: after each kali-yuga comes the dvapara-yuga, which is followed by the new treta-yuga, after which the krita-yuga begins.

There is yet another division possible. Every kalpa (that is, its day part) can be divided into fourteen periods, all of which are ruled by a divine being or a Manu. Such a period is called a manvantara and lasts for 308,448,000 years. Thus every manvantara contains 71 mahayugas.

To return to the four yugas, these take place in a continual sequence. After a kali yuga there is always a Krita yuga, with the exception of the very last time at the end of the day of Brahma. The periods are assigned different colours.

The Krita yuga or 'Golden Age' is the best one. People live for 400 years, are not sick and are calm and happy. Reproduction takes place through wishing and everything that one wishes for is successful. Truth and justice rule, there is no injustice, no gathering of riches, the vedas are known completely by all and people conform exactly to the rules of caste and life phases. People live according to true virtue and know the world of god.

Then comes the Treta yuga or 'Silver Age'. People live for 300 years at most. Law, justice and virtue decrease by one fourth. Theft, lies and deceit now appear. People do not adhere as closely to the rules, and sacrifices are not always made properly. Knowledge becomes imperfect. Barbarous peoples arise and the earth is occasionally shaken by disasters that affect people.

Then follows the Dvapara yuga or 'Copper Age'. People only live to be 200, reproduction now occurs through sexual contact, and law, justice and virtue decrease by another fourth.

Finally, there is the Kali yuga or 'Iron Age'. This is the least righteous of the four, and during this age things only get worse. People live only for 100 years at the most; there is discord, war and violence. Evil is very strong. People only have one fourth of the original knowledge, justice and virtue, and even that diminishes. People are almost spiritually incapacitated. Godlessness increases, sacrifices are no longer made, the caste rules are broken by all. The desire for the power and riches of kings becomes increasingly strong. More and more often, virtuous and pure people are persecuted and killed. The possessions of the individual are taken away and riches have become the religion, as it were, of this age. The desire for sex is strong, leading to the use of women exclusively as objects of lust. The earth is desecrated and exploited in many ways; there is no longer any respect for it. Religion has become purely external: empty words, a few rituals and pro forma worship. Overpopulation becomes acute, so that even desolate areas are occupied, leading to hunger and other afflictions. By the end of this age, people do not even live beyond 23 years of age.

Then, when the situation has become almost unbearable, the divine reality intervenes. In a Vaishnava family a certain Kalki or Kalkin is born — essentially an incarnation of the godhead. This Kalkin, who will reveal himself as a rider on a white horse, will act in judgement and bring order. He will destroy the thieves, sinners and outcasts, and will restore justice on earth. The spirits of those still living will awake, as it were, and become as clear as crystal. Thus they form the seed of a new generation of people who will now live in the new Krita yuga that is beginning.

In all the writings on the yugas it is very clear that the current age is the Kali yuga. We live in a very bad age that can only become worse. The current Kali yuga is often regarded as having begun about 5,000 years ago with the death of Krishna, according to the Indian method of counting in 3102 BC. Thus, the end is not as close as it seems.

We can see, however, that various new groups within Hinduism have their own ideas about how long the periods last. The Brahma Kumaris has greatly reduced the time cycle of the yugas. A cycle of the four ages lasts 5,000 years in total; thus we now live at the end of the kali-yuga. But the members of the Brahma Kumaris carry the seed of a new time, the 'diamond age'. This seed will be the beginning of the new krita-yuga which is coming. We find a different conception within the Self Realisation Fellowship, founded by Swami Paramahamsa Yogananda (1893-1952). His guru Sri Yukteshwar (1855-1936) declared that kali-yuga already ended in 1700. In his opinion the cycle was quite different. After the kali-yuga it is not the new krita-yuga but the dvapara-yuga that comes. The kali-yuga lasts 1,200 years. It began in AD500 and thus ended in 1700. It was succeeded by the new dvapara-yuga which will last 2,400 years.[3]

Furthermore, it is important to note here that more devotional Hindu branches strongly emphasize the only correct practice in this

3. Paramahamsa Yogananda, 1974, 193-94.

situation. Given the fact that humanity is so evil and so spiritually dead, the number of spiritual possibilities has greatly decreased. Krishna circles, including the Hare Krishna circles, see salvation as obtainable only through samkirtana, dancing before Krishna while repeatedly reciting his name. The Ananda Marga and the Radha Soami Satsang declare that their religious founder and leader is a specific incarnation of the godhead who has come into this black period to offer humanity enlightenment. The Divine Light Mission and the Brahma Kumaris see their founder and leader as a kind of Kalkin: he will restore justice and usher in the new age.

Kali Yuga Within Western Esotericism

It is obvious that the idea of the kali yuga became known in the West when the writings from India were translated in the previous century.[4] But the idea was not appropriated. It was taken up by Helena Blavatsky who, in her *Isis Unveiled* (1877), speaks emphatically of kalpa and kali yuga; and in her publication *The Secret Doctrine* she discusses this in even more detail. Although at no point does she give a systematic explanation of the entire yuga doctrine, it can be observed that, if we put together various fragments of her writings, we do indeed encounter Hindu eschatology. She has included almost the entire complex of ideas in her view of time and history. One of her disciples, G. De Purucker, has in his works systematically explained the entire complex of yuga and kalpa, basing his work on Blavatsky. Therefore, we can once again observe that in the first instance this specific Hindu eschatology is present in full.

On the one hand, this is understandable. After all, Theosophy assumes the one truth that can be found in all religions and Hindu

---

4. There is yet another issue to be settled. Already in classical antiquity, in Hesiod, we encounter a division into four ages. We could also recall Nebuchadnezzar's dream in the book of Daniel, where ages also play a role. The question now is which conception of the ages is older: that of Hinduism or that within Western culture? People tend to think that the idea of world ages moved from the West to the East. If this were true, it would mean that Western esotericism actually borrows an idea from the East that comes from its own Western tradition.

eschatology is the most elaborate, the most concrete and thereby the most convincing. This eschatology gives the impression of being scientific, which is a second reason why Blavatsky readily accepted this kalpa doctrine. In Western natural sciences it had become clear that the earth could not have been created only 5000 years ago but must have existed for many millions of years. The Christian idea that there will soon be a definitive end to this earth also becomes very unlikely. Due to modern science a perspective is offered of endlessly long time both in the past and in the future. The Hindu eschatology, which is worked out in such detail with its millions of year in the past and for the future, seems to be much more in keeping with modern science. Thus people within Theosophy readily accepted these ideas, all the more because the struggle to reconcile faith and science could also become clearly visible here.

On the other hand, it is still not understandable why Theosophy adopted the Hindu doctrine of kalpa. Basically, this doctrine is cyclical and assumes a continual retrogression and degeneration. There is definitely no progression to be found. It is possible to make a new beginning, but afterwards things always decline again. In contrast, Theosophy has a strong evolutionist tendency: there is a constant progress towards improvement, and backsliding is not possible. In principle, the earth, and with it humanity, evolves into higher levels. Ultimately, evolution has no losers but only winners, even though it is possible for individuals to be left behind. Thus the question is how Blavatsky and De Purucker could adopt this Hindu eschatology. Is this not a combination of two essentially contrary views?

De Purucker, once again in line with Blavatsky, has solved this tension in two ways. First of all, he posits, nothing is ever simply and solely 'decline'. Indeed, we could say that the Kali yuga is a period of retrogression, but then we must at the same time see that the Kali yuga is not one period but various shorter periods. Some of these shorter periods are clearly better than others and thus display progress after a decline in a previous shorter period. Nevertheless, the end result is good. Thus De Purucker comments:

Much is said about this dark age, the Kali yuga, but it is this tension and pressure that opens our heart and removes the curtain of our spirit. It is the Iron Age, a hard, rigid cycle, in which everything moves violently and is difficult;

but it is also the time in which very quick spiritual and intellectual developments can be made ...It is a strange paradox that the hardest and cruellest of
all yugas is that in which the quickest progress can be made. It is the time of
chance, the time of choice, in which the furthest advanced egos become the
seed of the following rootrace.[5]

But we must see this in a larger perspective, which we find, secondly, in the teachings of Blavatsky about the rootraces and their development. This development must be seen as the total development of
humanity. Obviously, humanity has not begun on the level at which
it is now to be found. Humanity is fairly developed and clearly has
more insight than before. Indeed, there are also negative things, but
they are also significant. Humanity, it is said, began simply: in the beginning, people were not aware of everything. Their understanding
and insight were not yet very developed. We could call this beginning period the 'Golden Age' but must be aware that it is something
like the period of childlike innocence and blessed ignorance. Thus the
beautiful Golden Age is not a higher phase, after which worse ages
follow; it is an earlier phase in which humanity had not yet developed completely. In the 'Silver Age' humanity therefore progresses a
step further, more aware of everything. And so it continues to the
next age. Then comes this current black period, which demonstrates
a very strong development of humanity, within which side effects are
also evident.

   In Blavatsky's philosophy a so-called 'rootrace' is connected with
every age. Such a race undergoes both progression and retrogression
in its age, but it does not decline completely. In previous ages there
were races such as the Lemuric and Atlantic races, whereas in our age
it is the Aryan race.

   The connection of the doctrine of the rootraces with Hindu eschatology is not entirely clear in Theosophy. Obscure and loose areas
remain. But it is clear that here the yuga doctrine should be viewed
in an evolutionary way as a history of development. Thus the question has become whether this interpretation of the yuga doctrine does
justice to its original intention. My opinion is that it does not. The

---

5.   De Purucker 1974, 186 (Dutch edition).

content has changed in an essential way. More strongly, I would suggest that we are faced with the same situation here as in the case of the karma and chakra ideas mentioned above. The original complex of ideas is changed in such a way that, in essence, it no longer bears any resemblance to the original idea.

If we continue to follow the development of Western esotericism we can observe that within this esoteric world the idea of kalpas and yugas are actually abandoned and that one continues along the lines of the doctrine of rootraces. This is best illustrated by Rudolf Steiner; most of the later esoterics in fact base their work on him. We find this model worked out in detail by the esoteric Schoenmaker. He assumes seven ages that follow one another sequentially on an evolutionary scale. Thus we find the Polar Age, the Hyperborean Age, the Lemuric Age and the Atlantic Age. We now live in the Post-Atlantic Age. There arose seven rootraces in the Atlantic Age. Some of them have disappeared; some of them still exist, though they have clearly remained less developed (such as the Accadian and Mongolian rootraces). Still others continued to evolve. Thus the Semitic rootrace arose in Atlantis and formed, as it were, the seed of the Aryan race, which is so important in the Post-Atlantic Age. This Aryan rootrace in turn has its sub-races, which develop alongside one another. With every new development the old race is left behind. Thus there was the Indian Age, the Persian Age, the Egyptian-Chalcedonian Age and the Greco-Roman Age. In AD 1400 the Christian Age — also called the Age of Piscus — began, which will end in AD 3500. Then the Age of Aquarius will begin,[6] and history will thus continue to develop for quite some time.

I have gone into such detail on this model in order to demonstrate that we are far removed from the yuga model here. There are indeed ages, but these occur within an evolutionary framework, in which every notion of retrogression has disappeared. We therefore also see that within the esoteric world elements of Hindu eschatology increasingly disappear and that even the word kali yuga is hardly ever used

6. I would like to point out the fact that in this view the Age of Aquarius, therefore, did not begin around the year 2000 and that accordingly the Age of Piscus did not begin about 2000 years ago. This is an idea that deviates from the prevalent ideas within the New Age world.

any more.[7] In short, the idea of kali yuga did not make it in the West and has disappeared. When certain Theosophists still use the term, this arises from a kind of dogmatism through which people wish to adhere to the literal text of what Blavatsky said. But in this case as well it functions in another way than was originally intended.

In short, the *idea* of kali yuga has reached a dead end in the West.

Kali Yuga Within New Age

The *term* kali yuga has, however, not disappeared. Even though one may speak of a dead end, the use of the term is not a matter of the past. Within various New Age groups we frequently encounter this term as a reference to our modern period. At times it is no more than mentioned, but elsewhere we also see a more elaborate view of the kali yuga.

This is the case with a Dutch author, whose starting point is evolution. He thus posits that the earth and humanity develop and that every phase is, as it were, a kind of evolutionary step. At times it seems to be going badly, as in our time, but then we must realize that we are dealing with a process that leads to a low point from which a slow climb begins. That descent was necessary in order to learn. In this way it can be said about our time that it is kali yuga, and that it is characterized by moral corruption, perversities, materialism, hardening, catastrophic ecological and economic policy, a decline in real religiosity, etc., but we must go through all of this. They are elements that will help us to grow and bring us to insight and repentance. For in this kali period or Iron Age we have developed a very strong consciousness of ourselves. That was also precisely the evolutionary intention. Only, this positive I-awareness has its negative aspects and they are often the first things that are visible. But they are, as we said, to be learned from and overcome. In short, it is a view that does not

---

7. Rene Guenon (1886-1951) also wrote on the subject of kali yuga. The impression sometimes exists that he is using the idea in the same sense as classical Hinduism. But we find the same elements here as we find in the rest of modern esotericism: evolution, the idea that everything becomes better and that the negative aspects can be overcome and integrated.

differ very much from later Theosophy, which is something to be expected within New Age. However, this author attempts to link Christian elements with Hindu elements and thus mentions Kalkin. The Hindu rider on the white horse is identified with a similar rider in the biblical book of Revelation (19,11-16). This Kalkin (who is the returning Christ), when he rides forth, will drive away the destruction and the godlessness, renew the creation and bring back purity. How things will go after that the author does not say.

We can see that in his view of humanity and the future he is completely in tune with esotericism. The use of the word kali yuga is a general reference for this negative period. It is interesting that he takes up the idea of Kalkin, an element that rarely plays a role in esoteric views. But Kalkin is so strongly interpreted in a Christian sense that there is nothing left but a formal aspect: he is the initiator of a new age.

Conclusions

When we survey the whole, we can establish the following.

— The term kali yuga was introduced into the West. Terms that accompany it, such as kalpa and Kalkin are also present, but noticeably used less often.

— Kali yuga is almost immediately placed into an evolutionary framework, through which the system of the world ages becomes a entirely different affair.

— The doctrine of kali yuga is still first linked with the doctrine of rootraces; we see that these later actually infiltrate the idea of the kali yuga.

— Various elements of Hindu eschatology, such as the decline of purity, the arrival of Kalkin, the various manvantaras, the interpretation of exactly what is bad and is retrogression, the returning cycle, the methods of attaining salvation in the kali yuga, the absolute decline of the world, etc., do not — or rarely — appear. In the beginning they do appear in Theosophy, but later hardly ever.

This has to do with the rise of another historical and eschatological model.

— When the term kali yuga is used with the modern spirituality of the West, it is no more than the use of a Sanskrit word to characterize the contemporary period. Basically, it is completely stripped down and, when it is used, has almost nothing to do with the original context and content. It has become simply a term.

— Perhaps we should say that it could not be otherwise, because the context of Hinduism is so completely different from that of the West that the adoption of this complex of ideas does not, in principle, have any chance of a long life.

Bibliography

Blavatsky, H.P. 1888. *The Secret Doctrine*. Den Haag: Edition Couvreur.
Blavatsky, H.P. 1877. *Isis Unveiled*. Den Haag: Edition Couvreur.
De Purucker, G. 1974. *Fountain-Source of Occultism*. Pasadena: Theosophical University Press.
De Purucker, G. 1981. *Occult glossary*. Pasadena: Theosophical University Press.
Dowson, J. 1982. *Hindu Mythology and Religion*. Calcutta: Rupa.
Frauwallner, E. 1953. *Geschichte der Indischen Philosophie*. Salzburg: Müller Verlag.
Gelberg, S.G. 1983. *Hare Krishna, Hare Krishna*. New York: Grove Press.
Hanegraaff, W.J. 1996. *New Age Religion and Western Culture*. Leiden: Brill.
Hummel, R. 1980. *Indische Mission und neue Frömmigkeit im Westen*. Stuttgart: Kohlhammer.
Judge, W.Q. 1996. *The ocean of Theosophy*. The Hague: Theosophical University Press.
Loosjes-Roelofs, M. 1977. *Antroposofie*. Zeist: Vrij Geestesleven.
Reinders, P.J. 1988. *De Brahma Kumaris*. Amsterdam: Free University Press.

Schneider, U. 1989. *Einführung in den Hinduismus*. Darmstadt: Wissenschaftliche Buchgesellschaft.

Schoenmaker, M. 1989. *A short occult history of the world*. Carfield, Victoria, Australia: ICA-press.

Singer, M. 1966. *Krishna: Myths, Rites and Attitudes*. Chicago: Chicago University Press.

Stolp. H. 1996. *Karma, reïncarnatie en christelijk geloof*. Baarn: Ten Have.

Wilkins, W.J. 1982. *Hindu Mythology*. Calcutta: Rupa.

Yogananda, Paramahamsa 1973. *Autobiography of a Yogi*. Los Angeles: Self-Realization-Fellowship.

Part III:

Religious Leaders

CHAPTER 7

Civilized Shamans: Sacred Biography and Founders of New Religious Movements

Robert S. Ellwood

Mircea Eliade, in his classic study *Shamanism: Archaic Techniques of Ecstasy* (1964) presents a paradigm of the ideal shaman's career.[1] The archetypal shaman experiences, perhaps early in youth, an 'initiatory psychopathology' in which he must contend with hearing the voices of the gods, and is perhaps virtually destroyed by the tumult within himself. Out of this, however, comes the shaman's call, for he realizes, or is told, that he now can never expect to live a merely normal life, but must respond by acquiring one spirit as his patron before the legion tears him apart. He must therefore undertake a formal initiation into the shaman's arcane arts, either under a master of the craft, or in deep isolation in the wilderness, or both. In the mythology of the people, the novice may be carried off by spiritual beings to the heights of the sky, or the depths of the earth, where the Supreme Being confers upon him shamanic powers. He may also be physically changed with, for example, his internal organs exchanged for organs of quartz.

The period of separation and isolation, when the candidate is withdrawn from the ordinary structures of society and for this very reason especially accessible to the other world of gods and spirits, and susceptible to receiving their gifts, is of considerable interest. An Eskimo shaman told the Danish explorer Knud Rasmussen, 'All true wisdom is only to be found far from men, out in the great solitude, and it can only be acquired by suffering. Privations and sufferings are

1. Eliade, 1964.

the only things that can open a man's mind to that which is hidden from others'.[2] Finally, after the skill and the patronage of a guiding spirit has been attained, the new shaman returns to his community in his or her fresh status, able to divine and heal. These stages of initiatory psychopathology, call, isolation, initiation, and reaggregation clearly represent a particular, individual case for the specialist of the three fundamental steps in initiation described by Arnold van Gennep and Victor Turner: separation, marginality or liminality, and reaggregation.[3]

In important respects the founders of many new religious movements are exemplars of aspects, at least, of this pattern. Scholars have frequently noted that the founders of the new religions of Japan, often women, are very like contemporary representatives of the *miko* or shamanesses who were powerful in ancient Japanese religion before Buddhism, and who have never entirely disappeared. Eliza M. Butler, in her classic study *The Myth of the Magus* has shown that a comparable type, which she calls the magus, has existed in the esoteric lore of the West at least since Hellenistic times.[4] E.R. Dodds, in *The Greeks and the Irrational*, has demonstrated a fairly direct link from the primeval shaman to the Hellenistic magus: The Greeks in the late archaic period came in contact with Scythians, and probably also Thracians, who possessed a central Asian type of shamanistic culture. From this time on, there appeared in Greece a series of *iatromanteis* seers, magical healers and religious teachers whose power was based on potent initiation, trance, magical flight (Abaris), and out-of-the-body travel like that of earlier shamans and later wonderworkers.[5]

Examples of the western magus range from Pythagoras and Apollonius of Tyana to the Paracelsus, Christian Rosencreutz, Saint Germain, and Cagliostro of popular legend. The magus will typically show evidence of strange powers and unusual calling from early childhood. He or she travels very widely, usually in Asia. He/she crisscrosses the world to meet sages and receive esoteric initiations. When the magus enters public work, the world is amazed by fab-

2. Cited in Lommel, 1967, 29.
3. Van Gennep 1960; Turner 1969.
4. Butler 1948.
5. Dodds 1951

ulous magical powers, but this wizard may feel that teaching is his/her most important work and it is less well understood. The disciples in turn will find their teacher puzzling, for he/she may go through unpredictable and extreme moods, even appear and disappear, in ways that are hard to comprehend yet are thought to be, in some mysterious way, a part of the teaching. He/she may not be moral or ascetic by conventional standards, even given to dissimulation, drink, sexual indulgence, or luxury, yet all this is accepted as part of his/her 'crazy wisdom'. The magus is neither a saint, nor a savior, nor a prophet. He/she is a shaman in civilization, and like most shamans is part fraud, part showman, part myth, and part extraordinary mystic. The magus's story is half legend, even in modern times, but the stories follow a similar line, and that story line is significant. For the magus's archetypal role as a great initiate who has received secret wisdom far beyond the ordinary, far more than that contained in ordinary religions, is what is important about him or her to friends and enemies alike. The followers of the magus characteristically report that, even more important than the metaphysical specifics of the teacher, is the way he or she enables them to see and experience the world in an almost indescribably fresh way, full of wonder and insight.

Three particularly striking modern cases may be suggested: Helena Petrovna Blavatsky of Theosophy, Georges Gurdjieff of the Gurdjieff groups, and L. Ron Hubbard of Scientology. Let us look at the outlines of their stories, for the present purposes suspending all critical response.

Helena Blavatsky (1831-1891), born in Russia of noble family, was unusual even as a child. She was headstrong, secretive, imaginative. She would hide in strange places for hours, and would tell her brothers and sisters marvelous tales of the fossils and animals in her grandfather's zoological museum, describing not only the animal's immediate life, but also its previous incarnations. She was married at sixteen or seventeen to N.V. Blavatsky, a widower more than twice her age who was vice-governor of Erivan. But she soon left him and began more than twenty years of wandering, ill-documented save for a trip to London with her father in 1851 where she said she first saw her 'master', a striking turbaned man of the East, and when she was back in Russia, amazing family and friends with remarkable psychic powers. During the years 1858-64 Blavatsky travelled widely over the earth, studying spiritualism and contacting shamans and masters of arcane lore in places as far apart as Egypt, Mexico, Canada and inner Asia, always seeking her ultimate goal, Tibet. She finally found it, spending the years 1864-67 in a Tibetan lamasery undergoing initiations with her Masters. She came to New York in 1874; and the following year, 1875, she and her American companion, Henry Steel Olcott, founded the Theosophical Society. She continued to produce remarkable 'phenomena', especially after she and Olcott moved to India in 1879; stories range from the production of a cup and saucer on a picnic to the transmission of the so-called Mahatma Letters from the esoteric masters guiding the evolution of the earth. Yet she was always controversial, and needless to say the wisdom in her massive and difficult tomes, such as *Isis Unveiled* and *The Secret Doctrine*, initially reached fewer souls than news of the wonders she performed.[6]

Another western magus is Georges Ivanovitch Gurdjieff (1872?-1949). He has probably influenced western esotericism more than any other modern figure except Blavatsky. He was born in the Caucasian region of the Russian empire, and even as a child would run away from home with the Romany, 'Gypsies', for days at a time, loving their wildness, mystery, and psychic powers.[7] As in the case of Blavatsky, according to his *Meetings with Remarkable Men*, it was the nineteenth century talk of Spiritualist phenomena such as table-tilting and mediumship that first engaged his systematic attention But in his exotic Transcaucasian homeland far more than parlor Spiritualism was available for investigation. He was determined to travel to seek out the meaning behind such phenomena as the Yezidi circle — legend had it that members of this sect inaccurately accused of devil-worship, could not leave a circle drawn on the ground. He also wanted to seek out the Sarman society, reportedly located near Mosul, which he had heard lodged supreme upholders of esoteric truth. So it was that, like Blavatsky, he claimed to have travelled widely in central Asia as a young person, and there to have met representatives of a

6. Blavatsky 1877; Blavatsky 1888. Cranston [Anita Atkins] 1993, is a sympathetic biography. Meade 1980 is more critical. See also the controversial Johnson 1994; and Gomes 1994, is an indispensable resource.
7. Bennett 1973, 20-21.

Hidden Brotherhood, probably Sufi, who preserved an occult tradition. Gurdjieff surfaced in Moscow on the eve of World War I, where
he met people who were later to write vividly about him, including
P.D. Ouspensky and Thomas de Hartmann. Lines from them incom-
parably delineate what it means to encounter a modern magus. Olga
de Hartmann, wife of Thomas, said:

> Mr Gurdjieff was an unknown person, a mystery. Nobody knew about his
> teaching, nobody knew his origin or why he appeared in Moscow and St.
> Petersburg. But whoever came in contact with him wished to follow him...
> He was a magus, and he presented a new way to the world.[8]

And Ouspensky said of the first meeting:

> I remember this meeting very well. We arrived at a small cafe in a noisy
> though not central street I saw a man of an oriental type, no longer young,
> with a black moustache and piercing eyes, who astonished me first of all be-
> cause he seemed to be disguised and completely out of keeping with place
> and its atmosphere... [He] in a black overcoat with a velvet collar and a black
> bowler hat produced the strange, unexpected, and almost alarming impres-
> sion of a man poorly disguised, the sight of whom embarrasses you because
> you see he is not what he pretends to be and yet you have to speak and
> behave as though you did not see it.[9]

The mystery of Gurdjieff did not end with first meeting. After an ad-
venturous escape from revolutionary Russia with such followers as
Ouspensky and the de Hartmanns, he established the well-known
'Institute for the Harmonious Development of Man' in Fontaine-
bleau, France. His disciples found stringent manual labour alternated
with lavish banquets and classes in Eastern dance, interpreted by
dialogue worthy of a Zen master. Gurdjieff would often play the role
of a cruel and unreasonable despot; he would order a project begun,
and then abandoned, or shout harshly at people for their stupidity, or
demand work be performed at top speed. At other times he might explain the reasons for these episodes. Not many stayed long, which

8. De Hartmann 1964, xiii.
9. Ouspensky 1949, 7.

seemed in fact to be the master's intention, and the centre was sold in 1933. But few who had ever been with Gurdjieff forgot their days with the magus, and many wrote about their experience in awestruck tones.[10]

L. Ron Hubbard, founder of the Church of Scientology, also exhibited characteristics of the modem magus. He was born in Tilden, Nebraska, in 1911. His father was a career officer in the U.S. Navy, and he was raised at his grandfather's Montana home in the area of Seattle, Washington. As with other magi, remarkable signs appeared early in life: by his own report he was made a 'blood brother' by the Blackfoot Indian tribe, was the youngest Eagle Scout on record, and at the age of twelve studied psychoanalysis under a student of Freud. Accompanying his father on tours of duty, as a teenager he journeyed to the Far East allegedly travelling from India to Japan and visiting monks and monasteries in inner Asia.[11] As a young adult, he entered George Washington University, studying the new field of nuclear physics. He participated in three ethnological expeditions to Central America and later to Alaska, did some pioneer flying, and became an accomplished sailor. His man vocation, however, came to be science fiction writing: he had published in *Astounding Science Fiction* by 1938, and for the next several years was remarkably prolific in this field. Certain of his stories suggest in embryo that imaginative and futuristic idealism which is expressed in developed Scientology. There is the concept that living men can be trapped in a writer's fantasy, or that the whole cosmos may be the fantasy of a single mind living in it. In later Scientological thought, we find that all sense of individual alienation, and all universes, stem from turbulence in theta or thought, which in its pure form, as 'static', is without motion or dimension and the ground of the universe. Keen perception can dissolve these enslaving veils; only that which is not directly observed tends to persist.

During World War II Hubbard was a Navy officer.[12] He said it was a matter of medical record that he was twice officially pronounced dead from combat injuries during that time, but returned to life —

10. Webb 1980; Bennett, op. cit. For resources see Driscoll, and the Gurdjieff Foundation of California, 1985.
11. Hubbard 1973; Miller 1987, 40-43.
12. Miller op. cit., 95-111.

the shaman's initiation. He was, by his report, once dead for eight minutes during an operation, and during this time received a vital message to impart.[13]

After the war, Hubbard resumed writing. He may also have been involved in the O.T.O., Aleister Crowley's magical order, in Pasadena, California, at that time; according to Church statements, he then broke up 'black magic' in America. By the end of the forties, however, had had taken up with another intense concern. In 1950 L. Ron Hubbard published his most famous book, *Dianetics*, in which he claimed that 'the hidden source of all psyche-somatic ills and human aberrations has been discovered and skills have been developed for their invariable cure'.[14] This volume was an immediate sensation, rating articles in the mass media, and discussion and practice groups. The next upshot was the Church of Scientology, founded in 1952, with Hubbard as its principal teacher. In the course of this role, Hubbard produced numerous books and made more claims of a shamanistic type: that he had visited heaven and hell and wore 'the boots of responsibility' for this universe. He told stories of his own past lives. Through the techniques imparted by his organization, as shamanic disciples his students realize results of shamanism for themselves, visiting their own remote pasts on faraway worlds to ascertain the distant causes of their present problems. L. Ron Hubbard died in 1986.

Founders like Blavatsky, Gurdjieff, and Hubbard are more than mythic figures; persons of our own times or the near past, they are as historical as any well known personalities of the nineteenth or twentieth century. Yet they have surely been reconstructed by themselves and their followers, the community at large, and not least their enemies, to conform in no small part to a mythic paradigm. In their present life-stories one can observe the mythmaking process that over the centuries has obtained in the case of the great religious founders, numerous saints, and holy men and women.

This is not merely a cynical observation. Myth necessarily says, in symbolic language things that are important about the subject and

13. Derived in part from Church of Scientology 1994, 'About L. Ron Hubbard', 783-87. See also memoirs in Hubbard, op. cit. For a critical biography see Miller, op cit. Many allegations in Miller's book are disputed by the Church of Scientology.
14. Hubbard 1950, ix.

the experience of others in relation to him or her. What a mythical narrative relates may not be literally true, but serves as metaphor to evoke the numinous or magical presence of the subject as she or he is remembered.

The mythopoeic (mythmaking) process can begin with a shaman, in these cases a shaman in civilization. Eliade has been criticized for glamorizing the shaman, and taking so seriously the shaman myth, as to lose sight of the reality that many shamans in primal societies are in fact charlatans, alcoholics or drug-takers — at the most entrepreneurs of spiritual wares no better than any other — rather than the lofty wizards and ascenders into heaven seen by assorted spiritual seekers.

Yes and no. Like most religious professionals, the shaman is a more complex person than appears on the surface. William Howells has this to say about shamans, and much the same could be said about many shamans in civilization, like those we are discussing:

The shamans know, of course, that their tricks are imposition, but at the same time everyone who has studied them agrees that they really believe in their power to deal with spirits. Here is a point, about the end justifying the means, which is germane to this and to all conscious augmenting of religious illusion. The shaman's main purpose is an honest one and he believes in it, and he does not consider it incongruous if his powers give him the right to hoodwink his followers in minor technical matters.[15]

Thus Franz Boas, in a famous study of Quesalid, a shaman of the Kwakiutl Indians of British Columbia, noted that this individual had started as a sceptic, and that skepticism was only enhanced as he teamed from senior shamans how to induce trances and fits, how to produce seemingly magical feats by sleight-of-hand, and much more. Nonetheless, he found that he could produce healings as well as anyone, and came to consider that this was accomplished because the sick person 'believes strongly in his dream about me', and apparently thought that *deceptions* were justifiable insofar as they helped people believe.[16] Clearly this is basically what shamans, like healers of all

15. Howells 1962, 132-33.
16. Boas 1930. Summarized in Levy-Strauss 1967, 169-73.

sorts — ancient and modern — do: create an atmosphere in which the illness, physical or mental, is interpreted and explained in terms of the worldview of that culture, whether this means attributing it to evil spirits, a lost or strayed soul, or germs. Then, with convincing dramatic gestures, the healer drives out of the evil, retrieves the soul, or does whatever is required, in terms of the same worldview. An important part of the scenario, of course, is the aura of authority created by knowledge of the shaman' a professional credentials, including his extraordinary initiation and supernatural assistants.

That brings us back to the sacred biographies of founders of new religious movements. The official biographies usually contain material that serves to create an aura of glamour, mystery, and extrasensory power about the person, as well as great charismatic appeal. Sometimes these accounts will raise doubts in the minds of outsiders, and understandably so. Yet it is important to realize why they are there; like perhaps some of the miracles of Jesus, they are emblematic of the power on other planes of the dramatic subject.

It is certainly legitimate and important for scholars to do their work and establish discrepancies between the actual lives of religious founders and the legend, even if, as is often the case, the founder himself helped construct the myth and perhaps came himself to believe in it. For memory is not a video camera but a creative art, as we are coming to realize more and more. Yet we need to see what the stories that memory makes are saying in their own language, as in the case presented by Albert Schweitzer of the Jesus of history and the Christ of faith.

Let us then outline characteristics of the standard sacred biography of the life of a founder of a new religious movement as a civilized shaman. Not surprisingly the stories of many of them fall into patterns resembling one another, and also into the shamanic paradigm; one also finds parallels to the lives of Hindu saints as argued by that caustic Austrian anthropologist, tantrist, and Hindu monk Agehananda Bharati, and of the mythic hero as presented by Joseph Campbell in *The Hero with a Thousand Faces*.[17] Here are some basic features of the life; they do not necessarily occur in this order:

17. Campbell 1949.

162 *Robert S. Ellwood*

1. There are signs in childhood of remarkable powers and exceptional achievements.
2. The candidate has an initial call, like Blavatsky's sight of her Master in London in 1851, Gurdjieff going out with the Gypsies, or Hubbard's experience during the eight minutes of 'death' in the hospital.
3. A break with the ordinary occurs: Blavatsky's marriage and wandering, Hubbard's crossing the Pacific.
4. The candidate travels to exotic places, especially in Asia and the East, where encounters with exceptional wisdom may be expected.
5. There is a time of isolation: Blavatsky in Tibet, Hubbard in the Naval hospital, Gurdjieff in his wanderings, allegedly also to the area of Tibet.
6. The candidate then returns, and takes up a more or less ordinary life.
7. Then comes an event of manifestation to the world: the founding of the Theosophical Society in 1875, Gurdjieff's appearance in Moscow and St Petersburg during the First World War; Hubbard's publication of *Dianetics* in 1950.
8. The founder gathers disciples, forming an incipient but still largely charismatic organization, which proceeds however to become institutionalized: the Theosophical Society, the Institute for the Harmonious Development of Man, the Church of Scientology.
9. There is then commonly a time of trial, like the 'deep sea journey' in Joseph Campbell's model: Blavatsky's troubles in 1883-84 concerning alleged fraud and the investigation by a representative of the Society for Psychical Research, Gurdjieff's escape from revolutionary Russia, later the end of the Fontainebleu centre and a serious automobile accident; the many legal problems that Scientology has undergone.
10. There is finally an apotheosis of the founder, when the troubles are somewhat overcome and his/her best work is done, such as Blavatsky's, *The Secret Doctrine* (1888) or Gurdjieff s greatest book, *All and Everything* (typescript ms. 1930; published 1950). It is followed by retirement, the last and most advanced training of the disciples who will be the movement's new leaders, the final words, and death.

Like the ancient shaman, the civilized shaman is a complicated mixture of substance and show, wisdom and foolishness. What can be said about them for certain is that they are extraordinary individuals, and for that reason they fascinate the rest of us. It has also been said that the primordial shamans were exceptional agents in the creation of human culture at its most primeval and basic levels, for they were makers in the realms of song, dance, costume, language, and story, as well as establishing basic paradigms of cosmology, religion, and, psychotherapy. It is not too much to hope that one or other shaman in civilization will do the same for our civilization.

Bibliography

Bennett, J.G. 1973. *Gurdjieff: Making a New World.* New York: Harper & Row.

Blavatsky, Helena Petrovna 1877. *Isis Unveiled: A Master-Key to the Mysteries of Ancient and Modern Science and Theology.* New York: J.W. Bouton.

Blavatsky, Helena Petrovna 1888. *The Secret Doctrine: The Synthesis of Science, Religion, and Philosophy.* London: The Theosophical Publishing Co.

Boas, Franz 1930. *The Religion of the Kwakiutl.* New York: Columbia. Contribution to *Anthropology*, 10, part 2, 1-11.

Butler, E.M. 1948. *The Myth of the Magus.* New York: Macmillan.

Campbell, Joseph 1949. *The Hero with a Thousand Faces.* New York: Pantheon.

Church of Scientology, 1994. 'About L. Ron Hubbard', *The Scientology Handbook: Based on the Works of L. Ron Hubbard.* Los Angeles: Bridge Publications, 783-87.

Cranston, Sylvia [Anita Atkins] 1993. *H.P.B. The Extraordinary Life and Influence of Helena Blavatsky.* New York: Tarcher/Putnam.

De Hartmann, Thomas 1964. *Our Life with Mr. Gurdjieff.* New York: Cooper Square.

Dodds, E.R. 1951. *The Greeks and the Irrational.* Berkeley: University of California Press.

Driscoll, J. Walter & Gurdjieff Foundation of California 1985. *Gurdjieff: An Annotated Bibliography.* New York: Garland.

Eliade, Mircea 1964. *Shamanism: Archaic Techniques of Ecstasy.* New York: Pantheon.

Gomes, Michael 1994. *Theosophy in the Nineteenth Century: An Annotated Bibliography.* New York: Garland.

Howells, William 1962. *The Heathens: Primitive Man and his Religions.* New York: American Museum of Natural History.

Hubbard, L. Ron 1950. *Dianetics: The Modern Science of Mental Health.* Los Angeles: American St. Hill Organization.

Hubbard, L. Ron 1973. *Mission into Time.* Los Angeles: American Saint Hill Organization.

Johnson, Paul 1994. *The Masters Revealed: Madame Blavatsky and the Myth of the Great White Lodge.* Albany: SUNY Press.

Levy-Strauss, Claude 1967. *Structural Anthropology.* Garden City, NY: Doubleday, 169-73.

Lommel, Andreas 1967. *Shamanism: The Beginnings of Art.* Transl. Michael Bullock. New York: McGraw-Hill.

Meade, Marion 1980. *Madame Blavatsky: The Woman Behind the Myth.* New York: Putnam.

Miller, Russell 1987. *Bare-Faced Messiah: The True Story of L. Ron Hubbard.* New York: Henry Holt.

Ouspensky, P.D. 1949. *In Search of the Miraculous.* New York: Harcourt Brace Jovanovitch.

Turner, Victor 1969. *The Ritual Process.* Chicago: Aldine.

Van Gennep, Arnold 1960. *The Rites of Passage.* Chicago: University of Chicago Press.

Webb, James 1980. *The Harmonious Circle: The Lives and Work of G.I. Gurdjieff, P.D. Ouspensky, and Their Followers.* New York: Putnam.

CHAPTER 8

Hagiography and Text in The Aetherius Society: Aspects of The Social Construction of A Religious Leader

Mikael Rothstein

Introduction

The historical facts surrounding religious leaders are often clouded by religious interpretations of the person and his or her life and achievements. Very often there is no easy access to plain facts, whereas legends, myths and theological elaborations on the religious leader's life, meaning and work are in abundance. Externally obtained data are similarly relatively rare. Brief biographies as those found in J. Gordon Melton's *Biographical Dictionary of American Cult and Sect Leaders* [1] give valuable scholarly information, but very often it is difficult to measure the validity of biographical details on religious leaders given by their own supporters.

This is very much the case with religious leaders or innovators of the past such as Muhammad, Siddharta Gotama or Jesus — to mention a few — but it is certainly also a common feature regarding religious leaders of the present. Most new or alternative religions will, providing they have a leader or founder of religious importance, be able to describe and explain all matters concerning the leader as long as it is of interest to the believers. Information of other kinds is very often more difficult to get at. A prominent example of this mechanism

---

1. Melton 1986. This book only deals with religious leaders who died prior to January 1st, 1983.

is Scientology's compassionate occupation with L. Ron Hubbard, his life and his work. Scientology has transformed the person of L. Ron Hubbard into a superior being of ultimate good and ultimate competence. He is not declared divine, but the way in which he is adored and understood among the believers of the Church's inner-movement, reveals a conceptualization of Hubbard which places him in a unique position, not only in the organization, but in the history of mankind. Maharishi Mahesh Yogi of Transcendental Meditation, Madame Blavatsky of The Theosophical Society and Sun Myung Moon of The Family Federation for World Peace and Unification (formerly known as The Unification Church) are but a few other recent examples of a somewhat similar kind.[2]

Although the actual historical and social conditions that surround religious leaders are of general relevance to the study of religion, they are not always of primary importance. If the scholarly attention is focused on the religious *interpretation* or the *making* of the religious leader, the need for precise biographical data is in certain ways of less importance. For instance, the historical facts surrounding Muhammad are of less interest than the legendary *hadith*-traditions if the intention is to understand the image of Muhammad as the ideal person in contemporary Islam, and the correct data regarding the birth of the historical Jesus is of no significance if we are interested in the mythological foundation of Christian Christmas celebrations or the understanding of the infant Jesus in Christian lore or iconography. Similarly the actual whereabouts of L. Ron Hubbard is of no paramount importance to the scholarly study of the *mythological* rendering of Hubbard, which has become increasingly significant among scientologists.

The image of the religious leader is generally a social construction, and the narratives about him or her will very often form a coherent hagiographic tradition. Studying the image of the religious leader or founder, therefore, will typically be an interrogation into comprehensive mythological narratives. However, very few historians of religions have taken up the challenge of analysing the sacred biographies

---

2. There are, of course, exceptions. The life of Bhaktivedanta Swami Pra-
   bhupada, guru and founder of ISKCON, for instance, has been described
   in great detail in several books written by his disciples.

of contemporary religious leaders as they appear in primary religious texts.[3] An indication of this lacking interest is found in the *Encyclopaedia of Religion*,[4] where the entry 'Biography' (which is explained to mean 'sacred biography') only refers to classical religions, and among those primarily to Christian traditions. There is no mentioning of the literally thousands of hagiographic traditions outside the realm of traditional Christianity, Islam, Buddhism and Confucianism. This article, however, aims at a hermeneutical investigation into religious texts in order to understand the 'sacred biography' of one relatively unknown modern religious leader.

George King in the Texts of The Aetherius Society

No real attempts have been made by scholars to go behind the official image of George King (1919-1997), the founder and (until his death) official leader of The Aetherius Society. Furthermore, as far as I am informed, all external descriptions of George King and his life are based on sources provided by his movement. A biographical note on King by sociologist of religion Eileen Barker, for instance, is solely based on information obtained from books issued by The Aetherius Society.[5] What is typically emphasized is the religious conceptualization of King. George King was not an ordinary man in the eyes of

3. See Dorthe Refslund Christensen on the hagiographic tradition surrounding Ron Hubbard (Refslund Christensen 1997a, 1997b, 15-27 and 1997c, 36-45) and Rothstein 1992 (in part) and 1993.
4. LaFleur 1993.
5. Barker 1991. Eileen Barker's biographical sketch of King reads: "Founder and President of The Aetherius Society, 'An International Spiritual Brotherhood'. He is known as the Metropolitan Archbishop, His Eminence Sir George King, OSP, PhD, ThD, DD. Sir George was born in Shropshire; his father was a schoolteacher, his mother a practicing spiritual healer. He became a London taxi driver and, a conscientious objector during the Second World War, he served as a section leader in the Fire Service. He practiced yoga and studied a number of Eastern and New Age philosophies. In 1954, he claims to have received the command 'Prepare yourself! You are to become the voice of the Interplanetary Parliament.' Sir George has since channelled numerous messages, especially from a Cosmic Master from Venus, known as Aetherius, and Master Jesus" (Barker 1991, 216).

his followers, and any biography should partly relate to the perception of the believers. The common description of King, whether internal or external, will therefore easily involve the same mixture of myth and historical facts that constitutes any sacred biography. Historian of religions William R. LaFleur writes:

Whereas mythology will usually tell only of random deeds of deities in a largely episodic and nonconsecutive manner, the subjects of a sacred biography will tend to be treated as persons whose life stories need to be told as discrete and continuous lives. The subject of a sacred biography will tend to be treated as someone whose life story can be told from birth to death and, to that degree at least, as it would be treated in a secular biography. The difference from the latter, however, lies in the degree to which such a subject will be represented as carrying out a divinely planned 'call' or visions authenticating such a mission, and having either infallible knowledge or supernatural powers.[6]

As we shall see, every aspect of this characterization suits the example of George King nicely.

In order to get hold of the tradition that developed around George King, the perspective of the believers becomes unavoidable. It is of no direct interest to us that King earned his money as a taxi driver until 1954 when his career as a religious leader began, but it is of great importance to understand that his former position as an anonymous taxi driver signifies something crucial to his followers: Their religious leader started out as nothing more than an ordinary man. Hence, the frequently reported detail on King's professional life prior to the beginning of his religious career. However, entirely 'normal' is not the proper description. In the pamphlets and books of The Aetherius Society it is stated over and over again that King, as he was approached by extraterrestrial beings of superior intelligence in 1954, was 'a Western Master of Yoga', or 'A Western Yoga Adept'. Further, due to the laws of karma, it is believed that King has passed through all sorts of development, and that many elementary stages of conscious-

6. LaFleur 1993, 220.

ness and knowledge have been left behind.[7] The image we get is that of a common man who raised himself to a point where he had reached superior insight into all sorts of spiritual knowledge and practice. King is depicted as the 'self realized' man who attained what all humans may potentially qualify for — but what is accomplished by only a very few. It is occasionally suggested by members of The Aetherius Society that King was in fact a Cosmic Master himself, but this idea has never been officially confirmed.[8]

In the various texts issued by The Aetherius Society, King is introduced in more or less the same standard phrases. The emphasis is always laid on his unique personal qualities, and the immense importance of his spiritual task, but only little is mentioned about his life prior to the time when his religious interest and subsequent religious duties changed his life. A rather typical official presentation of George King by The Aetherius Society reads:

His Eminence Sir George King. Primary Terrestrial Mental Channel.
His Eminence Sir George King was born on January 23rd 1919, in Wellington, Shropshire, England. His father was a schoolmaster and his mother a noted clairvoyant and Healer. From a very early age, he showed a profound interest in Religion — at that time, orthodox Christianity.

7. Usually this is not stated explicitly, but the principle is often emphasized, for instance in *Aetherius Society* 1982, 15, where it says: ' [the law of karma] will place each individual exactly where he belongs; exactly what he has earned will be given him...'.
8. When members of the group were asked about the status of George King, a common answer was the following: 'A lot of people think that he is an adept, but it has never been verified by his Eminence himself' (Bang 1996, 48). When King is titulated Master this consequently means 'spiritual leader' rather than Cosmic Master. Elsewhere (concerning Claude Vorilhon (Rael), the leader of The Raelian religion) I have pointed to the fact that religious leaders often will avoid discussing their spiritual status (Rothstein 1993, 143). During the process of 'charismatization' (Barker 1993) they will often leave it up to their followers to come to their own conclusions. This is the case with Rael, Maharishi Mahesh Yogi of TM, Sun Myung Moon of the former Unification Church, and Jesus of course through the discourse known to theologians as the 'Messiasgeheimnisse'.

The World War II years were spent in the London Fire Brigade, battling the effects of the Nazi Luftwaffe incendiary and high-explosive raids on London and surrounding areas. During this time he learned personally and deeply of man's inhumanity to man — as well as much about man's capacity for self-sacrifice and bravery.

His interest had turned by this time to the more profound Truths of advanced metaphysics and he became a student of Yoga — practising ever more difficult and challenging Yoga exercises for up to 10 hours daily. His own psychic abilities became very pronounced, including his ability to project into the Higher Realms to pursue his intense search for the highest Truth, with the assistance of advanced intelligences there. By 1954 he was deeply engrossed in Spiritual Healing and had already received advanced Initiations on the Higher Planes.

It was in this year that he received the well-known 'Command' to prepare himself to become the voice of Interplanetary parliament and was soon shown, through a series of highly specialized exercises, how to bring about that elevated state of consciousness absolutely necessary to establish a mental rapport with the Beings Who inhabit the other Planets. He mastered the science of Raja, Gnani and Kundalini Yoga until he could consciously attain the state of Samadhi. It was then the Cosmic Masters of the Solar System began using him as Primary Terrestrial Mental Channel.

Early transmissions from the Cosmic Masters indicated the wide diversity of Their deep interest in and compassion for mankind. The Master Aetherius from Venus gave a series of simple exercises for mental and physical health which were published as The Practices Of Aetherius. This Great Being also announced the beginning of the Magnetization Periods during which a huge Spacecraft, satellite No. 3, sent powerful Spiritual Energies through all those on Earth who performed acts of selfless Service. The Cosmic Master Mars Sector 6, who was in control of Satellite No. 3, also delivered many profound Messages, with frequent reference to the terrible dangers of nuclear experimentation. The great Master of Love from Venus, the Master Jesus, also spoke often in words of gentle, yet profound Wisdom to humanity.

Upon the Master's instructions, His Eminence founded The Aetherius Society in London to help propagate Their Teachings. The Society was extended to the United States, where he became an Ordained Minister. He later earned many degrees, including Doctor of Divinity, and was created an Archbishop in 1980, founding The Aetherius Churches.

At this time he was recognized by Orders of Chivalry worldwide for his outstanding humanitarian accomplishments and became a Knight of many Orders, and in 1981 he was Crowned His Serene Highness Prince George King de Santorini.

To Members of The Aetherius Society throughout the world His Eminence Sir George King is acknowledged Primary Terrestrial Mental Channel for Interplanetary Parliament and recognized as their Spiritual Master in these latter days before the dawning of a New Age upon Earth![9]

In several additional texts, King's many achievements are described in more detail, and the many prices, awards, titles and other sorts of acknowledgements he, according to The Aetherius Society, has received, are mentioned in detail. An addenda to the 1982 version of the book *The Age of Aetherius* [10] is a good example. The actual information will not be questioned here.[11] Rather I shall concentrate on the way it is presented:

Long-deserved recognition of the outstanding abilities and achievements of Doctor George King began to arrive in 1977, when the academic degree of Doctor of Philosophy was conferred upon him. Soon to follow were other degrees: Doctor of Sacred Humanities, Doctor of Literature with an appointment as Professor in Human Relations at North-West London University, a well-established and highly-reputed one in England, also issued to the Author [King], on the recommendation of several outstanding European scholars who had reviewed his works, a Citation mentioning the Author's publications, You Too Can Heal, The Day The Gods Came, and The Nine Freedoms, as well as his research thesis entitled 'The Behaviour of Humanity and the Pyschological Approach to Humanity'.

9. Abrahamson 1994, 14-15.
10. King and Avery 1982.
11. The book gives a line of references, but only to other Aetherius Society publications or texts of a similar kind. I have not had the opportunity to go through these documents.

From the Academy of Science in Rome came the Gold Medal of Merit in Science and the Medal of Honour with Collare Grand Croce d'Onore al Merito con Bandia d'Italia Marce Tuillo Cicerone, together with the Diploma Solenne in Science confering the title, 'Immortal of Rome'.

The nobility and royalty of the world also began to take note of his humanitarian achievements and he was soon invested in Knighthood in many Orders of Chivalry in Europe[12]

Further in the text, among many other things, it is described how George King was crowned by His Royal and Empirial Highness Prince Henri III Paleologue (who was apparently King's cousin), and bestowed with virtually all sorts of orders and titles. Following this information, King's own successful efforts to establish new orders of chivalry is described, including his enthronement as Prince Grand Master of his own order, The Mystical Order of Saint Peter on June 20th, 1982. King's authority as Archbishop and Metropolitan Archbishop of The Aetherius Churches is also stressed. But more — many more — distinctions are listed, including the appointment of Honorary Consul-at-Large, Minister of State and Special Adviser to the President of the Republic of Free Poland (in Exile) [sic.], from where he also was honoured with 'its highest awards including Virtuti Militari and the Grand Cordon of the Order of Polonia Restituta'. George King was, according to this text, voted Minister of the Year for 1981 by the International Evangelism Crusades, and received the Prize of Peace and Justice, with the rank of Knight of Humanity in 1981 from UNICEF and the UCCI. A comment in the text reads: '...this Prize being only somewhat less prestigious than the famed Nobel Prize'.[13]

The text ends with the following:

Honours and awards too numerous to list here have been received from all over the Western world where the humanitarian works, Spiritual abilities and insight of this outstanding Master of Yoga have begun to win the recog-

12. King and Avery 1982, 77-78.
13. King and Avery 1982, 77-78.

nition which they have so long deserved. Others are sure to follow and will be added to the addenda of future editions of this book.[14]

An ultimate accolade was awarded George King at his 78th birthday (January 23, 1997). The Aetherius Society invited all mankind to partake in a Cosmic Tribute to King at that specific time. He has, the invitation reads, received many 'temporal and divine' recognitions, but on this day, 'a heavenly tribute will be bestowed!'. The occasion was explained as a very special astrological alignment of the planets of the solar system.[15]

But King is also shown as a unique religious leader in other ways, not least by associating him with divine or semi-divine beings. In one text, for instance, King himself describes how he met with Master Jesus face to face at the top of a mountain, Holdstone Down, in Devon on July 23th, 1958. A text which explains the details of a photo of the site where the meeting allegedly took place reads: 'The small pile of boulders in the foreground marks where Master Jesus stood on this historic occasion [...] Thousands of pilgrims have followed our Master to this spot [...]'.[16] In other texts the elevated Masters themselves acclaim that King is of a special kind. In the publication *The Twelve Blessings*, which, according the The Aetherius Society's mythological rendering, was delivered by the Master Jesus through George King, there is a two page note, stating (among other things) that 'Jesus blessed this book'. In a spacecraft commanded by a being known as Mars Sector 8, George King's mother, Mary, met with Jesus on his request. She had mentally been instructed to bring the book: 'This must not be touched by any [...] save our Mental Channel', a cosmic voice had told her. The spaceship, after a wonderful journey, entered a 'Mother Craft' and Mary King was approached by Jesus: 'Give me the Book', he said, and took it in both hands. Then he exclaimed:

Oh Supreme Master of all Creation
Higher than Highest

14. King and Avery 1982, 79.
15. From the The Aetherius Society's home page on the Internet, December 28th, 1996.
16. Abrahamson 1994, 22.

Mightier than the Mightiest
Greater than all Greatness
We bring to Thee this offering in Love and Humility
From our beloved brother of Earth — George,
The one Whom Thou didst choose to be a Leader
Among men of Earth, in this their New Age[17]

George King is 'a beloved brother', he is called 'a leader among men' and certainly, he has been chosen by no less than the Supreme Master of all Creation, apparently the same entity called by the name of God. The authority here is none less than Jesus, the single most authoritative figure in Western religion (however theosophically transformed in this context), and the statement is not rendered by King himself. Contrary to the channelled messages, this vital information is provided through the memory of Mary King, George's mother, who went to the far end of the Solar System with the Cosmic Masters. Hence, it is somebody else who tells of King's unique qualities — not himself — a fact that will obviously strengthen his credibility (see note 19).

After this, we are informed, Jesus placed the book in a box, and Mary King heard beautiful music fill the whole room. She was very affected, and wept aloud. After a few moments of 'cosmic music', Jesus turned and these were his words:

Blessed is he, who reading this Book doth understand.
But exalted is he, even among Angels,
Who reading this Book, doth take it to his heart
And follow its precepts.
Tell my Son, that this Book is now and forever — Holy[18]

The last sentence is obviously that of greatest interest to us. Jesus is talking directly to Mary King, and there is no doubt that 'my son' is George. There are no indications of actual family-bonds, and prob-

17. The Aertherius Society 1974, 11.
18. The Aertherius Society 1974, 12.

ably the meaning is symbolical.[19] However, what we have is the explicit mentioning of a close relation between Jesus and George King, and none less than George's mother serves as the mediator. Although the theological composition is different, the word 'son' points to Christian conceptualizations, and King is more or less paralleled to the figure of Jesus Christ in Christianity. In Christian mythology Jesus is the 'son of God', and in this text King becomes symbolically the son of Jesus. The important thing is that King thereby is positioned as some kind of saviour, as a chosen one with the position of Jesus in Christian myth as the matrix. The hagiographic tale of King meeting with Jesus on a mountain is another example of the same type of Biblical analogy. The phenomenological structure equals that of Moses on Mount Sinai, and the myth of the transfiguration of Christ on a mountain as well: George King, then, encounters the divine in the same manner as prominent figures from Jewish and Christian myths. In this perspective King may be seen as a representative of the Biblical tradition of prophethood and, simultaneously, through the notion of Cosmic Masters of a superior spiritual standing, as embedded in an easily recognizable theosophical tradition.[20]

All in all the text affirms George King and his teaching as unique and of utmost value. Further, the book contains minute descriptions of how George King is supposed to react during 'overshadowing', thus forming a matrix for his actual performance as the leader of the

19. Another UFO-prophet, Claude Vorilhon (Rael), claims, on the contrary, that his mother — whose name is also Mary (Marie) — was once abducted into a spacecraft and inseminated with sperm from the leader of the Planet of the Eternals, Jahwe. Later on Claude was born as the child of an earthly mother and a celestial father — who had never had sex. When mature, during a visit to his father's home, he was informed of this, and he was introduced to his half-brother, Jesus, whom he embraced warmly (Vorilhon 1989, 114). In The Raelian religion this myth of origin serves to consolidate Vorilhon's image and authority, just as George King's position is consolidated by the myth recalled here.

20. George King's teaching legitimizes itself through Christianity in other ways as well. The Twelve Blessings given to humanity by the Master Jesus, are, for instance, seen as an extension of Jesus' Sermon on the Mount, which, thanks to George King, according to the believers, now also 'includes a Cosmic concept'.

group's rituals. Consequently George King's religious behaviour is also legitimized in sacred texts. Finally, we may observe that the language of the Master Jesus is similar in style to the 1950's traditional Biblical language; not because Venusians read the King James' version of the Christian scriptures, but because that kind of language signals religious authority to those (time and place taken into consideration) listening to it or reading it. An easily recognisable idiomatic tradition is very apparent in The Aetherius Society. In that sense the texts of The Aetherius Society are quite traditional. Cosmic Masters etc. tend to prefer older forms of English whenever they approach mankind.

Further Examinations of the Texts

A brief examination of texts, such as those cited above, reveals several characteristic features:

1. When introduced, George King does not speak for himself. He is described by his closest associates in the organization — although he himself may well be the actual author or editor of the books wherein the texts are found. Hence, he is promoted by others, by his followers. Actual self-promotion by King, however, also occurs, namely in direct connection to discussions of the religious goals and preconditions and the ritual practice of The Aetherius Society. Sometimes he is acclaimed by the Cosmic Masters in the messages channelled by himself, but this kind of recognition is more powerfully expressed through others: In one case, as we have seen, he is promoted by his own mother.

2. King is praised through a list of formal recognitions, although most titles and awards refer to institutions beyond the knowledge of the average reader outside The Aetherius Society.

3. King is depicted not only as a superior spiritual leader and expert of various spiritual techniques, but also as an outstanding intellectual and humanitarian. The mentioning of his time as a child where the foundation for future greatness was laid, resemble numerous of similar childhood narratives in sacred biographies.

We do not learn of many specific details, but the indication that King was of a remarkable kind since his birth is clear.[21]

4. King is perceived not as the only contactee, but certainly as the most important and most competent, a fact astrologically expressed in the anticipated correlations of the planets on his very birthday,

5. Finally, it was anticipated that future rewards of all kinds would come as a natural consequence of George King's efforts and achievements.

At this point we may refer to The Aetherius Society's Internet home page, which of course also contains presentations of George King. The text is basically the same as in the printed materials, but certain pieces of information are added. For instance it is stated that King had abandoned 'all business interests and materialistic ambitions', and that he was 'acting upon instructions from Cosmic Authority'. Further, several new titles and marks of honour are mentioned including 'the international Prize of Peace and Justice from H.H. Prince Pensavalle, President of the International Union of Christian Chivalry' in 1981, and the event in 1991 when King was '...presented Letters Patent of Armorial Bearings also known as a Grant of Arms, by Bluemantle Pursuivant, a Herald of Her Majesty's College of Arms in England'.[22]

As it appears, the presentation of George King, which has been much the same throughout the entire history of The Aetherius Society, serves insiders more than outsiders. The hagiographic texts are not a means for making people join the society. Rather the texts provide those already engaged in the society's work with stimulating information. Indeed the texts cited above are from books meant for people already interested in George King's teachings. The texts do not explicitly aim at presenting convincing arguments in the line of missionary work, and they do not refer to specific accomplishments

21. For comparisons to the legends of L. Ron Hubbard, see Refslund Christensen 1997.
22. From the Internet December 28th, 1996.

by George King. Rather, King's virtues seem to be presupposed and his greatness can simply be stated. If the reader is somewhat acquainted with the beliefs of The Aetherius Society, the description of King becomes religiously meaningful and potent, but if not, most people will probably find it over-exposed or even ridiculous. More than anything, therefore, these texts are statements of faith written by leaders of the movement to the average member. The texts communicate the message of George King's unique importance and the general meaning of The Aetherius Society's work, and the repetition of these statements serves to institutionalize a specific image of the man and internalize the hagiographic details as unshakable facts in the minds of the believers. The hagiographic material adds to the internal solidarity rather than providing ammunition for missionary work.

According to Eileen Barker, the tales of the former Unification Church's Sun Myung Moon's divine qualities are of direct relevance only to the believers, while outsiders will find them hard to accept, to say the least.[23] I take this to be a common feature in all small religious groups which form a more or less secluded cultic milieu around their leader — but in fact also a well known mechanism in larger social contexts: The person of Jesus, for instance, is of no immediate relevance to non-believers in Christian environments. In The Aetherius Society, the outsiders' lack of deference to and understanding of George King is (at least among certain members) turned into something positive. During my talks with members of the Aetherius Society in London in 1993, two women told me that the skepticism of non-believers was perfectly understandable, and that no one should be expected to understand George King 'just like that'. However, learning about him, would — as they saw it — lead to a natural awe for his person. As I understood these women, their special (we might say esoteric) knowledge of King, was a strong force in their religious commitment. They had access to knowledge and resources unknown to the general public, and thus the ignorance of the surroundings was of no personal burden to them. If this interpretation is correct, indeed if my informants are representative, it appears that the hagiography about George King, as an expression of insiders' narratives, serves an

23. Barker 1993, 194.

important purpose. It helps the believers to identify themselves as opposed to those who are not initiated into the special knowledge of King's organization. Hence, internal social stability may be gained through a somewhat restricted communication to people outside the society whether potential converts or the general audience. The partly esoteric beliefs among members of the society's inner-movement includes a special evaluation of King, and, therefore, limited knowledge about him on the part of outsiders points to the believers' special position and may thus add to the self esteem of the inner-movement members.

In accordance with this differentiation between believers and non-believers, external communications are carried out in very different ways than internal communications. During 1996, for instance, The Aetherius Society conducted a lecture tour throughout the United Kingdom where 18 major cities were visited, but the message carried on those occasions did not promote George King as the central figure. 'Public information' on UFOs and the destiny of our planet, i.e., more principle elements of faith, were in focus. Spokesman of The Aetherius Society in London, Richard Lawrence, said: '...what we want is to get the message out to as many people as we can [...] It's a matter of getting the message out to people and letting them decide'.[24] As a matter of fact, The Aetherius Society does not seem to be too interested in gathering a larger membership: 'We will always say to people; don't join us unless you really know what we are'.[25] The importance of George King is unquestionable among the believers, but The Aetherius Society is perfectly able to see that not everyone may feel the same. Why, then, jeopardize a positive interest in the society's work by emphasizing the importance of a specific individual?

In a message on The Aetherius Society's home page on the Internet, which is probably visited mainly by those already acquainted with the society, a paragraph shows how King's influence, according to the believers, is seen everywhere, although not everyone on Earth

24. Charles Abrahamson interviewed by Mel Richards in the magazine *Encounters*, Issue 12, October 1996, 64. A small book was issued on that occasion: King and Lawrence 1996.
25. Charles Abrahamson interviewed by Mel Richards in the magazine *Encounters*, Issue 12. October 1996, 64

is able to realise it. A four pages presentation of King ends with the following:

Indeed is the legacy created and built by Sir George a massive and almost un-believable one. He is truly an inspiration to all on Earth, most especially to those interested in working to bring in The New Age on Earth. For Sir George has shown us the Way for these modern days [...]. By living amongst the many, contacting the Spark of God within and then returning to teach, heal and uplift mankind in all ways possible.[26]

This brief text, just as those cited earlier, is addressed to inner-mem-bers. Texts addressing the general public hold quite another perspec-tive. The overall soteriological importance of George King is neglected in favour of a much more restrained rhetoric. In a flyer advertising a series of lectures delivered by Aetherius Society leaders in London during a 'Festival for Mind, Body and Spirit', King is presented in the following way:

[...] It [The Aetherius Society] was founded in August 1956 by Western Mas-ter of Yoga, His Eminence Sir George King, who has produced many books and cassettes on a wide variety of metaphysical and occult subjects.[27]

To outsiders the books and cassettes mentioned may seem bizarre, naive or all too complicated, but to the initiates everything becomes clear due to the fact that George King, who channelled the basic parts of the society's literature, was in permanent tune with beings of spir-itual superiority. In short: A precondition for wholly appreciating The Aetherius Society's publications is the acknowledgement of George King as a unique religious authority.

Religious Leadership

Having discussed the appearance of George King in a selection of The Aetherius Society texts, we may be able to establish some kind of

26. From the Internet, December 28th, 1996.
27. Leaflet published on the occation of The Festival for Mind, Body and Spirit, The Royal Horticultural Hall, London 20th-29th May 1995.

external categorization. One possibility is to analyse the case of George King along Max Weber's classical conceptualization of religious 'prophets'.

Weber distinguishes between two types of prophets, the emissary type and the exemplary. In short the emissary type refers to a religious preacher, who believes he or she has received a message of general or specific importance, and that it is his or her task to communicate it to others. The emphasis lies somewhere else regarding the exemplary type: His or her religious authority is based on his or her own experience, which serves as an example to others.[28]

Probably most leaders of contemporary new religions are of the exemplary type, but certainly not all. Some are emissaries from divine beings, and George King appears to be a mixture.

The way in which he is described and understood in The Aetherius Society refers to three distinct functions:

1. He is the especially chosen Primary Terrestrial Mental Channel who receives and communicates concise and decisive information from highly authoritative 'Cosmic Masters'.
2. He is, however, also the self-made expert of all sorts of metaphysical techniques, and thus glorious due to his own personal achievements.
3. Finally, George King is described as a great and unique person in the ordinary sense of the word, a great humanitarian, a self-sacrificing and trustworthy man.

In other words, George King unites the two standard types of religious leadership suggested by Weber. He communicates messages from powers beyond, and he personally serves in all possible ways as a beacon to his followers. The Aetherius Society's texts always point to the fact that King's spiritual development went before the 'Command' to act on behalf of the super human beings. Thus, we get the impression that the Cosmic Masters chose him because of his self-established qualities. On the other hand, his authority as a religious leader is very much based on the position given him by the Masters. In this way the two dimensions of his religious authority (as defined

28. Weber 1963, 46ff.

by Weber) melt together forming a unity of 'emissary' and role model.
In the track of Weberian sociology on religious leadership, more
recent scholars have developed ways of approaching leaders of new
religious groups through the concept of charisma. Sociologist of religion Roy Wallis made the following comment on David Berg,
founder and leader of the Family (formerly known as the Children of
God) until his death in 1994, emphasizing that Berg's charisma was
constructed in the process of social interaction:

It emerges out of a particular structure of social relationships in which an exchange takes place of mutual attribution of status and worth. The putative
charismatic leader emboldened by this flattering recognition of the status
and identity to which he aspires, then seeks to realize in his behaviour the
powers and status with which he has been credited: to live up to the image
with which he has been endowed. In the process others are elevated with
him as intimates or lieutenants. Their significance derives from him. Having
been raised up, and recognized as special by him, they add to the recognition
of the leader, endowing him with still further significance as author of the
movement and their own fortunate condition, leading him to take ever more
seriously the conception of himself as someone out-of-the-ordinary.[29]

The books issued by The Aetherius Society are entirely in the hands
of George King and his 'intimates and lieutenants'. Either the close
associates have written the books alone or in cooperation with King
himself, or they have served as editors of King's texts. As a matter of
fact only two or three names come up again and again. At the time of
his death George King himself was, as far as I can judge, never approached by others than those chosen few. Prior to his death it was
quite often mentioned that King was not too well, and that his hard
work had affected him.[30] This, of course, made the contributions of
the assistants even more needed, and their position even stronger.
These individuals have, according to King: 'dedicated all their essen-

29. Wallis 1993, 172. Wallis is quoting himself from: 'The Social Construction
    of Charisma' which originally appeared in Wallis and Bruce (eds.): *Socio-
    logical Theory. Religion and Collective Action*, Belfast 1986, 129-54.
30. King himself explained how the process of channelling the messages
    from the Cosmic Masters was of great danger to his health. King and
    Avery 1982, 52-53.

tial energy to the cause of World Peace and Enlightenment', and he adds: 'These few, under my personal direction, are responsible for a staggering work load which benefits all life on Earth in a very direct manner'.[31] In return they propagated George King as a religious ideal when he was among them, and they continue to do so after his death.

In this way the texts of The Aetherius Society reflect the general social mechanism described by Wallis. The image of King was being socially constructed through the relations and interactions between George King himself, his closest associates and those of a more peripheral position in the organization, and in the years following King's death the process continues. The books published by The Aetherius Society are in fact the tangible result of a complex hagiographic process which is experienced by the believers in terms of their devotion to George King. At the same time the literature of the movement is a resource in that process. The status of King is confirmed in the texts, and additional power is added to the process of devotion and enthusiasm.

A concrete example of how texts serve as hagiographic resources is the internal interpretation and description of George King's 1959 appearance on British television (BBC May 21st, 1959). According to internal texts, George King demonstrated 'a Yogic Samadhic trance so that a Cosmic Master from another Planet could actually speak to Britain!'. The event is called 'unique and historic', and it is said that it was 're-broadcast again and again through ensuing years' due to its popularity. The fact that King reached national television in 1959 is still (some 44 years later) looked upon as a great accomplishment, so great that it is recorded in the most recent written updates regarding the society. In reading about the society's prior achievements, enthusiasm and good spirits in today's work is encouraged. Commentator on the UFO-debate, Jerome Clark, however, refers to several other instances where George King arouses everything but pleasure in the media. A newspaper in London speculated that The Aetherius Society might be a Communist front, and during a radio interview in New York, King was straightforwardly called a charlatan.[32] This was

31. King and Avery 1982, 50-51.
32. Clark 1992, 15.

also in the late 1950s. It is obvious that an old success is still embraced and recapitulated again and again, while the controversies of the same period have disappeared into oblivion. A former success on television has been turned into a hagiographic text, which has been reproduced many times over the years, thereby transgressing the time boundary of the original event. King's appearance on TV has become a static event, not something that happened at an earlier point in history. In exactly the same way King's former achievements during the 1950s and 1960s (for instance the charging of 19 mountains with spiritual energy) are analysed and discussed again and again.[33] The constant meditation upon King's previous achievements, bring his deeds into the present, which is nourished by the tales.

In this perspective we may see the sacred narratives about George King as a part of the foundation myth of the whole society and, indeed, as a founding feature of The Aetherius Society's historiography in general. What is experienced today is directly derived from the events in these semi-mythological times. The Aetherius Society has added religious meaning to mundane events of no obvious importance. In doing so, in conceptualizing the historical past in mythological terms, this religious group is doing exactly what many religions have done in the past.

Adding to the charisma discussion, Eileen Barker has pointed to the fact that recognition of the religious leader's charisma must be learned. Charisma describes a certain relation between the devoted believer and the leader, and thus it signifies a process of socialization. Following Barker, who developed her theory through studies of Sun Myung Moon and The (now former) Unification Church, this process may be termed 'charismatization':

The argument is that charismatic authority can result, at least in part, from social processes that take place within the group which is headed by the person who is accorded the authority. [...] It is not until they are in the movement that the followers learn to re-cognize the charisma of their leader and thereby come to accept that he should have a virtually unlimited say in how they live.[34]

33. Abrahamson 1994.
34. Barker 1993, 184.

As we have seen, only those really interested in George King's work and organization get the opportunity to enter the process of 'charismatization'. Among those, though, only few have had the opportunity to establish a personal relationship with George King. Even when he was still alive, many members would not meet with him. This, of course, was to some extend due to Kings poor physical state which meant that he lead a rather secluded life in his old days, but presumably it was of no great importance to his followers to be in his physical presence. Most members of any new religious movement will never have met their Master in person. They may have been in a big audience while he or she was present on a stage, but a personal rendezvous is usually rare to the average member.

Referring to Weber once again, we may safely conclude that the charisma of George King is by now embedded in his writings. This 'routinization' of charisma implies that his followers meet him as a social construction, as a symbol of meaning, in the movement's literature.[35] The 'routinization' of King's charisma takes the form of 'textualization' or 'scripturalization': He primarily appears in authoritative texts.

The hagiographic depicting of King along with his own writings provides all that is needed for believers to feel comfortable. Needless to say, the 'intimates and lieutenants' are key-persons in that process. Our main observation therefore is that the religious authority of George King in the years leading up to his death was a social construct which was based on the mythological rendering of his life, and on the books and pamphlets of The Aetherius Society rather than George King in person. King's death has not indicated a decline in the effects of that mechanism. From a comparative point of view this is not a surprising development at all: For thousands of years Christians and Buddhists (just to mention two remarkable examples) have enthusiastically followed their respective religious leaders, whom they have never met outside the context of sacred scripture and ritual. Jesus and the Buddha are easily considered individuals, but as persons they are only accessible through the narratives and rituals of the religions built upon them. The cult of Jesus, consequently, only in-

35. Weber 1975, 89-104.

directly has a person at its centre. Rather, it is the narrative featuring this person that holds the central position. George King is, in a similar way, being transformed from 'person' to 'narrative' or 'text'.

A part of the hagiographic dealing with King is intensely occupied with his actual feats in the earlier days of his movement's life. Many books describe in detail what King did, where, how and when. A prominent and relatively recent example is the book on 'Operation Starlight', which tells the story of how King and a few followers had a line of mountains charged with spiritual healing energy from the Cosmic Master's spacecrafts.[36] In this way the history of King and the society, through the texts, is integrated into the minds of current members. At an earlier stage King was, in person, the centre of the movement, but in the years leading up to his death the relation between leader and disciples declined, and today, in the years following his death, it is the institutionalized memory of George King that is at work.

This sociological oberservation will probably not be accepted by the believers. And neither should it. When King was old and sick he was still serving as Primary Terrestrial Mental Channel to the Cosmic Masters and his physical absence from the organization's everyday life had, from a believers' standpoint, nothing to say.[37] Now, after his death, the legend about his person is developing, and due to an on-

36. Abrahamson 1994. The front cover of this particular book gives a beautiful example of the iconographic promotion of George King as the Master of the Society. Standing on the top of a rock in full mountain climbing atire, a beam of light is entering him from above. On the black/white photo the light forms a corona around his head and shoulders. The light, of course, is interpreted as healing spiritual energy beaming out from the spacecraft high above Earth. A note in the book explains that the picture is no fraud, and that similar beams of light were seen around George King during the entire climb. Otherwise King is only shown in old photographs — sometimes as a mountaineer, sometimes in full bishop's gown, but usually as a thoughtful and serious man in plain clothing.

37. In this article I have restricted the issue to religious texts. However, George King, although physically absent to most believers, is also perceived in other ways. A line of tape recordings with King has been issued, and photos of him, when he was much younger, may be purchased through the society's offices.

going process of 'charismatization', he is just as vital a symbol as ever.

George King and Other Contactees

At this point we may ask whether the concept of UFOs, which is at the heart of George King's teachings, has anything to say with regard to the making of King as a religious leader. Why, one may ask, was the concept of UFOs at all integrated into George King's religious thinking? Why was he approached by extraterrestrials aboard UFOs and not by theosophical Masters of a more familiar or traditional kind?

The question is probably answered when we take time and place into consideration. During 1954 a major capital of the English speaking Western world (London) provided a perfect frame for King's experience. In the specific case of George King it is of great relevance to observe that his initial contact with Master Aetherius of Venus took place at a time when the most famous contactee of all times, George Adamski (1891-1965), had just come forward. In 1953, the year before King had been contacted by the cosmic Masters, Adamski and co-writer Desmond Leslie had issued the best seller *Flying Saucers Have Landed*[38] simultaneously published in New York and London (Werner Laurie in London and British Book Centre in New York).[39] Adamski's book was immediately discussed, and anyone with an interest in the paranormal would hear of it.

The similarities between King's experiences and those of Adamski are remarkable. Both encountered spiritual Masters from Venus, these entities are described much in the same way, and the messages given to the chosen mediator are of the same principal kind. The contactee is chosen for a certain mission with one primary objective; to teach humanity how to live in love and peace. Further, as is well known, George Adamski had been occupied with various kinds of spiritual and occult endeavours prior to his meeting with the 'Space Brother' Orthon in the Californian desert on November 20th, 1952,[40]

38. Adamski and Leslie 1953.
39. Further bibliographic details may be found in Eberhart 1986, vol. II, 831ff.
40. Clark 1992, 1.

and according to The Aetherius Society's information, King was also very much occupied with all kinds of spiritual training and reading when he was approached by the superior intelligence from beyond.[41] Finally, of course, both men claimed to be taken aboard flying saucers and given unimaginable tours to other worlds.

Considering the vast amount of later contactees who, deliberately or not, assimilated Adamski's philosophy (among others George van Tassel, who told of the Asthar Command, Guy Ballard and the I AM Movement, Pauline Sharp (known as Nada-Yolanda) of Mark Age, Tuella of Guardian Action and Ruth and Ernest Norman of the Unarius Academy of Science), it is hard to ignore the possibility of a direct influence upon King from Adamski's and Leslie's book.[42] The official claim of The Aetherius Society is that others may also have had some kind of contact similar to that of George King, and that other groups work along the same lines. No organization, though, holds the same position as The Aetherius Society.[43] Hence it is not totally ruled out by King's followers that the Cosmic Masters may have sought contact with others prior to their interest for King. However, it is stated in a perfectly clear manner that no one in the world has had the same intense and decisive contact as George King since 1954. In the words of the reverend Charles Abrahamson of The Aetherius Society in London:

41. Abrahamson 1994, 14 & King 1974, 7.
42. For further comments on the heritage from Adamski/Theosophy in contactee-movements, see Robert Pearson Flaherty 1990, chapter 5. I have only come across one reference to Adamski in Aetherius-material. Under the heading: 'A Miraculous Healing. A Personal Discovery' on the homepage of The Aetherius Society, a woman tells of how she miraculously overcame severe illness by mentally contacting healers on Venus. Her inspiration was Adamski's book, which is explicitly mentioned. I take this to be an indication of good will towards Adamski and one of his subsequent organizations, IGAP.
43. The Aetherius Society has argued for its special value in all sorts of ways, for instance, through a numerological and astrological analysis of the organization. Hence divination forms an important part in the construction of The Aetherius Society's image (see for instance The Aetherius Society 1982, 15-42)

We are not saying that he is the only contactee at all, but we do think he has a unique role. We don't think there is anyone else who for over 42 years has consistently been in contact on a weekly basis without a break. I don't think there is anyone in the world to even claim that, or who has built up an organization which has done as many things as we have.[44]

In other words: George King is partly incorporated into a well known religious tradition, namely Theosophy. It is never mentioned straightforwardly, but the religious foundation of his teachings is well known. It is a fact that most religious innovators in the wake of the Theosophical Society, each within the frames of his or her special organization, have formed special alliances with special representatives of the group of superhuman beings (variously known as Adepts, Masters, members of the Hierarchy etc.), who are at the heart of theosophical mythology. Much in the same way, George King has made his own path through a consistent UFO-related theology and through special affiliations to specific Masters such as Master Jesus, Mars Sector 6 and, of course, Master Aetherius. Only Master Jesus is known to other channels or contactees. This taken into consideration it is safe to say that George King has developed his idea of Theosophy and the theosophical inspired ufology, in the tradition of Adamski, with just the right emphasis. The construction of King as a religious leader, therefore, is partly based on the general acceptance of the theosophical doctrines and the tradition (which has flourished since the days of Madame Blavatsky) of bestowing religious leadership upon those in direct contact with the Adepts. George King is venerated because of his personal accomplishments, but also because he has placed himself in a tradition where religious leaders automatically are looked upon as something special, simply because no theosophically inspired leader or religious innovator can function without personal contact with the superior beings of realms beyond ordinary human reach. The fact that the Cosmic Masters or Adepts use huge space crafts and other sorts of alien technology in their struggle for a spir-

---

44. Charles Abrahamson interviewed by Mel Richards in the magazine *Encounters*, Issue 12. October 1996, 64-67.

itual revolution among human beings[45] simply shows that they are keeping track of developments on Earth.[46] The mythological framework of Theosophy has been considerably modernized, not least by the adoption of a symbolic language with close links to modern technology (mythologized in the shape of space crafts). Basically, though, the channelled data are phenomenologically of the same kind as those previously received by Madame Blavatsky and her successors. George King does not stand alone. The sacred biography surrounding him is a natural effect of his particular religious engagement.[47]

Conclusion

The ideal of George King legitimizes his religious belief system as well as The Aetherius Society as an organization. By invoking George King as the most important human being ever, and as the prime source for the salvation of humanity, the believers are placing themselves within the same sphere of authority as the one attributed to their leader. This socially constructed mechanism is obviously of great importance to the very existence of the Society as a social unit. Through the religious texts, not least the texts describing the life and achievements of George King, the members of the group are included in the life and work of their leader.

At the same time King may be interpreted as a devotional object: He is revered as the ideal human being, and it seems fair to see him — rather than the extraterrestrial Masters — as the actual subject of devotion in the Society. Through The Aetherius Society's texts the believers will encounter not only the insight and results gained by

---

45. The Aetherius Society and George King have developed various contraptions designed for storing 'spiritual energy', so-called Prayer Power Batteries. Whenever needed — if a war is breaking out or other disasters are happening — the energy may be released, and thus the problems diminish.
46. Most, if not all, aspects of this development are dealt with in Flaherty 1990.
47. Future research, therefore, should address the question of Theosophical hagiography in general to find similarities and differences in the various narratives about various Theosophical leaders.

George King, but also minute descriptions of what kind of person he was. King appears as the believers' bridge to a higher spiritual level, and he definitely occupies the position as humanity's saviour in times of dire straits, even if dead.

Although no formalized worship of King is explicitly suggested, it seems as if the hagiographic rendering of King in the Society's texts is the precondition to the wider range of theological, philosophical and ritual positions of the group. If it was not for George King, then nobody would know of the extraterrestrials' plan regarding Earth, and nobody would have the chance to raise themselves to higher levels. Thus the tales of the religious leader, in this example, serves the same function as in most other religious groups: The religious teachings and ideals are legitimized through the ideal founder and leader.

The qualities of George King are succesfully defined within the internal traditions, but to outsiders the understanding of the religious leader cannot escape stultification. This is probably why the Society will often approach non-believers without highlighting George King too much. This does not mean that the importance of King is limited in this situation. Rather, it is a matter of missionary strategy. To the believers the Society will indefatigably promote George King, and during the process of conversion a new member of the group will gradually learn to appreciate the qualities of King. The focus on the religious leader, in this way, serves sociological as well as epistemological purposes.

Bibliography

Abrahamson, Charles (ed.) 1994. *The Holy Mountains of the World — Charged in Operation Starlight*. Hollywood: The Aetherius Society.

Adamski, George and Desmond Leslie 1953. *Flying Saucers Have Landed*. London/New York: Werner Laurie & British Book Centre.

Aetherius Society 1974 (1958) [No author]. *The Twelve Blessings. The Cosmic Concept For the New Aquarian Age as given by The Master Jesus in His Overshadowing of George King*. Hollywood: The Aetherius Society.

Bang, Sturla 1996. 'The Truth is Out there. UFO som del av en religiøs verdensforståelse'. Unpublished thesis, University of Bergen, Norway.

Barker, Eileen 1991. 'King, George'. In: John R. Hinnels (ed.), *Who's Who in World Religions*. London: The Macmillan Press, 216-17.

Barker, Eileen 1993. 'Charismatization. The Social Production of "an Ethos Propitious to the Mobilisation of Sentiments"'. In: Eileen Barker, James A. Beckford and Karel Dobbelaere (eds.), *Secularisation, rationalism and Sectarianism*. Oxford: Clarendon Press, 181-202.

Clark, Jerome 1992. *The UFO Encyclopedia Vol. 2. The Emergence of a Phenomenon: UFOs from the Beginning through 1959*. Detroit: Omnigraphics.

Eberhart, George M. 1986. *UFOs and the Extraterrestrial Contact Movement: a bibliography. Vol. I (Unidentified Flying Objects). Vol. II (The Extraterrestrial Contact Movement)*. New York/London: The Scarecrow Press, Metuchen.

Flaherty, Robert Pearson 1990. 'Flying Saucers and the New Angelology: Mythic Projection of the Cold War and the Convergence of Opposites'. Non-published dissertation, University of California.

King, George 1974 (1963). *The Nine Freedoms*. California: The Aetherius Society.

King, George and Richard Lawrence 1996. *Contact With The Gods From Space. Pathway To The New Millennium*. California: The Aetherius Society.

King, George & Kevin Quinn Avery 1982 (1975). *The Age of Aetherius*. California: The Aetherius Society.

La Fleur, William, R. 1993 (1987). 'Biography'. In: Mircea Eliade (ed.), The *Encyclopedia of Religion Vol. 1*. New York: Macmillan, 220-24.

Melton, J. Gordon 1986. *Biographical Dictionary of American Cult and Sect Leaders*. Garland Reference Library of Social Science (vol. 212). New York/London: Garland Publishing.

Refslund Christensen, Dorthe 1997a. 'Legenden om L. Ron Hubbard — et eksempel på en moderne hagiografi. Om konstruktionen af et mytologisk livsforløb og brugen af det i Scientology', *Chaos*, 28. Copenhagen: Museum Tusculanum, 53-76.

Refslund Christensen, Dorthe 1997b. *Scientology. En ny religion*. Copenhagen: Munksgaard.

Refslund Christensen, Dorthe 1997c. *Scientology. Fra terapi til religion*. Copenhagen: Gyldendal.

Rothstein, Mikael 1992. 'Videoer og vismænd: Traditionel og moderne kanon i de nye religioner', *Chaos* 18. Copenhagen: Museum Tusculanum, 83-112.

Rothstein, Mikael 1993. 'Helliggørelse og religiøs argumentation. The International Raelian Movement og Claude Vorilhon', *Chaos*, 20. Copenhagen: Museum Tusculanum, 137-47.

Vorilhon, Claude 1989. (Rael), *Let's Welcome our Fathers From Space. They Created Humanity in Their Laboratories*, AOM Corporation, Tokyo.

Wallis, Roy 1993. 'Charisma and Explanation'. In: Eileen Barker, James A. Beckford and Karel Dobbelaere (eds.), *Secularization, Rationalism and Sectarianism*. Oxford: Clarendon Press, 167-79.

Weber, Max 1963. *The Sociology of Religion*. Boston: Beacon Press.

Weber, Max 1975. *Magt og byråkrati*. Oslo: Gyldendal Norsk Forlag.

CHAPTER 9

South African New Age Prophets: Past and Present

Christine Steyn

The New Age movement is alive and flourishing in South Africa. Indications are that the movement is growing at a rapid pace. This is
not to be wondered at, given the unique conditions in South Africa.
However, this article will deal with some very interesting material on
the early and mostly unknown South African heralds of the movement. Long before the advent of the movement, there were these
shining lights in South Africa that were almost totally ignored, but in
retrospect, it is clear that they were propagating some of the central
concepts of New Age thinking a long time ago. In their footsteps have
followed a procession of further prophets who have also aspired to
influence the movement as a whole. We shall first briefly explore the
concept of 'prophet', and then examine the prophecies and teachings
of a fascinating woman called Johanna Brandt. Thereafter, we shall
analyse the metaphysical implications of the scientific theories of
one-time Prime Minister of South Africa, Field Marshall Jan Christiaan Smuts, and lastly pause to consider the prophesies of one
Joseph Busby, self-proclaimed mystic.

 In Western society, the term 'prophet' conjures up visions of
bearded men in flowing garb who stand up alone and defiant against
kings and nations to deliver messages from God. These messages
were frequently unpopular and unwelcome messages of doom and
damnation, but sometimes also of salvation and redemption. This
image is derived from the prophets of the Hebrew Scriptures and the
Old Testament who were recipients of communications from God,
which they then proclaimed to the nation. The use of the term 'mes-

senger of God' is still the most common, and our first case study falls into this category. But there are other ways in which the term 'prophet' can be used, for instance, in the case of someone with particular vision and insight into reality, and this is the manner in which it will be applied to Jan Smuts. The last 'prophet' for consideration, Joseph Busby, can be described as a prophet only insofar as any contemporary channeller can be labelled as such, since he was said to have channelled messages from an Ascended Master of the Spiritual Hierarchy. Of vital importance in this case is the prophetic task of prediction. All three 'prophets' discussed in this paper can be described by Reid's definition of a prophet as 'someone who challenges us to live responsibly in the teeth of history, on the edge of a new tomorrow which we hopefully choose'.[1]

Johanna Brandt (1876-1964) was born into a family with a long line of missionaries and ministers. She was in her twenties during the Second Anglo-Boer War (1899-1902) and wrote two books about her own and her mother's experiences in assisting the Boer commandos during the war, and on the wartime concentration camp at Irene, near Pretoria, where she worked as a nurse for a short time. In 1902 she travelled to Holland where she married a Dutchman, Louis E. Brandt, who was a minister of the *Nederduitsch Hervormde Kerk* — one of the Dutch Reformed Churches still present in South Africa. She soon convinced him that there was vitally important upliftment work to be done in South Africa in the aftermath of the recent war,[2] and by 1904 they were permanently back in South Africa. The Rev. Louis Brandt was to become the Moderator of his church in Africa — a position which he held for 21 years. When Mrs Brandt started publishing what the church regarded as her 'heretical' writings, her husband was asked to dissociate himself from her views, which he did, and at the time no further action was taken against her. One can only assume that she was tolerated for the sake of her husband and probably also because the voices of women were typically regarded as irrele-

---

1. Reid 1980, 16.
2. Since the English had followed a scorched earth policy in the war, concentration camps were set up where 26,000 women and children of the tiny Afrikaner nation had died as a direct result of the poor conditions in the camps.

vant at the time. Considering the ultra conservatism of this church, it is remarkable that Mrs Brandt was tolerated at all.[3]

In 1916 at the deathbed of her mother, Mrs Brandt had a vision in which a Messenger conferred on her the gift of prophecy. Days later the Messenger visited her again and she received prophetic revelations of the future in a series of mystic visions. These visions were so compelling, and the call to inform the nation so urgent, that she wrote a volume called *The Millennium*.[4] In it she described her vision of the earth at the brink of great things — 'old conditions are passing away and in the pangs of unendurable agony we see the light rising of an altogether new epoch'.[5] The Great War was, however, only the beginning of humanity's agonies — revolutions, pestilence, civil wars, famines, storms and earthquakes would follow before the Light could predominate.[6] The Millennium, she wrote, 'will be the gradual and irresistible revival of the Mystic Powers' — those powers which serve as a channel between the seen and the unseen worlds.

With reference to South Africa, she was shown that the country would be swept by a tornado of relentless fury — a veritable hurricane of passionate and relentless wrath — devastation, blood, and ruin — everything brought about by hatred, violence, injustice, jealousy, animosity, hypocrisy, oppression and deceit. She was told that in South Africa, more than any other quarter of the globe, there was need of harmony — but also that through the darkness which was descending on this land, harmony would be born.[7] When she enquired why South Africa was singled out for the start of this process, she was told that 'South Africa [was] a pearl in the eyes of the Lord' and that 'in South Africa the first great miracles of the new age of mystic revelation will be performed'.[8]

3. In 1933 it became known that Mrs Brandt had had herself re-baptised sixteen years previously, and this the church could not accept. As a result, her husband was asked to resign from his congregation and Mrs Brandt was asked to resign as a member.
4. Brandt 1918.
5. Ibid., 1.
6. Ibid., 90.
7. Ibid., 100.
8. Ibid., 121.

Later in 1916, as a result of these visions, Brandt founded The World Harmony Movement. The aims of the Order were to promote harmony on earth — 'Harmony between races; the sexes; religion and politics; spirit and matter; mysticism and intellect; faith and reason; nature and science … Harmony in one word, between God and Man'.[9] The Order was a universal peace movement, non-political, non-racial, non-sectarian and having for its basic principle the establishment of a universal brotherhood through international friendship. It was, said Brandt, a Union of Reformers whose first aim was to reform themselves and to create the harmony of health and perfection in their own bodies, their homes and immediate environment, as the only means of bringing harmony in this troubled world. The movement also taught that a pure spirit should live in a healthy body. Brandt proposed seven healing methods, namely the fasting cure, water treatment, fresh air, sunbathing, spinal adjustments, the fruitarian diet and mind exercises. Members of the Order strived to live in obedience to the laws of nature and they waged 'peaceful war against evil' such as the vivisection of animals, the sale of foods with added chemicals, the sale of intoxicating liquor, the production of armaments and last — but not least — the compulsory vaccination of children.[10]

She also discovered the healing properties of grapes and claimed to have healed herself from cancer through the Grape Cure — a diet of only grapes. This she felt was so important that she left her husband and seven children and sailed for New York to spread the message and also establish chapters of the World Harmony Movement there. During her stay in the States the medical profession gained an injunction against her which forbade her to treat patients, but also sought to deport her as an undesirable person. The American School of Naturopathy, however, conferred an honorary doctorate on her for her contribution to the field of natural remedies. After two years in the States, she returned home to continue her work in South Africa.

Brandt taught that vice, disease and death were necessary phases in the evolution of humanity which would not be overcome by denial, but by the understanding of their nature. By overcoming the lower

9. Brandt op. cit., 1.
10. Ibid., 2.

with the higher. Besides, all seeming evil was impermanent, though none the less real while it lasted. This was known, she wrote, as the Science of Transmutation and was based on the Law of Vibration. As one of the Hermetic principles states: 'He who understands the Principle of Vibration has grasped the sceptre of Power'.[11]

The Order furthermore taught that the earth was now in the transition phase between the Ages of Pisces and Aquarius and that new teachings were being sent to earth and that a new rate of vibration was being established. Brandt went further and proclaimed that the Age of Aquarius was the age of the water bearer, which was the life-bearer and therefore the Mother. She maintained that the New Age would bring about the realization of the non-duality of body and soul, the interrelatedness of humans and nature, of the balance of male and female principles and of the benefits of a vegetarian diet. She subscribed to the notion of reincarnation and the divinity of humankind,[12] she believed that the kingdom of God was within the human being and within this reality,[13] she believed that the universe was in a process of evolution and that humanity was evolving towards godhood.

In 1936 she published a book entitled *The Paraclete or coming World Mother* in which she gave further details of the original visions which the world was not ready to receive at the time. All religions, she claimed, were expecting different avatars to deliver humanity from earthly woes. In the New Age the Holy Spirit, namely God-the-Mother would come to earth as the Comforter, which Jesus had promised. There has always been, she said, a dreadful blank in the Universe in the absence of a mother in the divine household. What humanity has not understood, however, was that no quality could exist without its opposite — no positive without negative, no masculine without the feminine, no thought without action, and so on. The Mother was always there, but was simply not recognized.[14] The Mother would first

11. Brandt, op.cit., 4.
12. Brandt 1921, 14-5.
13. Brandt 1918, 114.
14. Brandt revealed that in December 1925 she had a vision in which 'the Mother came in great power and glory and explained much to me' and since then she no longer called on Christ, because 'it was always the Mother Who responded to my cry' (1936, 29).

Christine Steyn

be experienced by the women of the world, but through them the
whole of humanity would develop the qualities of intuition, imagination and mysticism. In the New Age, every one of all creeds, colours,
sexes, and ages would be united because all were children of God.
The coming of the Cosmic Mother would herald the Age of Fulfilment — fulfilment of all earthly desires for peace, rest, and the emancipation of poverty and disease.[15] But it would also bring fulfilment
of spiritual gifts and power. It would be the age of self-development,
self-control and self-healing. Once the Mother had taught humanity
to do the will of the Father, a total transformation would take place
and humanity would enter upon the Path of Divinity and claim its
heritage as Sons and Daughters of the Most High.[16]

Although Brandt claimed that this all came to her in mystic visions, she did refer to the work of Anna Kingsford (1846-1888) who developed a feminine theology of the Holy Spirit and founded the Hermetic Society in 1883, and she had most probably been in contact
with Theosophical teachings of some kind.

This very short exposition of the teachings of Johanna Brandt
shows clearly that she regarded herself as a revealer of the will of
God and felt compelled to proclaim it, first in South Africa and then
to the rest of the world. We see in her a clear example of a prophet in
the Old Testament mode. But, despite all her best efforts, she had
only a small following and was almost totally disregarded and ignored by the establishment, so that nothing of her work had survived
until a couple of years ago when she was rediscovered and interest in
her work revived, albeit on a small scale. It is clear that some of the
central New Age principles were being expounded in South Africa as
early as 1916 and the term 'New Age', usually attributed to Alice
Bailey, was used much earlier by Johanna Brandt.

The second 'prophet' for consideration is Jan Christiaan Smuts
(1870-1950) who would certainly not have seen himself as a prophet
of God, and despite his enduring optimism he also did not have a
vision of a new age dawning in the near future. He was, however, a
pioneer and compelling advocate for a new view of life which included a principle that was said to lie at the heart of our reality. Unlike

15. Brandt 1936, 23.
16. Ibid., 23.

Johanna Brandt, he was a respected and revered international states-
man, but also his philosophical views were mostly ignored in South
Africa, and when noticed, often led to severe criticism from his con-
servative nation.

Smuts was born of Dutch stock and grew up on a farm near Cape
Town. He was first sent to school at the age of 12 where he learnt English and High Dutch (Afrikaans being his mother tongue), and within a mere four years he was ready to enter the University of Stellen-
bosch. At the age of 21 he entered Christ College at Cambridge (he
was to become Chancellor of this very University some fifty years
later).[17] He returned to South Africa in time to serve as a general for
the Boers during the Anglo-Boer War at the turn of the century. After
the war he entered politics and became Prime Minister in 1919 — a
position he held until 1924 and then again from 1939 to 1948.[18] He
was responsible for drafting the constitution of the League of Nations
and his draft of the Preamble to the Charter for the United Nations
Organization was adopted with only very minor changes. His major
contribution to the area of New Age thought is, however, to be found
in his book *Holism and Evolution* (1926).

It was not his intention to propose a system of philosophy, but
rather to write a scientific treatise in which he attempted to pull together many currents of thought into a larger holistic viewpoint.[19] In
a culture where scientific interests have dominated and the spiritual
interests of humankind have been neglected, a new direction was
needed in which these elements could be synthesized.

For Smuts there were two main forces in life: an ultimate synthet-
ic, ordering, regulating and controlling force, for which he coined the
term 'holism'; and a growing, generating and developing force,

17. He studied Law and his achievements were so impressive that the *Encyclopaedia Britannica* described them as 'unprecedented'.
18. Smuts was Minister of Defence in the first Union of South Africa Cabinet
1910-1919, Member of the (British) Imperial War Cabinet 1917-1918, Leader of the Opposition 1924-1933, and Deputy Prime Minister 1934-1939. He
was appointed Field Marshall in the Allied Forces during World War II.
19. Smuts was elected president of the British Association for the Advance-
ment of Science in the organization's centenary year, 1931. He regarded
this as the crowning honour of his life, since the invitation came from
scientists and not politicians.

namely evolution. Together the two resulted in the emergence of ever-increasing complex wholes.

Evolution was the gradual development of wholes, stretching from the inorganic beginnings, through matter, organisms, plants, animals, humans, then mind and consciousness, and then reaching further to the highest levels of spiritual creation, namely goodness, truth and beauty. Evolution was thus the 'manifestation of a specific fundamental, universal activity'.[20] At the core of this process there was holism, the unifying power which generated ever more complex wholes. Thus holism was matter and energy at one stage, organism and life at another, and it was mind and personality in the latest stage. 'Thus', wrote Smuts, 'the four great series in reality — matter, life, mind and Personality — apparently so far removed from each other, are seen to be but steps in the progressive evolution of one and the same fundamental factor, whose pathway is the universe within us and around us'.[21]

At this stage, the human personality was the supreme holistic achievement. This whole with its conscious reason and soul was at present the 'highest embodiment of that spiritual Principle which we believe is at the heart of the universe'.[22] However, in future far greater advances would be made. Life was yet young, and, said Smuts, 'I don't believe that we, the human beings, are the acme of the universe. I believe there will be evolved far higher forms of spiritual wholes than we see before us today'.[23] The way of reform and salvation in this troubled world 'lies through the fostering, the purification, the enrichment of the human personality. There the Divine light shines most clearly in this dark world'.[24]

With regard to reality, Smuts postulated that its fundamental characteristic was activity and the physical stuff of the universe was action. 'The universe is a flowing stream in Space-Time, and its reality is not intelligible apart from this concept of activity'.[25] All things were more than their structures — inner action transcended outer struc-

20. Smuts 1926, 325.
21. Ibid. 320.
22. Smuts 1951, 164.
23. Smuts 1944, 132.
24. Smuts 1951, 165.
25. Smuts 1926, 326.

tures and all things went beyond themselves. These overflowing actions form fields around things and these fields interpenetrate and interact with one another and thus open the way for creative evolution.

Smuts emphasized that this process was not merely a combination or grouping or an unfolding of implicit pre-existing elements, but a genuine process of generation and creation. The result then, was that this was a whole-making universe. 'It is the fundamental character of this universe to be active in the production of wholes, of ever more complete and advanced wholes, and that the Evolution of the universe, organic and inorganic, is nothing but the record of this whole-making activity in its progressive development'.[26] Limited freedom in the early stages of evolution expanded and widened so that at the human stage, freedom took conscious control of itself and began to create the free ethical world of the Spirit.[27]

The worldview that emerged from this was neither Naturalistic nor Idealistic. Holism did not deny matter, but 'affirmed and welcomed and affectionately embraced it', but when naturalism became purely materialistic and denied the creative element which produced spirit, Holism had to break from it. Concomitantly, although holism celebrated the spiritual as a relatively recent arrival in the evolutionary order of things, when Idealism claimed the pre-existence of Spirit, which was now merely unfolding, Holism had to dissent. Smuts wrote:

To view the ideal or spiritual element in the universe as the dominant factor is to ignore the fact that the universe was before ever the ideal or spiritual had appeared on the horizon; that the ideal or spiritual is a new and indeed recent creation in the order of the universe, that it was not implicit in the beginnings and has not been reached by a process of unfolding; but that from a real pre-existing order of things it has been creatively evolved as a new factor; and that its importance to-day should not be retrospectively antedated to a time when the world existed without it.[28]

26. Ibid. 326.
27. Ibid. 139.
28. Smuts 1926, 330.

Spirit and mind were, therefore, not at the beginning but at the end of the process, but 'Holism is everywhere and all in all'.[29]

Matter and Nature were not devalued in this view; indeed, Smuts was an eminent nature lover — a true son of the veld — and a keen and knowledgeable botanist. He remarked that humans were 'indeed one with Nature' since 'her genetic fibres run through all our being; our physical organs connect us with millions of years of her history; our minds are full of immemorial paths of pre-human experience. ... The intimate *rapport* with Nature is one of the most precious things in life'.[30] However, this did not mean that we should make unwarranted assumptions of animism and thus invest nature with soul.

For Smuts therefore, neither a group, a family, a society, an organization, the world, nor the universe, were real wholes. Although they were a group of wholes where the wholes were mutually exclusive, their fields interpenetrated and reinforced one another and thus created the appearance of a new organism or whole. This was, however, misleading because although such groups were very powerful and displayed the characteristics of organisms, they were organic, but not organisms in the real sense. Similarly, in Nature there was also an interpenetration of fields of wholes, which created a certain spirit or atmosphere. This could impact so strongly on humans that they tended to personify it, or even deify and worship it. 'But the sober fact is', wrote Smuts 'that there is no new whole or organism of Nature; there is only Nature which becomes organic through the intensification of her total field. In other words, Nature is holistic without being a real whole'.[31]

With regard to the question of direction, Smuts observed that evolution had always moved in one general direction. Did this therefore mean, that there was a grand inner purpose or cosmic teleology or transcendent Personality or Mind behind this process? The facts, said Smuts, did not warrant this assumption. The essence of a whole was that it always transcended its parts and its character could not be inferred from its parts. Thus to infer the existence of a supra-mundane Mind from the parts that made up reality, would mean that this Mind

29. Ibid., 335.
30. Ibid., 336-37.
31. Ibid., 340.

was still of the same character and order as its parts. Although holism shaped, directed, regulated and controlled, it worked through the wholes at various stages and in the different variations which creatively arose from them. To infer more was to 'make the mistake of spiritual Idealism and to apply later human categories to the earlier phases of the evolutionary process'.[32] The belief in a Divine Being, said Smuts, must necessarily rest on different grounds and this he said was not the subject matter of this book.[33] Thus, he neatly evaded the issue.

He went on to point out that nature and the universe with all the interpenetrating fields had a holistic character and the environment that was created in this way was the home of all the family of the universe 'with something profoundly intimate and friendly in its atmosphere. In this Home of Wholes and Souls the creative tasks of Holism are carried forward'.[34] Despite all the suffering and strife, said Smuts, 'we come in the end to feel that this is a friendly universe'.[35] It was a universe in which we were very far from the goal to which holism pointed, but a universe where humans were earnestly groping towards the light. He wrote of the universe:

Its deepest tendencies are helpful to what is best in us, and our highest aspirations are but its inspiration. Thus behind our striving towards betterment are in the last resort the entire weight and momentum and the inmost nature and trend of the universe. ... The groaning and travailing of the universe is never aimless or resultless. Its profound labours mean new creation, the slow, painful birth of wholes, of new and higher wholes, and the slow but steady realization of the Good which all the wholes of the universe in their various grades dimly yearn and strive for. It is the nature of the universe to strive for and slowly, but in ever-increasing measure, to attain wholeness, fullness, blessedness. ... The rise and self-perfection of wholes in the Whole is the slow but unerring process and goal of this Holistic universe. [36]

32. Ibid., 343.
33. Ibid., 342.
34. Ibid., 343.
35. Ibid., 343.
36. Ibid., 344-45.

In summary, Smuts' thought can therefore be said to show major similarities with certain trends in New Age thought. First, his aim with the introduction of the concept of holism was to overcome the prevailing dualism between matter and spirit. Secondly, Holism as the driving and directing force behind evolution had resulted in the emergence of the human personality and it was through the further development and self-realization of this that a contribution could be made to the ongoing evolutionary process. Thirdly, the world was, therefore, not only whole-making, but also soul-making and freedom that was one of the major characteristics of the human personality made it possible for humans to become the masters of their own destiny. Fourthly, although Smuts, in contrast with much New Age thinking, dismissed the idea of nature, the world, and the universe as wholes, he saw it as permeating and influencing (through its fields) the human personality. Fifthly, the process of evolution, while open and truly creative, was also seen as in an upward motion towards ever-higher spiritual values.

Smuts regarded *Holism and Evolution* as a scientific treatise and therefore declined to discuss metaphysical implications and specifically the role of God in this process (the existence of which, he said, rested on different arguments). He was severely criticized for this and a large section of the nation believed that he was an atheist. Although the relationship between Holism and God was never made clear, it is particularly interesting that while in his earlier work he wrote that the spiritual element in the universe was a recent creation in the order of the universe,[37] in the preface to the German edition of his book in 1938 he wrote that the organism with conscious reason and soul was the highest embodiment *of that spiritual Principle which we believe is at the heart of the universe,*[38] and that it was in the human personality that the Divine light shined most clearly. Here we find an indication for the unusual use of the word 'Holism' — Smuts presented his book as science, but ultimately 'holism' was, in fact, a divine spiritual principle.

He was loath to discuss his religious convictions but in his private correspondence we find some clues to his thought. In a letter written

37. Ibid., 330.
38. Smuts 1951, 164.

a couple of months before his death he described a beautiful day after good rain on his farm, and added:

> It is at such times that one becomes aware of the Divine, not as something beyond, but as the soul and essence of nature and oneself ... The mystic whole is all the time with us and in us, but we understand it only in flashes of high experience.[39]

Although we know very little about what Smuts believed to be the ultimate source of reality, there are indications that suggest that holism could be seen as an immanent Divine principle, but this aspect requires further research of his private papers. Evolution, in Smuts' opinion, can be categorized as what Hanegraaff calls an 'open-ended', creative linearity.[40] Linear, because it starts from nature and describes consciousness as emerging from nature; creative, because it is not merely an unfolding towards a telos that is implicitly present from the beginning. Open-ended, because evolution is governed by a tendency of self-organization where every system strives towards ever-increasing complexity, and the result to which the process will lead is unpredictable.

Although Smuts is virtually unknown in New Age circles, his thought on evolution and holism is obviously a precursor to some of the most prevalent New Age views. And although he is not a prophet in the strict sense of the word, he always felt that he had made a valid scientific contribution that would, in time, be recognized.

The last 'prophet' for consideration is Joseph Busby (1916-1996). To call him a prophet is to use the term freely, since he claimed to be a channeller for an ascended master who spoke through him. He was, therefore, merely the channel through which the wisdom and messages reached humankind. Busby was born in England where he taught esotericism for many years. He and his wife organized many international S-U-N (Spiritual Unity of Nations) Conferences in several countries. In 1972 they founded the Sun Centre School of Esoteric Philosophy in South Africa where they lived until their deaths in 1996 and 1997. In contrast to Brandt and Smuts, Busby was acknow-

39. Beukes 1991, 55.
40. Hanegraaff 1995, 106ff.

ledged and honoured for his teachings. For him there was not the isolation of Brandt or the scorn that Smuts had to suffer for his philosophical ideas from his own people. Busby's work was not original,
but simply represented the ancient wisdom teachings as it had become known over the last hundred years. The interesting aspect of
his work is his predictions for the future of South Africa which reson-
ated in many people's hearts. In 1985 he channelled the following
message:

A great Light is radiating here and now over South Africa. A flood of cosmic
power is being transmitted into the subtle ethers from the higher spiritual
planes of Being. The soul of the people is awakening to a new age divine
effulgence. Here, there and everywhere, people are responding to the call of
the soul to raise their consciousness and come up higher.

The dynamic challenge of the living Creative Fire of the Absolute is piercing
through the veils of human ignorance — inherited, conditioned and self-
imposed ignorance — of the truths of Being. The very centre of Man's inner-
most self is exploding into the new age Light.

Aquarius, the sign of the Son of Man, is breaking across the horizon of the
human mind revealing a new age vision of resplendent beauty, high spiritual purpose and glorious promise.

South Africa is destined to ride the crest of the wave of testing and prove herself to be triumphant. The Soul of the people of South Africa will arise to
heights of achievement and fulfilment beyond the wildest dreams of its most
enlightened sons and daughters. No matter what the current situation, this
land, this corner of the African continent, is destined to shine forth like a multifaceted diamond of truth radiant in promise for all its people.

Press on, O, soul of my people, your goal is high and noble, your destiny
great. Keep your inner eye clearly focused upon eternal spiritual verities. Let
not your hearts be troubled — you are stronger than you think — your souls
are greater than your personalities. There is no time for sleep, no time for
waiting, no room for lethargy, and no need for procrastination. Your time in
eternity has come.

Arise now, O, stirring soul —
Awake, my people of South Africa — AWAKE!

In a taped interview in November 1990 (after Nelson Mandela had been released from jail, but before the democratic general elections in 1994) the master teacher who channelled through Busby proclaimed that South Africa had a tremendous future. This had been divinely ordained, and it was the special concern of those who guided the souls of the nations. Mighty forces were said to be at work behind the scenes. A psychological war was being waged between the forces of light and the forces of negation, but eventually the light would be triumphant. Right leadership had been brought about and those of the old guard who could not change would be removed. South Africa had been appointed to be a guardian and to initiate plans that would prove to be a shining example to the rest of the world.

Esotericists in South Africa were encouraged to raise their efforts to bring about a rise in consciousness and were reassured that seldom in the history of the world had there been such a direct shaft of light from Hierarchy shining on a nation. This, however, had been earned by South Africa because the people had transcended so many trails and tribulations. This light had been directed at leaders with powerful visions and some of them had captured something of the hierarchical intensions. South Africans were urged to take courage and go forward with confidence, since a mantle of protection and love had been spread around the land — protecting and guiding its appointed leaders. The battles were not over, but the negative forces had their backs against the wall and would soon surrender.

With the eyes of the world on South Africa during recent times, with the adoration of the world for the South African president Nelson Mandela, and with people commonly referring to the 'miracle' that had taken place in South Africa, Busby's messages surely seemed prophetic. Whether the intention was that these messages were to be interpreted politically, is a moot point. When compared to the intelligence and depth of the philosophic work of Smuts, Busby's work seems a facile repetition. Compared to the personal courage that was required of Brandt to spread her unpopular message in a hostile environment, his adoring audiences gave him a warm reception. Perhaps this reflects different aspects of the New Age movement. Some sections of the movement are characterized by deep and creative philosophical thought. Other sections are characterized by personal courage to criticize traditional religious, social, and political conventions, while there are others that ride the crest of the wave to popular applause.

None of these 'prophets' were particularly influential. Brandt's work had disappeared completely until it was rediscovered in recent years. Smuts, while he will always be a major factor in the history of South Africa, will not be remembered for his philosophical musings in a country where many people still object to the teaching of evolution theory on religious grounds. And although Busby has had a smoother reception for his teachings, his school has, in the months since his death, undergone a metamorphosis and much of what he held dear is being done away with. It seems that the old adage that the prophet is not honoured in his or her own land, still holds true.

Bibliography

Beukes, P. 1991. *The holistic Smuts: a study in personality.* Cape Town: Human & Rousseau.

Brandt, J. (nd) *The Order of Harmony. Founded at Pretoria 1916.*(s.l.)

Brandt, J. 1918. *The Millennium: a prophetic forecast.* Bloemfontein: De Nationale Pers.

Brandt, J. 1921. *The fasting book: a book on the creation and redemption of the body.* Bloemfontein: De Nationale Pers.

Brandt J. 1929. *The grape cure.* South Africa: The Order of Harmony.

Brandt, J. 1936. *The Paraclete or coming World Mother.* (s.l.): Brill Bros.

Cameron, T. 1994. *Jan Smuts: an illustrated biography.* Cape Town: Human & Rousseau.

Hanegraaf, W. 1995. *New Age religion and Western culture: esotericism in the mirror of secular thought.* D.Th. thesis. Utrecht University.

Reid, D.P. 1980. *What are they saying about the prophets?* New York: Paulist Press.

Smuts, J.C. 1944. *Toward a better world.* New York: World Book Company.

Smuts, J.C. 1951. *The thoughts of General Smuts.* Compiled by P.B. Blanckenberg. Cape Town: Juta.

Smuts, J.C. [1926] 1987. *Holism and evolution.* Cape Town: N & S Press.

Part IV:

Social Aspects of the New Religions

CHAPTER 10

Making History: Memory And Forgetfulness in New Religious Movements

Judith Coney

> *You think that just because it has already happened the past is finished and unchangeable? Oh no, the past is cloaked in multicoloured taffeta and every time we look at it we see a different hue.*[1]

Introduction

This chapter focuses on the ways in which emerging religious movements construct their group histories, and takes as its starting point the idea that in new religious movements we can see 'history in the making'. By saying this, I do not mean that, because they are contemporary, we have the facts to hand and can record a true, factual account of the beginnings of a religion. Instead, I am referring to the opportunity to witness at close quarters the ways in which human beings selectively and collectively create histories.

William Bainbridge has argued that 'cult is culture writ small',[2] and made the point that exclusive NRMs provide perfect conditions for the study of larger social processes, in that their boundaries, entry and exit points are usually well defined. This makes them easy to locate and scrutinize.[3] Similarly, I am suggesting that emerging religions — whose direction is not yet clearly articulated, whose leadership often behaves in inconsistent ways, who often undergo radical

1. Kundara 1994.
2. Bainbridge 1985.
3. See also Barker 1995.

change and discontinuity, and who take time to establish coherent identities — provide perfect conditions for charting the dynamics involved in the formation of history.

Because of these conditions, and although they are small, emerging NRMs contain a diverse set of individual, public and 'small group' histories. These histories are not created in a vacuum, but always emerge in relation to other histories and accounts, and are structured in terms of an Other. Some aspects of these histories may overlap, or even appeal to each other as a form of legitimation. Others compete with each other, as well as with preceding versions of events, for dominance. The construction of a history, therefore, is never separated from issues of power.[4] Histories always privilege certain elements over others, and always express social power relations:

Power and knowledge directly imply each other...there is no power relation without the correlative constitution of a field of knowledge, nor any knowledge that does not presuppose and constitute at the same time power relations'.[5]

Foucault has usefully drawn attention to two types of subjugated knowledge, the first being buried or disguised and the second disqualified and marginalized. Both 'contain and exemplify histories of hostile encounters that either buried one form of knowledge or pushed it to the margins'.[6] The first type is knowledge belonging to an elite that is re-interpreted to fit with the prevailing interpretive framework. It is the Other which is interwoven with the dominant version as a way of legitimating the latter.

The second is ordinary knowledge, which may be discomforting to recall, and which is suppressed and managed. This is the Other which is usually systematically eradicated or separated out over time, because it cannot exist alongside or within the dominant version of history. We will see examples of this type when we turn our

4. As the character Mirek in a Kundara novel comments poignantly: 'The struggle of man against power is the struggle of memory against forgetting'. Kundara 1996, 4.
5. Foucault 1977, 27.
6. Bond and Gilliam 1994, 10.

attention specifically onto NRMs. It is enough to say here, however, that the two versions are usually irreconcilable.

Implicit in what has been said is a further point about history which should be made explicit: a history is not usually a permanent version of events, but is one which undergoes continual revision. As Mary Douglas has noted, this:

... revisionary effort is not aimed at producing the perfect optic flat. The mirror, if that is what history is, distorts as much after revision as it did before. The aim of revision is to get the distortions to match the mood of the present times.[7]

Summing up the argument so far, the way in which history is being understood here is not as a narrative whole, a complete and unexpedited version of events. Instead, it is a socially negotiated version which is invested in by a group and which is always a partial representation. Moreover, this negotiation is ongoing, and is inextricably linked to power.

But if this is history, then what is memory? A model of memory as an individual faculty lodged in the skull of each person, which acts as a simple device for recording and recalling information, sits uneasily with the idea of history I have outlined. In this chapter, however, I propose a rather different model of memory, along the lines suggested by Radley: 'Memory is not the retrieval of stored information, but the putting together of a claim about past states of affairs by means of a shared cultural framework'.[8] This 'putting together' is necessarily selective.[9] The context in which these processes take place, moreover, provides more than a social background that creates tendencies to organize the past along certain lines. Instead, context is 'the substance of collective memory itself, contestively established in talk'.[10] Memory is social, therefore, not simply because our thoughts are expressed through language which is learnt socially, but because it is established and re-established through social negotiation. Rather than being a faculty located in the skull of an individual, then, it is

7. Douglas 1987, 69.
8. Radley 1990.
9. Bartlett 1932, 296.
10. Middleton 1990, 11.

very much constructed in relationship with others and is no more a permanent record of events than history itself.

Although, so far, it is the selective aspect of memory which has been emphasized,[11] it is important to stress another aspect of memory. This is that, although social memory is often distorted and inaccurate, it can also sometimes be a vehicle through which memories, once they have been constructed, are preserved with tremendous accuracy, despite numerous retellings. Furthermore, social memories can be reawakened after they seemed to have been lost entirely. This is especially the case when recall is prompted through the senses and by association — by seeing old photographs, hearing old tunes, smelling evocative scents, and so on. Again, we shall look at specific examples of these kinds of memory preservation and recall when we focus more closely on NRMs.

For the moment it is enough simply to state that it is memory that makes us what we are — you could not, for instance, agree or disagree with any of what has been said so far without it — and to point out that the other side of memory is forgetfulness, and that this is similarly socially organized. We collectively forget for different reasons. A practical reason is that there is simply too much information to remember. Information that is either repetitious or unexceptional tends, therefore, not to be carried forward. At other times, forgetfulness is the result of repressing an uncomfortable Other. Bartlett, as early as 1923, hypothesized that

when there are conflicting impulses seeking expression, none 'operates entirely by itself', but they are organized into their own distinct 'spheres of influence' *in relation to each other* — with one sphere, however, usually dominant over the other, with, in particular, anything *fearful* being repressed.[12]

11. By making these points about selective interpretations, I am not claiming that histories are not 'true'. Instead, all histories are true, in so far as each contains within it reference to other histories and the social dynamics on which it has been formulated. As Fentress and Wickham have observed: '...the issue of whether or not a given memory is true is interesting only in so far as it sheds light on how memory itself works...all that matters is that it be believed'. In Fentress and Wickham 1992, xi.
12. Summarized in J. Shotter in: Middleton and Edwards 1990, 130-31. Italics in original.

This repression leads to a social amnesia, which is reflected in the removal of support for the alternative discourse. However, in certain instances such repression also has implications for the discourse that is left, as was noted by Portelli in his description of the story of a witness

... who gave what proved to be a fantasy version of events which had sadly tested his loyalty, along with many others. He had, without any conscious deception, come to present a 'what might have been' story, perhaps because he could not acknowledge to himself the contradiction in which he had been involved.[13]

and repressed memories can return to haunt the margins of a discourse and continue, despite their apparent absence, to influence its structure.

Most often, what is forgotten is forgotten because it no longer fits in with the current version of events, especially one constructed by an elite group. Sometimes, indeed, leaderships systematically destroy unwelcome memories. In such situations, whether deliberately manufactured or the result of 'drift', human beings no longer have the ability to retrieve the memories, since they cease to make collective sense: 'If events do not fit into the frameworks provided by one's social institutions — into which one has been socialized — then they are not remembered'.[14]

The Dynamics of History Construction in NRMs

This chapter has been written in the light of over fifteen years of contact with new religious movements in the UK. As anyone with that length of experience will attest, it is almost impossible not to notice how the discontinuities that accompany the development of most groups become ironed out or 'explained', and de-emphasized in favour of a strong, continuous storyline.[15] Similarly, certain aspects of

13. Summarized in Tonkin 1992, 114.
14. Shotter op cit., 131.
15. Unless these discontinuities are played upon to reaffirm the trust of members in the leadership and the rejection of social hierarchies and regulation as, for instance, in the Family. See Wallis 1984.

the history of a movement are often either deliberately concealed or unconsciously forgotten, whilst other aspects are brought to the fore and highlighted. On what basis does this selection occur?

The argument was put forward earlier that histories are not made in vacuums, but are structured in response to other histories. Sometimes these are the accounts of 'mainstream' society about NRMs, especially of those who attack such groups for destroying family values or for practising mind control.

In tracing back such accounts, however, more deeply embedded discourses become apparent. One such discourse, for example, gives rise to our view of ourselves as 'singular individuals' who are either active or passive in relation to separated 'social forces'. Once this assumption is accepted, as it is generally in the West, it becomes a reference point for the structuring of various histories which then revolve around the issue of whether members of NRMs are free agents, or vice versa. Another revolves around the dangerous nature of marginal religious groups who either explicitly or implicitly challenge the status quo.

But this sort of history-making involves the public face of a movement as its leadership attempts to present a history about the NRM which can compete successfully over time with others in the public arena, and which will therefore minimize conflict and legitimate the group's claim to authenticity. What of all the competing histories within a movement as well? These are present for numerous reasons, including the fact that members join at different stages of an NRM's development, and so have different experiences on which to found their understandings, and because charismatic leaders are notoriously capricious and inconsistent, so giving rise to diverse interpretations of their teachings. Multiple histories also grow up because as a movement expands there is less personal interaction with the leadership, and more room for other interpretations of 'what is going on' to develop. Significant differences will normally occur between the understandings of leaders and those of ordinary members, as the latter are not privy to specialized forms of information. Lastly, different versions also arise in the different locations in which a group establishes itself. International groups are clearly influenced by different cultural assumptions, but even regional and national characteristics lead to diverse understandings of 'what is going on'.

Sometimes these different histories vanish with their owners. As a number of scholars have shown,[16] NRMs have a high turnover of members in the early years, or if there is a crisis of confidence in the leadership. A good example of the erasure of memories that can accompany the departure of old members and an influx of new members is that of ISKCON (Hare Krishna) in the USA. In ten years or so, the public image of the movement has become transformed from that of a cult attracting drug users with a track record of unscrupulous gurus and manipulative financial practices, to that of a primary exemplar of Hinduism in the West. This transformation has occurred through its strong support from sections of the South Asian community, and as a result of the departure of many former members. Its previous identity is fading from view, as the recollections of mostly American hippies and drop-outs are replaced with the social memories of mostly middle-class Gujuratis, with the blessing of the current leadership. Here, too, is evidence of a history being fashioned by reference to others. Thus, ISKCON, although founded in the late 1960s as an organization, cites a historical lineage going back to Chaitanya, the sixteenth century Bengali saint, in an effort to distance itself from a pejorative identification as an NRM.

As well as the transformation that can accompany voluntary membership changes and a re-alignment of the movement by the leadership, some histories are deliberately excluded because they compete directly with that of the leadership. In such cases, the relevant malcontents are likely to be expelled and their accounts ridiculed or erased. At other times, competing versions of events are submerged or buried within a dominant account. More often, historical facts, which are perhaps embarrassing or salacious, are simply not referred to by the leadership and gradually cease to be part of the group repertoire of memories. It is also characteristic of a number of NRMs that the name of either the leader or the group changes to suit the new mood of the times. Memories associated with the previous designation tend to recede with its disappearance from usage, and new memories are produced in their stead. In thirty years time, for example, how many members of their respective movements will

16. See, for instance, Barker 1984; Galanter 1989.

recall memories associated with 'Bubba Free John', or the 'Children of God', or 'est'?

Versions that directly contradict the dominant account also tend to be submerged. It is as if they are remembered but not articulated, until they rise again to the surface of the collective memory. Rajneesh-ism in the early 1980s is a case in point. Rajneesh's teaching of spon-taneity, naturalness and freedom was utterly at odds with the in-creasing centralization of power in the movement and the imposition of uniformity and regulation throughout its communes. The ethos of the teachings became a latent feature, articulated only by those on the periphery, until the downfall of Rajneeshpuram when spontaneity and freedom were resurrected as important motifs within the movement.

Forgetfulness in NRMs

Inevitably, an examination of the construction of histories is, as we have seen, also an examination of what is forgotten as well as what is remembered. It is time, however, to briefly focus more closely on the ways in which memories are forgotten in movements, as this occurs both unconsciously and consciously.

An instance of unconscious forgetfulness is the ways in which members of NRMs tend not to be able to recall those who leave, or can only recall the conflict that led to them leaving. This forgetfulness is exacerbated by the fact that most leavers tend to severe their con-nections entirely,[17] and by the emotions associated with apostasy. Yet, unless the member has been expelled, she or he is not likely to have been consciously and systematically erased from social memory. In-stead, attention simply shifts from that individual until their details are obscured. Unconscious forgetting also tends to occur particularly around embarrassing claims that cannot easily be reconciled with the dominant history. In Sahaja Yoga, for example, early beliefs included the idea that members were guaranteed immortality and that they were transforming into angels. No such transformation has yet taken

---

17. As Wright has noted in relation to departure from new religions, 'even in cases in which exiting is not viewed negatively, it is difficult for ex-members to sustain relationships when interests and daily activities be-gin to diverge from those of group members'. Wright 1993, 126.

place, however, and some members, including one very devoted to the leader, have died. These days, devotees will express surprise that such beliefs were ever in common currency.[18]

But there are also numerous examples of conscious forgetfulness. The Neo-Sannyas movement of Mohan Chandra Rajneesh provides a particularly poignant example of such a process. In the mid-1980s, in the aftermath of the downfall of Rajneeshpuram, Rajneesh changed his name from Bhagwan (God-Realized) to Osho and returned to India. He died in 1990, by which time the Poona leadership had already recast him as a Zen master, a far cry from his roots in Tantra and his early followers' interest in radical Western psychotherapies. The previously published literature of the movement is now being systematically revised.

Early *'darshan* diaries' with Bhagwan are being re-issued under the title *Osho*, as are all his other books from that era. Those republished by Element Books declare that all the titles were copyrighted in 1977 by 'Osho International Foundation', although there was no such Foundation at that time, the new designation of Osho not having been adopted until about a decade later. New videos using selected footage from old films are also being produced to portray a highly selective image of Osho.[19] In short, it is eerie to witness, as a long-time observer of the movement, the withdrawal from view of a vital and rebellious human being who seemed to thrive on controversy, called Bhagwan, and his public replacement by a tamed and copyrighted entity called Osho who was 'Never Born and Never Died'.[20]

18. Such forgetfulness is a necessary part of dealing with the inevitable cognitive dissonance occurring in NRMs. Cognitive dissonance has been described by Festinger et al. as 'the experience of competing, opposing or contradictory attitudes, thoughts or actions leading to a feeling of tension and a need to achieve consonance'. Festinger et al. 1956, 10. Consonance is most satisfactorily provided, they argued, by group explanations which are reinforced by social contact.
19. It is also of interest to note that the name 'Osho' does not have the traditional South Asian associations of 'Bhagwan'. Not being 'fixed', it provides the perfect vehicle for whatever historical representation of Rajneesh seems appropriate.
20. So reads the commemorative inscription on his marble plaque where his ashes rest at the Poona ashram, India.

Structures for Remembering in NRMs

There are also structures in place, however, in NRMs which facilitate recall. Two, in particular, are significant enough to warrant inclusion in this short chapter. The first is the role of 'miracle stories' within NRMs. Miracle stories are tales of either miracles or extraordinary events. They are usually connected to the founder or current leader, or are cited as by-products of following the spiritual practices of the NRM. They are an important part of the oral tradition of a group, and are often patterned in characteristic ways. Being part of the oral tradition, these stories are always articulated and exchanged in a social setting, and various versions of them will spread quickly through the social networks of an organization. Miracle stories can be seen as especially enduring and resilient memories, because of their structure, which are incorporated into what might be termed the hagiographic repertoire of the movement.[21]

The second concerns the role of artefacts in remembering. The ways in which photographs, images and scents can awaken buried memories has already been commented upon. Such recollection takes place through the senses and can have a powerful emotional effect. The implications of this for NRMs are several. Radley has noted that there are objects which are made specially in order that they might help us remember. But he has also pointed out:

Objects do seemingly present themselves unexpectedly to 'evoke' memories, but they are also very much part of the material world ordered to sustain certain myths and ideologies, both about people as individuals and about particular cultures.[22]

---

21. Some studies have concluded that spiritual leaders become progressively divine in the decades and centuries after their death. However, it may be that their miraculous aspects are preserved through the tales which circulate during their lives, and that these over time — and because of the enduring qualities of oral tales — often rise to the surface to be incorporated in the hagiography of a religious figure.
22. Radley op cit., 51.

Two examples can be offered to illuminate the pertinence of his observations for NRMs. One concerns the evocation of memories in a follower. When a favoured Western devotee of Sathya Sai Baba glances at his wrist and sees the Rolex watch which his Master produced out of thin air, the image stimulates recall. This recollection is not just of the miraculous incident but of his feelings for Sathya Sai Baba, and his identification of this guru with his own spiritual development. The artefact, then, becomes a condensed symbol of his relationship to Sathya Sai Baba which triggers a renewed appreciation in the present of that remembered relationship each time it is noticed.

The other involves the recall of memories in a collective religious setting, especially when those present are engaged in ritual practices. Rituals are commonly strewn with artefacts of one kind or another. These, through their ability to stimulate associative recall, enable the participants to 'get in touch with' and so renew their sense of connection with the ethos and values of the group, as well as their fellow members. A common observation by participants is: 'I felt very present'. It may be that this is because the release of forgotten, socially constructed memories provides a much more richly textured experiential understanding than filtered everyday memory management allows.

Research Implications

It has been argued that an appreciation of the social structures of memory and forgetting is part and parcel of a study of history construction in NRMs. Similarly, however, memory and forgetting also have an impact on the sorts of studies we carry out. Scholars, too, contribute to the making of histories, through the ways in which we select what we deem to be relevant, what fits in with our intellectual presuppositions, and the points we are trying to make.

Robbins, for instance, has noted how academics with an interest in NRMs exclude certain versions by refusing to accord them legitimacy. He has drawn attention to the ways in which the results of studies are:

... predetermined by 'epistemological exclusionary rules' whereby a class of respondents such as committed converts or recriminating apostates are treated a priori as incapable of valid insights while another class is assumed to have a monopoly of truth.[23]

Others have commented on the ways in which scholarly accounts are structured in line with the assumptions of prevailing discourses. We have seen, for example, how the social theories that assume the existence of an individual separate from society inevitably lead to debates over agency and passivity. The effect is that these issues come to assume overriding consideration and are selected for inclusion in most studies on NRMs, especially since this discourse also structures the ways in which marginal groups are perceived in the public arena. Moreover, notwithstanding our assiduous recording of data, we still forget some and remember other elements of our engagements with NRMs. This selective process feeds back into future interactions with the group, and in turn is reflected in the data produced.

Enough, it is hoped, has been said to indicate the significance of an appreciation of history construction to NRMs for our understanding of such movements. However, there is also a problematical ethical issue to be faced in a study of features such as the nature of memory in NRMs, which is not easily overcome. By what right do I and others have to rummage around, attempting to trace these social processes by uncovering memories which have been forgotten in a NRM, usually for good reason? This ethical consideration impacts on our ability to include some of the kinds of data crucial to such a study, especially when it is associated with historical revision by an elite group.

Nevertheless, studies of history construction are both possible and desirable, as long as their focus of interest is clear. Smaller social groups, elite groups and large collective occasions can all be examined in order to illuminate the social aspects of such processes. It may be particularly fruitful to concentrate attention on discontinuities and the ways in which these are explained, and on schism, where two competing versions can no longer co-exist harmoniously.

23. Robbins 1988,14.

Conclusion

This paper constitutes a tentative first exploration on my part of the social aspects of history construction in NRMs. It has shown that what is remembered and forgotten in these movements are both important. What is remembered is recalled either because an elite grouping supports its recall, or — though these two points are not easily separated — because the social environment lends support to the persistence or retrieval of certain types of memories. Artefacts and oral tales both have significant roles to play in such recollection. What is forgotten, moreover, although it is hidden from view, can continue to make its unspoken presence felt in the ways in which articulated memories are socially patterned and can shed light on intentional and unintentional aspects of NRMs.

This is not, however, an easy subject to explore, as can be seen in Bartlett's work in the 1920s and 1930s. As Mary Douglas has pointed out, he too fell prey to processes of forgetting in his own research.[24] Thus, by the second decade he had reversed his understanding of memory as a social phenomenon, and gone back to couching its investigation in terms of it being an individual faculty. Musing on this ironic twist, Shotter has suggested that there is something to be feared in the theory itself.[25] One can speculate that simply paying attention to these processes can be anxiety-provoking and lead to selective amnesia on the part of the researcher, since they run too close to our own, largely unconscious behaviours for comfort. After all, as social animals we are all involved in the construction of histories. Without paying such attention, however, we will miss a valuable opportunity to study these processes in NRMs.

Bibliography

Bainbridge, W.S. 1985 'Cultural Genetics'. In: R. Stark (ed.) *Religious Movements: Genesis, Exodus, Numbers.* New York: Paragon House.

Barker, E. 1984. *The Making of a Moonie: Brainwashing or Choice?* Oxford: Blackwell.

24. Douglas op cit.
25. Shotter op cit., 131.

Barker, E. 1995. 'Plus ca change...'. *Social Compass*, vol. 42(2), 165-80.

Bartlett, F.C. 1932. *Remembering: A Study in Experimental and Social Psychology*. London: Cambridge University Press.

Bond, G. and A. Gilliam 1994. *Social Construction of the Past: Representation as Power*. London: Routledge.

Douglas, M. 1987. *How Institutions Think*. London: Routledge & Kegan Paul.

Fentress, J. and C. Wickham 1992. *Social Memory*. Oxford: Blackwell.

Festinger, L. et al. 1956. *When Prophecy Fails*. New York: Harper Torch Books.

Foucault, M. 1977. *Discipline and Punish*. Harmondsworth: Penguin.

Galanter, M. (ed.) 1989. *Cults and New Religious Movements: A Report of the American Psychiatric Association*. Washington, DC: Committee on Psychiatry and Religion.

Kundara, M.1994. *Life is Elsewhere*. New York: Penguin.

Kundara, M. 1996. *The Book of Laughter and Forgetting*. London: Faber and Faber.

Middleton, D. and D. Edwards. 1990. *Collective Remembering*. London: Sage.

Radley, A. 1990. 'Artefacts, Memory and a Sense of the Past'. In: D. Middleton and D. Edwards, *Collective Remembering*. London: Sage.

Robbins, A. 1988. *Cults, Converts and Charisma*. London: Sage.

Shotter, J.1990. 'The Social Construction of Remembering and Forgetting'. In: D. Middleton and D. Edwards *Collective Remembering*. London: Sage.

Tonkin, E. 1992. *Narrating Our Pasts*. Cambridge: Cambridge University Press.

Wallis, R.1984 *The Elementary Forms of the New Religious Life*. London: Routledge & Kegan Paul.

Wright, S. 1993 'Leaving New Religions'. In: D.G. Bromley and J.K. Hadden (eds.), *Religion and the Social Order*, vol. 3B. Greenwich: JAI Press.

CHAPTER 11

Les Témoignages de Convertis et D'ex-Adeptes

Jean Duhaime

On peut lire ou entendre assez souvent des convertis qui racontent avec enthousiasme leur quête spirituelle et leur découverte du mouvement ou du courant religieux qui a transformé leur vie. Mais les médias et les associations dites 'anti-cultistes' ou 'contre-cultistes' nous relaient aussi un autre son de cloche, celui d'ex-adeptes déçus qui viennent dire comment ils ont été attirés et manipulés dans des groupes religieux dont ils sont sortis à temps. Que penser des témoignages de convertis et d'ex-adeptes? Comment se fabriquent-ils? Que signifient-ils? Quelle valeur peut-on leur accorder? J'ai choisi d'aborder ces questions à partir des sciences sociales, en particulier des travaux des sociologues sur les témoignages des convertis et des ex-adeptes. Dans l'exposé qui suit, je résume d'abord la recherche sur les récits de conversion; je me penche ensuite sur trois témoignages d'ex-adeptes dont je cherche les points communs et la signification pour les personnes et la société.

Les témoignages de convertis

L'expérience de conversion

On désigne habituellement l'adhésion d'une personne à une nouvelle religion par le terme 'conversion'. Comme le note Hervé Carrier,[1] la

---

1. Carrier 1966, 67.

Jean Duhaime

conversion est un phénomène complexe, impliquant l'intervention de facteurs psychologiques, de références collectives et d'éléments de croyance. Elle résulte d'un processus assez élaboré, dont une observation attentive peut dégager la séquence type comme l'ont fait Lofland et Stark[2] à partir de l'observation, en 1962-63, du groupe millénariste des Divine Precepts (D.P. — un pseudonyme pour l'Église de l'Unification). Selon les auteurs, 15 des 21 convertis aux D.P. partageraient sept caractéristiques similaires:

1. Tension: Ces personnes auraient toutes la perception 'as a felt discrepancy between some imaginary ideal state of affairs and the circumstances in which these people saw themselves caught up'[3] (d'un décalage entre un ordre idéal des choses et les circonstances dont elles se voient captives). Elles aspirent par exemple à la richesse, au savoir, à la renommée et au prestige ...
2. Recherche de solution religieuse: Une personne qui perçoit de telles carences dans sa vie peut recourir à trois sortes de solutions: psychiatrique, politique, religieuse. Dans la perspective religieuse, la personne tend à localiser dans un monde invisible la source et la solution de ses problèmes. Les futurs convertis auraient écarté les solutions religieuses traditionnelles à leur problèmes, mais 'they retained a general propensity to impose religious meaning on events'[4] (ont gardé une tendance générale à octroyer une signification religieuse aux événements).
3. Attitude de quête (Seekership): Ces personnes en sont venues à se définir comme 'en recherche religieuse' et ont entrepris diverses démarches fondées sur deux postulats: elles croyaient en des esprits ou entités surnaturelles agissant dans le monde matériel; elles croyaient que tout a été créé dans un but précis. Leur quête consiste à chercher à entrer en contact avec le monde spirituel pour y découvrir le sens de l'existence, ce qu'elles ont trouvé dans les D.P.
4. Le point tournant: Tous les futurs convertis avaient atteint ou étaient sur le point d'atteindre, 'shortly before, and concurrently

2. Lofland and Stark 1965.
3. Ibid., 864.
4. Ibid., 868.

with their encounter with the D.P., all pre-converts had reached or were about to reach what they perceived as a 'turning point' in their lives'[5] (*peu* avant, et *concurremment* à leur rencontre avec les D.P. ... ce qu'elles on perçu comme un 'point tournant' dans leur vie). Ce point tournant serait généralement associé à un changement de situation personnelle: déménagement, perte d'emploi, abandon scolaire, etc. Cette situation stimule le désir de changement, tout en le rendant possible.

5. Liens affectifs avec un ou des membres du groupe: Le contact avec le groupe des D.P. survient à cette étape. Pour que la conversion puisse se produire, il semble nécessaire que s'établissent (ou se consolident) des liens affectifs avec un ou plusieurs membres du groupe: 'In a manner of speaking, final conversion was coming to accept the opinions of one's friends'[6] (La conversion finale, pour ainsi dire, a consisté à accepter les opinions d'un ami).

6. Liens affectifs avec les personnes de l'extérieur: La plupart des convertis entretenaient peu de relations avec l'extérieur, en particulier à partir du 'point tournant' déjà mentionné. Les liens affectifs externes des autres personnes étaient ténus et les conflits affectifs ont été neutralisés.

7. Interaction intense: La combinaison des six facteurs précédents a conduit jusqu'à la conversion verbale, celle de la personne qui proclame son adhésion au groupe et est considérée comme sincère par les principaux membres du groupe. Seuls sont ensuite passés à une conversion totale, manifestée dans leur engagement concret, ceux qui se sont livrés à une intense interaction avec les autres membres, en particulier en s'installant dans les locaux du groupe, bénéficiant ainsi d'un support constant dans leur nouvelle identité.

Les principaux éléments de ce modèle se vérifient assez fréquemment. Cependant les expériences de conversion sont plus diversifiées. Dans une étude synthèse, Killbourne et Richardson distinguent des conversions où la personne a un rôle plutôt passif (elle est convertie) et celles où elle a un rôle plutôt actif (elle se convertit) et, dans chacune

5. Ibid., 870.
6. Ibid., 871.

de ces deux catégories, les conversions qui reposent surtout sur des facteurs internes à l'individu (expérience mystique, recherche intellectuelle) et celles ou les facteurs extérieurs (manipulation, expérimentation) ont un plus grand rôle.[7]

Les récits de conversion

L'expérience de la conversion n'est accessible que par ce que le converti en dit par ses paroles et ses actions, et principalement par le réncit de sa propre conversion. Comment de tels récits sont-ils fabriqués, que contiennent-ils, à quoi servent-ils? La recherche d'A. Billette permet d'éclairer ces questions.[8] Estimant que 'la conversion n'est peut-être pas tant un changement que l'interprétation (religieuse) d'un changement', Billettte s'est intéressé au récit de conversion lui-même,[9] qui serait, selon lui, tributaire de quatre dimensions constitutives:

1. Des faits d'histoire: 'Il y a eu dans le passé une séquence d'événements et souvent un événement de sens, instaurateur d'un changement personnel'; mais cet événement, riche de signification, 'est ouvert à des reprises successives dans le temps selon les multiples situations nouvelles'.[10]
2. Des conditions actuelles de productions: 'C'est le présent qui reconstruit le passé en fonction de l'agencement commandé par la situation actuelle'[11] La sélection et l'arrangement des événements s'effectue 'à partir des conditions immédiates de l'énonciation et surtout de la projection de l'identité actuelle du converti sur son passé'.[12]
3. Des manières de raconter: Dans le récit de conversion, les souvenirs d'événements sont agencés 'selon certaines 'formes' déjà existantes, de perception, de sélection et d'interprétations, conscientes ou inconscientes'.[13] Billette identifie quatre *patterns* prin-

---

7. Killbourne and Richardson 1989.
8. Billette 1975.
9. Ibid., 27.
10. Ibid., 205-6.
11. Ibid., 206.
12. Ibid., 207.
13. Ibid., 209.

cipaux: la structure de *salut*, la structure *vocationnelle*, la structure *intégrative*, et la structure *cosmologique*.[14]

4. Des actes de paroles: Le récit de conversion n'est pas seulement un rappel interprétatif du passé. C'est un acte qui s'inscrit dans la suite logique de la conversion et contribue à la consolider. La conversion racontée n'est jamais complétée au moment de la raconter. Le récit en anticipe l'accomplissement: 'La conversion est d'abord un phénomène de parole (...) qui dans sa forme même engage l'avenir, elle est (...) le premier changement, celui de la parole, de la confession, de la profession'.[15]

Les témoignages d'ex-adeptes

Les ex-adeptes et leur 'sortie'

A l'exception de ceux qui sont nés dans le mouvement religieux qu'ils ont quitté, les ex-adeptes ont été des convertis. Leur situation est cependant différente, puisqu'ils ont quitté. Tout comme les convertis, ils ont changé d'univers et réinterprètent maintenant leur biographie à la lumière de leur situation actuelle. Celle-ci est déterminée en partie par la manière dont la personne a quitté le groupe; cet 'exit' peut prendre plusieurs formes:[16]

1. Kidnapping: La personne est 'enlevée' au groupe, contre sa volonté, par des parents, des proches ou des professionnels qui considèrent qu'elle a été victime d'un lavage de cerveau et la 'déprogrammment'. Si l'opération réussit, on peut s'attendre à ce que le témoignage de l'ex-adepte endosse le cadre d'interprétation proposé par ceux ou celles qui l'ont arrachée au groupe.

2. Expulsion: La personne est rejetée par le groupe pour diverses raisons. Selon la manière dont cette exclusion s'est effectuée et les raisons qui l'ont motivée, la personne pourrait en parler avec nostalgie et aspirer à y retourner, ou au contraire le dénoncer et en parler avec agressivité.

14. Ibid., 210-11.
15. Ibid., 217.
16. Compare Wright 1987, 67-73.

3. Départ volontaire pacifique: La personne quitte le groupe de son plein gré, discrètement ou non, sans que son départ ne crée de controverse majeure. La personne constate que le groupe lui a apporté beaucoup, mais ne répond plus à ses nouveaux besoins, ou qu'il n'est plus ce qu'il était au moment où elle l'a joint; elle en parlera éventuellement en décrivant ce qu'il y a eu de positif dans son expérience, tout en expliquant pourquoi elle n'y est plus satisfaite. Dans les meilleures conditions, elle peut le faire avec l'accord des responsables, qui lui procureront les moyens de se réinsérer dans un autre milieu. Son témoignage sera plutôt positif et elle hésitera à qualifier d'échec son séjour dans le groupe et à porter des accusations envers ses dirigeants, préférant demeurer en bons termes avec ceux qui l'ont aidé à traverser une étape dont elle cherche à intégrer les meilleurs éléments.

4. Départ fracassant ou fuite: La personne constate que le groupe est ou est devenu une supercherie et qu'elle s'est 'fait avoir'; le leader dérape et la vie dans le groupe devient insuportable ou dangereuse, à son point de vue. Elle confronte les dirigeants et cherche à négocier sa sortie, mais se heurte à un refus de l'écouter, à des manoeuvres pour essayer de la retenir, voire à de la répression physique. Finalement, après une ou plusieurs tentatives, elle réussit à fuir cet 'enfer'. On peut s'attendre à ce qu'elle donne une image négative du groupe et qu'elle mette en garde quiconque serait tenté de le joindre, et qui pourrait à son tour être manipulé ou détruit.

Les témoignages des ex-adeptes

Vers la fin des années 1970, on a beaucoup entendu parler des opérations de kidnapping et elles ont été largement médiatisées. Elles mettaient souvent en scène de jeunes adeptes 'enlevés' à leur famille par des groupes totalitaires et 'récupérés' avec le concours de professionnels qui les déprogrammaient.[17] Ces opérations ont donné lieu à des controverses judiciaires et il en est de moins en moins question.[18] Les témoignages d'ex-adeptes les plus médiatisés actuellement sont,

17. Beckford 1985; Bromley, Shupe and Ventimiglia 1983; Shupe and Bromley 1981.
18. Bromley and Shupe 1995.

me semble-t-il, les histoires d'horreurs de gens qui ont fui leur groupe ou l'ont quitté de manière fracassante. Trois témoignages de ce type ont été publiés au Québec récemment:

— *L'église de Scientologie. Facile d'y entrer, difficile d'en sortir...*, par J.P. Dubreuil.
— *Le 54ᵉ*, par T. Huguenin, qui aurait dû être la 54ᵉ victime dans l'hécatombe de l'Ordre du Temple solaire en octobre 1994.
— *L'alliance de la brebis*, de G. Lavallée, ex-adepte de la secte de Moïse Thériault.[19] Ces trois témoins ont en commun de s'être échappés de leur groupe après avoir réalisé à quel point il s'agissait d'une escroquerie ou d'un 'enfer'. Ce sont des 'histoires d'atrocités', pour reprendre l'expression de Shupe et Bromley:

By an atrocity story we refer to the symbolic presentation of actions or events (real or imaginary) in such a context that they are made flagrantly to violate the (presumably) shared premises upon which a given set of social relation-ships should be conducted. The recounting of such tales is intended as a means of reaffirming normative boundaries. By sharing the reporter's disap-proval or horror, an audience reasserts normative prescription and clearly locates the violator as being beyond the limits of public morality. [20]

(Par une histoire d'atrocités, nous entendons la représentation symbo-lique d'actions ou d'événements (réels ou imaginaires) dans un contexte tel qu'ils paraissent constituer une violation flagrante des principes (présumés) selon lesquels un ensemble de relations sociales devrait se dérouler. Le fait de raconter de tels récits a pour but de consolider les limites qui sont norma-tives. En partageant la désapprobation ou l'horreur de la personne qui fait le récit, l'auditoire réaffirme les prescriptions normatives et situe clairement ceux qui les violent en dehors des limites de la moralité publique).

Les trois récits sont construits sensiblement de la même manière et comportent tous plus ou moins les éléments suivants:

1. L'enfance et l'adolescence: En rappelant son enfance et son adole-scence, le témoin identifie une carence: absence d'affection ou

19. Dubreuil 1994; Huguenin 1994; Lavallée 1994.
20. Shupe and Bromley 1981, 198.

d'attention de la part du père ou de la mère, peur, manque de confiance en soi, etc. Il évoque aussi son idéal ou son rêve qui peut prendre une forme religieuse ou spirituelle.

2. La quête: La personne cherche à combler son besoin par ses aventures amoureuses, son dévouement à une grande cause, des changements à son mode de vie, l'exploration des ressources 'spirituelles' disponibles, etc.

3. La découverte: La personne est mise en contact avec le groupe ou son chef, par hasard ou par l'intermédiaire d'un proche. Elle est amenée progressivement et subtilement, à un engagement de plus en plus exigeant et exclusif.

4. La période rose: La personne a le sentiment de progresser, de s'épanouir, d'être prise en considération; les relations sont bonnes, même si le régime de vie est exigeant et autoritaire.

5. La période noire: La personne commence à douter ou à perdre ses illusions: le comportement du chef change, l'atmosphère se transforme, on relève divers signaux d'alarme qu'on ne parvient parfois à décoder qu'après coup. On est enfermé dans un régime tyrannique, autoritaire qui ne laisse aucune disponibilité, épuise les forces physiques et psychiques. On est coupé totalement de l'extérieur, sauf pour soutirer de l'argent à ses proches, etc.

6. Les premières tentatives de sortie: Un événement ou une accumulation d'événements conduisent la personne à tenter de quitter le groupe. Cependant, elle revient pour diverses raisons: chantage affectif, promesses, incapacité d'abandonner le leader ou le groupe malgré ses travers, peur de vivre en dehors de la communauté de salut.

7. Le départ: Un événement décisif fait 'déborder le vase', la personne finit par surmonter ses craintes et elle quitte définitivement. Éventuellement, elle tente d'être indemnisée pour les services rendus ou l'exploitation dont elle estime avoir été victime.

8. Le témoignage et la situation présente: La personne fait part de son expérience pour dénoncer le groupe et mettre les gens en garde contre des manipulations semblables. Elle dit sa difficulté de refaire sa vie, affirme ses valeurs présentes et sa manière de les mettre en pratique de façon moins idéaliste, elle parle du support qu'elle reçoit dans cette entreprise.

Le style de ces récits

Les trois récits se présentent comme le compte-rendu sincère de ce que la personne a vécu dans le groupe. Ils ont le ton du témoignage direct, qui veut livrer la vérité sans secret ni pudeur. Ils sont souvent dramatiques. Les scènes-clé sont décrites de manière impressionnante, avec des détails frappants. Le portrait du leader se transforme progressivement à mesure que le masque tombe et que sa véritable personnalité se dévoile. Le témoin décrit ses émotions et celles du groupe: enthousiasme initial, frustration, déception et peur qui s'installent graduellement, colère qui monte, sentiment d'impuissance, etc.

Au plan informatif, on apprend finalement assez peu sur le groupe, son origine, son histoire, ses doctrines, son organisation, son financement. Le témoin ne peut en révéler que ce qu'il en a connu au moment de son appartenance ou ce qu'il en a découvert après coup. Plus l'organisation est importante et complexe, plus ces données lui échappent. Par contre, on apprend beaucoup sur la vie quotidienne dans le groupe, les activités auxquelles le témoin s'est adonné de gré ou de force et celles qui l'ont touché directement: la routine quotidienne épuisante et les brusques changements de programme, les décisions imprévisibles du chef, etc.

Le témoignage paraît vraisemblable parce qu'il fait voir l'ambivalence des situations: la 'victime' est apprivoisée progressivement avant de s'engager totalement dans le groupe. Au fur et à mesure que l'engagement devient plus exigeant, il est compensé par des gratifications ou des promesses. Au moment où la personne commence à exprimer des doutes et considère la possibilité de quitter, l'étau se resserre autour d'elle, ou encore elle se voit entourée de marques d'estime et d'affection qui la neutralisent. Lorsqu'elle tente de quitter ou fait une fugue, elle se laisse persuader de revenir soit par peur du monde extérieur ou du châtiment qui l'attend, soit parce qu'elle a encore des intérêts dans le groupe (elle ne peut se passer de son 'guide' spirituel, même s'il lui a menti ou s'est montré brutal envers elle), ou parce qu'elle croit la promesse d'un changement d'attitude ou d'une amélioration de la situation.

Crédibilité et fonctions de ces récits

— Du côté du témoin: Certains chercheurs rejettent comme non-crédibles ce qu'ils appellent les 'témoignages d'apostats'.[21] Je serais personnellement plus nuancé. Il me semble que des témoignages comme ceux de Dubreuil, Lavallée et Huguenin ne peuvent être écartés simplement parce qu'ils ne sont pas objectifs. Mais ils doivent être pris pour ce qu'ils sont: le récit que fait, avec sa sensibilité actuelle, une personne qui a été déçue par un nouveau mouvement religieux. La vérité de ces récits ne porte pas d'abord sur les faits 'objectifs' qu'ils pourraient contenir. Comme dans le cas des récits de conversion, la vérité des récits d'ex-adeptes porte aussi sur leur sélection et leur interprétation d'un certain nombres de faits à partir de leur situation actuelle. L'ex-adepte adopte aussi, on l'a vu, un modèle assez 'standard' qui circule dans la culture. Enfin, son témoignage sert aussi à dire à quel point sa blessure a été profonde et comment sa convalescence se dessine. Il y a 'de la vérité' à tous ces niveaux, et pas seulement à celui des événements rapportés; il y a 'de la vérité', mais pas nécessairement 'la vérité, toute la vérité, rien que la vérité'.[22]

En donnant un tel témoignage, la personne met de l'ordre dans sa vie et dans son expérience. Son témoignage confirme publiquement la séparation définitive de son ancien groupe d'appartenance. Il lui permet de tracer son programme de vie, de clarifier ses valeurs actuelles et de consolider sa volonté de les mettre en pratique. La personne sollicite également la solidarité et le soutien d'un nouveau groupe d'appartenance, plus diffus, sans doute, mais tout aussi réel, qui se fera solidaire de sa réinsertion sociale.

— Du côté de la société: Au plan social, les témoignages d'ex-adeptes sont des avertissements. Ils équivalent à peu près aux publicités-choc contre l'acool au volant ou la violence conjugale, qui dénoncent avec des images très crues des excès ou des comportements que la société ne tolère pas parce qu'ils créent des situations jugées dangereuses: elles ne peuvent en aucun cas servir de description du comportement du conducteur ou du conjoint 'moyen'. Les ex-adeptes qui témoignent veulent nous mettre en

21. Wilson 1994.
22. Cf. Beckford 1985, 146.

garde contre les abus potentiels de certains groupes religieux et nous sensibiliser aux signaux de danger ou de dérapage. Dans un essai intitulé 'Sur l'autoroute des religions', B. Ouellet mentionne quelques-uns de ces signaux, en particulier le monopole de l'autorité par le leader du groupe, le rapport obsessif à l'argent, la coupure totale avec la société.[23] De tels traits se retrouvent dans les témoignages des ex-adeptes. Il est probable qu'ils se retrouvent effectivement dans certains groupes religieux et les individus aussi bien que les instances sociales doivent effectivement se montrer vigilants et ne pas hésiter à intervenir lorsqu'il peut être démontré que les règles sociales couramment admises sont transgressées de manière abusive.

Les témoignages d'ex-adeptes ont cependant quelques inconvénients: ils peuvent nous amener à généraliser à l'ensemble d'un mouvement, à un type de mouvements ou à tous les nouveaux mouvements religieux sans distinction la situation décrite par le témoin. La recherche sur les nouveaux mouvements religieux a démontré sans équivoque que c'est une infime minorité d'entre eux qui constitue un danger potentiel. Même s'ils sont sincères et même s'ils contiennent une part de vérité, ces témoignages offrent une image tronquée du paysage. Un discernement s'impose donc, à défaut de quoi on en viendra éventuellement à dénoncer toute forme de spiritualité ou de religion comme une vaste supercherie.

Les témoignages d'ex-adeptes génèrent également des problèmes au niveau du dialogue inter-religieux. En publiant une image négative des nouveaux mouvements religieux, ils encouragent non seulement la prudence, mais parfois la méfiance ou même l'hostilité envers ces groupes. En réaction à cette attitude, des groupes prennent le maquis ou développent un syndrome de persécution. Il devient alors très difficile d'entrer en dialogue avec ces groupes pour qu'ils puissent faire connaître le type d'expérience religieuse qu'ils proposent, de manière transparente, et qu'ils s'intègrent dans le tissu social contemporain en respectant les valeurs communes. Ce problème est assez complexe et l'expérience du dialogue inter-religieux montre que la confiance est beaucoup plus longue à établir qu'à détruire.

23. Ouellet 1995.

Conclusion

Les témoignages de convertis et d'ex-adeptes sont des composantes importantes du paysage religieux contemporain. Ils reflètent généralement la perception sincère et l'interprétation rétrospective qu'une personne fait de son cheminement religieux, à partir de sa situation actuelle et des modèles de discours disponibles. A ce titre, ils comportent une part de vérité, mais qui demande à être appréciée de façon critique pour ce qu'elle est et non pour 'la vérité' factuelle et objective sur une situation passée. Ils ont une fonction importante de consolidation de l'identité actuelle du témoin, aussi bien qu'une fonction sociale de transmission de son expérience et, dans le cas d'ex-adeptes, d'incitation à la prudence. On peut cependant déplorer que les témoignages d'ex-adeptes se réduisent trop souvent aux 'récits d'atrocités'. Il serait sain, me semble-t-il, aussi bien au plan social qu'au plan religieux, que la diversité des témoignages soit plus étendue et qu'on dispose ainsi d'une image moins distortionnée des expériences vécues dans les nouveaux mouvements religieux.

Bibliography

Beckford, J.A. 1985. *Cult Controversies: The Societal Response to the New Religious Movements*. London: Tavistock.
Billette, A. 1975. *Récits et réalités d'une conversion*. Montréal: Les Presses de l'Université de Montréal.
Bromley, D.G. and A.D. Shupe 1995. 'Anti-Cultism in the United States: Origins, Ideology and Organizational Development'. *Social Compass*, vol. 42, 221-35.
Bromley, D.G., A.D. Shupe and J.C. Ventimiglia 1983. 'The Role of Anecdotal Atrocities in the Social Construction of Evil'. In: D.G. Bromley and J.T. Richardson (eds.), *The Brainwashing/Deprogramming Controversy*. Lewinston NY: E. Mellen, 139-60.
Carrier, H. 1966. *Psycho-sociologie de l'appartenance religieuse*. Rome: Université Grégorienne.
Dubreuil, J.P. 1994. *L'Église de Scientologie. Facile d'y entrer, difficile d'en sortir*. Sherbrooke: [private edition].
Huguenin, T. 1995. *Le 54ᵉ*. Paris: Fixot.

Killbourne, B. and R.T. Richardson 1989. 'Paradigm Conflict, Types of Conversion, and Conversion Theories'. *Sociological Analysis*, vol. 50, 1-21.

Lavallée, G. 1994. *L'alliance de la brebis. Rescapée de la secte de Moïse.* Montréal: Club Québec Loisirs.

Lofland, J. and R. Stark 1965. 'Becoming a World Saver: A Theory of Conversion to a Deviant Perspective'. *American Sociological Review*, vol. 20, 862-74.

Ouellet, B. 1995. 'Sur l'autoroute des religions'. *L'Église canadienne*, vol. 28, 106-10.

Shupe, A.D. and D.G.Bromley 1981. 'Apostates and Atrocities Stories: Some Parameters in the Dynamics of Deprogramming'. In: B.R. Wilson (ed.), *The Social Impact of New Religious Movements*. Barrytown NY: Rose of Sharon Press, 179-215.

Wilson, B.R. 1994. 'Apostats' (Summary of a lecture delivered at Oxford on Dec. 3 1994).

Wright, S.A. 1987. *Leaving Cults: The Dynamics of Defection.* Washington DC: Society for the Scientific Study of Religion.

CHAPTER 12

New Age Participants in Sweden: Background, Beliefs, Engagement and 'Conversion'

Liselotte Frisk

Introduction

The concept of 'New Age' has become a wide designation for a more or less religious subculture inspired mainly from sources outside the Judeo-Christian tradition. In many ways it is a continuation of a long existing occult and metaphysical tradition, but it also differs somewhat by traits characteristic of our time. Some of these traits are inspired by the American Human Potential Movement of the 1960s, and other currents of a more or less psychological nature.

In connection with a study I undertook in 1995, I distributed a questionnaire to some of the New Age groups in Sweden.[1] However, as New Age is a phenomenon full of nuances and difficult to define, it was problematic to decide exactly *which* New Age environments to choose. Therefore, in accordance with a study I made in 1993 based on an advertisement magazine called *Energivågen*,[2] I tried to keep to the 'mainstream' of New Age. However, as that magazine did not contain a great deal of advertising for shamanism and native religions, these currents in the New Age environment were not represented in my 1993 study. Information was therefore obtained from questionnaires issued to:

1. The study was financed by the Research Council of the Swedish Church.
2. Frisk 1997.

1. 36 people attending a lecture on 'Channelling'.
2. 33 people attending a weekend course in 'Rebirthing'.
3. 19 people attending 'A course in Miracles'.
4. 108 people from a lecture, a class and a 2-day course on 'Healing' (with Matthew Manning from Great Britain, who shows healing practices, but also talks a lot about common New Age themes like positive thinking, etc.).
5. 19 people from a class with an 'energy group' with some kind of theosophical inspiration, with beliefs in New Age, UFOs, spiritual Masters, Jesus/Sananda, etc.

In total, 215 questionnaires were completed. The response frequency varied from 60-85% depending mainly, I think, on the attitude of the leader and a willingness to let me present my project. One group refused to participate because I was working for the University and because the Swedish Church was financing the project. The group considered the University and the Church to be the worst institutions in our society, working against the coming new age.

It was possible to break down the material into smaller units/ groups according to, for example, gender, degree of engagement (attending lectures, classes, weekend-courses), and urban area/country area. I sometimes used this possibility, but of course the sub-units became very small.

The Questionnaire

The questionnaire centred mainly on five questions:

1. Who is engaged in the New Age environment: gender, age and education.
2. How is one engaged: beliefs and practices.
3. 'Conversion', or how one is socialized into the New Age-environment: previous perspective, worldview of parents, contact way.
4. Lifestyle: vegetarianism, use of alcohol, tobacco, drugs.
5. Politics and Society: voting, or not voting, in political elections.

Only a few of the questions were of an open nature, and only some of the data obtained will be described here. In some cases I make comparisons with the EVSSG[3] study from 1990, as well as other general studies on Swedes, and in other cases comparisons are made with a study that I conducted from 1981-83 of members of new religious movements in Sweden.[4]

Results

Who is engaged?

The average age of respondents was 42 years. In comparison it should be mentioned that in the study conducted 13 years earlier that members of new religious movements were on average 27 years old. This means that both groups showed a predominance of people born in the early 1950's. This generation is also called the post-war generation, or the baby-boom generation. These are the people who were young during the 1960's and experienced the hippie-movement and the Vietnam War. Many studies show that this generation, due mainly to structural changes of society, were not socialized into the religion of their parents as earlier generations were.

Concerning gender, as many as 83% of the respondents were women. But in the sub-groups there were variations from 74% in ACIM[5] to 97% in the channelling group.

With regard to education, some 48% of participants in the New Age group reported university education (37% exam, 11% courses). About the same figures were given by participants in the new religious movements (30% exam, 20% courses). There were some differences between different groups, however; in the ACIM, for example, 74% had some kind of university education.

3. EVSSG = European Value Systems Study Group.
4. This study was financed by the Riksbankens Jubileumsfond. See Frisk 1993.
5. ACIM = *A Course in Miracles.*

How is engagement expressed?

Beliefs:

Below are some of the results obtained after questioning New Age participants about their beliefs. These results are compared with other studies of Swedes in general. The tables are followed by a discussion.

Table 1. Belief in God
(The New Age material and the EVSSG study[6] in percent. All answers recorded).

	N	Personal God	Spirit/ life force	Don't know	Person-al spirit[7]	Don't believe	Other
New Age material	214	20	63	2	14	1	1
EVSSG	997	16	46	18	-	20	-

Table 2. Belief in life after death
(The New Age material and Swedes in general[8] in percent. All answers recorded).

	N	Yes, absolutely	Yes, maybe	No, probably not	No, absolutely not	Don't know
New Age material	211	77	16	3	1	3
Swedes in general	511	18	27	20	24	12

6. Unpublished material kindly submitted by Thorleif Pettersson, Uppsala University.
7. Both alternatives were marked, not only one as expected.
8. Sjödin 1995, 92.

Table 3. Belief in reincarnation
(The New Age material and the EVSSG study, in percent. All answers recorded).

	N	Yes, believe Yes	Yes, partly	No, do not believe	Hesitant, don't know
New Age material	213	67	-	21	6	7
EVSSG	881	20	-	80	-

Table 4. Belief in the possibility of contact with deceased
(The New Age material and Swedes in general,[9] in percent. All answers recorded).

	N	Yes, absolutely	Yes, maybe	No, hardly	No, not at all	Don't know
New Age material	213	52	34	5	1	8
		Agree completely	Agree partly	Dissociate partly	Dissociate completely	Don't know
Swedes in general	511	7	25	30	36	2

Table 5. Astrology: Belief that the position of stars at birth influences how one's life will develop
(The New Age material and Swedish youth,[10] in percent. All answers recorded)

	N	Agree completely	Agree partly	Dissociate partly	Dissociate completely	Don't know
New Age material	211	33	39	6	6	16
Swedish youth	1480	5	15	23	47	9

9. Ibid., 84.
10. Ibid., 95.

Table 6. UFOs: Belief that extraterrestrial beings sometimes visit earth
(The New Age material and ordinary Swedes,[11] in percent. All answers recorded)

	N	Agree completely	Agree partly	Dissociate partly	Dissociate completely	Don't know
New Age material	210	47	25	8	6	14
Ordinary Swedes	511	7	17	24	48	4

Table 7. Belief in a new age
(The New Age material in percent. All answers recorded)

	N	Agree completely	Agree partly	Dissociate partly	Dissociate completely	Don't know
New Age material	209	40	29	6	6	19

Discussion

It is clear that all the above-mentioned components are often included in the worldview of the New Age participant. Most central is belief in God, with a strong emphasis on God as spirit/life force rather than a personal God. The belief in life after death also seems to be important. Traditionally these two factors have been seen as indicating religiosity. Following this, the New Age environment is clearly a religious environment.

Strikingly, however, there seems to be a great deal of uncertainty concerning beliefs, with a vast space for 'maybe' and 'partly'. 'Partly' may of course also indicate that a more personal worldview is central, and that the formulation of the question simply does not completely correspond to the belief of the individual.

The worldview elements which characterize the New Age environment, such as belief in God as spirit/life force, reincarnation,

11. Ibid., 82.

and astrology are — according to the EVSSG-survey and other studies of ordinary Swedes — also firmly established among the general
public. Concerning the possibility of coming in contact with deceased
people, from 1980 to 1994 there was an increase from 21% to 32% in
the number of Swedes answering 'yes'.[12] As James R. Lewis suggests,
the New Age phenomenon is maybe only one visible part of a significant cultural change. Some parts of New Age are no longer a marginal phenomenon, but more or less 'mainstream'.[13]

Many beliefs are much more central than belief in a new age. The
concept — from which the whole subculture has gotten its name — is
of course not totally peripheral, but it could be questioned if it is representative for the subculture and if it is appropriate.

Beliefs and gender:

Table 8. Belief in life after death
(The material classified according to gender, in percent. All answers
recorded)

	N	Yes, absolutely	Yes, maybe	No, probably not	No, absolutely not	Don't know
Males	35	66	17	6	3	9
Females	175	79	15	3	0	2

12. Ibid., 101.
13. Lewis 1992, 4.

Table 9. Belief in reincarnation
(The material classified according to gender, in percent. All answers recorded)

	N	Yes, believe	Yes, partly believe	No, do not believe	Hesitant, don't know
Males	36	53	19	17	11
Females	176	70	21	3	6

Table 10. Belief that the position of stars at birth influences how one's life will develop
(The material classified according to gender, in percent. All answers recorded)

	N	Agree completely	Agree partly	Dissociate partly	Dissociate completely	Don't know
Males	35	20	34	3	17	16
Females	175	36	40	6	3	14

Table 11. Belief that extraterrestrial beings sometimes visit earth
(The material classified according to gender, in percent. All answers recorded)

	N	Agree completely	Agree partly	Dissociate partly	Dissociate completely	Don't know
Males	35	37	17	9	14	23
Females	174	49	27	8	4	12

The gender-related differences concerning beliefs are vast. More females than males are engaged in the New Age environment and, on the whole, females *believe* to a much greater extent than males and it would seem that the males who do participate are much more sceptical than the females.

Practices:

The New Age participants were also requested to mark the practical acitivites in which they had participated. The result follows in Table 12.

Table 12. Number of people in the New Age material who reported to have participated in the following activities
(In percent. N = 215)

Massage	84
Meditation	77
Healing	62
Acupuncture	52
Tarot	51
Rebirthing	42
Yoga	36
Acupressure	31
Reiki	31
Channelling	30
Crystal therapy	27
ACIM	20

It is clear from the material that all these activities are very popular. Although New Age activities derive from different traditions from all over the world, and could be very different from each other, it seems that through the practitioner they are united. Often the individual practises many things, even if the phenomena have no connection with each other. Somehow, through the individual, it seems to be meaningful to talk about New Age as a continuous subculture.

There seems, however, to be a type of pattern, according to which one chooses how to engage oneself in New Age. My material indicated that it is possible to differentiate between an 'occult-intuitive' pattern, including channelling, chrystal therapy and tarot, and a 'therapeutic/intellectual/Eastern' pattern, including massage, yoga, meditation, ACIM, acupuncture and rebirthing. The occult pattern — to a greater extent — attracts women, and — to a lesser extent — highly educated people, whilst men and highly educated people find the therapeutic pattern more attractive.

It is also interesting that the most popular activities — massage, meditation and healing — are, all three, possible to practice on different levels; for physical aims, mental aims and spiritual aims.

An independent question about affirmations was also asked. More than three-quarters, or 78%, answered that they used affirmations — at least from time to time. About 60% of these answered that they used affirmations for wisdom and realization; 60% for love and relationships, about 49% for health, and 27% for economy and materialistic goals (it was possible to mark one or many of the aims).

Another question concerned the frequency of attending lectures, classes or weekend-courses. To my surprise, the typical New Age-participant seldom frequented such courses. Only 9% said that they attended lectures once a week or more often, while 47% attended lectures once a year at the most. About 85% went to classes twice a year at the most, and only 13% said they attended weekend courses once a year or more often.

My conclusion is that New Age is very much a 'private' type of religiosity. The engagement is expressed through reading books, discussing with friends and sporadically practising something together with other people. While New Age beliefs may apparently be on their way to the man in the street, the willingness to attend lectures and courses is much lower. It also seems that there are far more 'producers' in the environment than necessary to accommodate the number of willing 'consumers'. Although I participated in many events during my research, at least three of the planned events were cancelled due to lack of interest.

'Conversion'

'Conversion', or how (and to what degree) one enters into a (more or less) new worldview, is an important question for the sociology of religion and the psychology of religion. There are many theories around this question, some of which could be related to unconventional religiosity.

Whether or not one wants to use the notion of 'conversion' to explain the change of worldview that participants in the New Age have most likely gone through, this change is very interesting for the scientist, but of course very difficult to illuminate through a short questionnaire. However, in spite of this, my intention was to try to shed some light on at least some parts of the 'conversion' process by means of the questionnaire.

Worldview of parents:

This table is based on two open questions where the participant was asked to characterize the worldview/religion of their mother and father in one or two sentences.

Table 13. The worldview of parents
(The New Age material in percent. All answers recorded)

	Atheist, Materialist	Passive Christian	Nonconformist	Alternatively religious	Christian	Belief in God	Other answers
Mother (N'177)	36	25	6	7	16	4	6
Father (N'170)	42	25	6	4	15	3	5

Participants' own previous worldview:

An open question concerning what kind of worldview/religion the respondent had before coming into contact with New Age thought was also included in the questionnaire. The answers were registered in different categories.

Table 14: Own previous worldview
(The New Age material in percent. All answers recorded)

N	Seeker	Diffusely Christian	A 'little' Christian	Belief in God	None, agnostic	Same as today	Atheist	Other
165	7	14	15	26	16	9	8	7

Most of the respondents say that they have had some kind of religious faith, but with diffuse characteristics. About 29% relate their earlier worldview loosely to Christianity: a little Christian or diffuse Christian, Christian but not a regular churchgoer, religious but not going to church, etc. Another 26% reported a belief in God, goodness, a higher power, a universal intelligence or a higher energy. About 9% said that they had never changed faith; they always had the same beliefs as today. About 7% characterized themselves as seekers.
First contact:

Two questions dealt with ways of contact; one with how one came into contact with the present lecture/course, and one with how the respondent came into contact with similar thoughts the first time.

Table 15: First contact with present course and first contact with similar ideas
(The New Age material in percent. All answers recorded)

	N	Friend	Family	Advertisement program	Book, media	Course	Own interest	Other
Present	207	37	15	21	9	16	-	4
First Contact	199	33	20	4	16	9	15	5

In accordance with earlier studies of alternative religiosity,[14] we can establish the significance of earlier existing social networks, i.e., family and friends. More than half of the respondents had come into contact with both the present course and New Age thoughts in this way.

Another interesting fact is that about 15% of respondents marked the square 'other way' when answering the question about how they came into contact with New Age thoughts for the first time, and continued to describe that there was in fact no 'first time', as their interest had developed from *within* or had always been there. As this alternative did not exist on the questionnaire itself, this percentage was fairly high.

About 59% stated that they had come into contact with New Age for the first time later than 1986, while another 18% stated that the contact took place during the 10-year-period before this.

As many as 59% marked the square 'seeker' as the reason for their first contact with New Age thought, while 56% marked the square 'problem, crisis' as the reason for their first contact.

Discussion

The background (religious/non-religious) of New Age participants is of course rather varied. Around a third seem to have had a non-religious, atheistic childhood, whilst slightly more than one out of five seem to have had a Christian background. However, it seems that even if parents had a religious worldview, the children were not very well socialized into it. The generation born in the early 1950's is also well known for insufficient socialization.

There are no signs of sudden conversion to the New Age environment. Most of them report having had some kind of religious worldview before the first contact with New Age, a worldview which in all aspects (retrospectively at least) does not seem to agree with conventional Christianity. Many emphasize that they never had a worldview different from the present one. Through friends or parents they then seem to have been introduced to parts of the New Age, at a time of life when they had some kind of problem or were searching for a worldview. It was at that time that their previous diffuse worldview seems to have become clearer.

14. Frisk 1993.

Life style

One out of five New Age participants report that they are vegetarian, with another one out of five claiming to be 'almost' vegetarian. This seems to be an important feature in at least some parts of New Age. Vegetarianism seems to be related to 1) the ideology of the group; 2) the degree of engagement (more vegetarians with increasing engagement); and 3) residential area (more vegetarians in the cities).

With regard to tobacco and alcohol, there does not seem to be a big difference between New Age participants and other people. About 80% say that they drink alcohol. In the EVSSG study it is 87%.

One conclusion could be that ascetic currents are not very common in this subculture, even though such currents also exist. Comparatively few in the survey mentioned having used any kind of drugs.

Table 16: Reported previous use of drugs
(The New Age material and members of new religious movements.[15] In percent, both groups).

	N	Hashish/marijuana	(Often)	Heavier narcotics
New Age material	200	18	13	7
New religious movements	237	62	24	30

In comparison with members of new religious movements, the conclusion could be drawn that New Age thought appeals more to 'ordinary people' than new religious movements, which seem to have attracted people with a more rebellious or experimental character.

Politics and society

Most of the participants in New Age — 86% — say that they usually vote in political elections. This is significantly more than in the new religious movements, where the number was 66%. This also indicates that the New Age environment is much more of a popular movement than the new religious movements.

15. Ibid., 278.

Bibliography

Frisk, L. 1993. Nya religiösa rörelser i Sverige. Relation till samhället/världen, anslutning och engagemang. Åbo: Åbo Akademi.
Frisk, L. 1997. 'Vad är New Age? Centrala begrepp och historiska rötter'. *Svensk religionshistorisk Årsskrift*, vol. 6, 87-97.
Lewis, James R. 1992. 'Introduction'. In: James R. Lewis and J. Gordon Melton (eds.), *Perspectives on the New Age*. Albany: State University of New York Press, ix-xii.
Pettersson, Thorleif 1990. EVSSG-study, (Unpublished Paper), Uppsala University.
Sjödin, U. 1995. *En skola – flera världar. Värderingar hos elever och lärare i religionskunskap i gymnasieskolan*. Stockholm: Plus Ultra.

CHAPTER 13

Students in Ramtha's School of Enlightenment: A Profile from a Demographic Survey, Narrative, and Interview

Constance A. Jones

Introduction

Ramtha's School of Enlightenment was founded in the late 1980s in Yelm, Washington, by J.Z. Knight (b. 1946), who had emerged as the modt popular of a new wave of channellers that arose in the West along with the New Age movement. In 1977 the spiritual entity Ramtha appeared to Knight, then a housewife in Tacoma, Washington, and introduced himself as the Enlighted One. The next year, Knight began to channel Ramtha publicly. She initially held weekend sessions called Dialogues, where she would channel Ramtha. The Dialogues were held around the United States and increasingly in several foreign countries, and many of these sessions were later transcribed and published as books or made available on videotape. However, in 1988 the decision was made to discontinue the Dialogues and to concentrate on developing a body of students who wished to go more deeply into the process of actualizing the enlightenment about which Ramtha had spoken.

According to the channelled message, Ramtha is a thirty-five-thousand-year-old warrior, who at the height of his power was almost killed. He found enlightenment during his time of recovery and eventually ascended to a spiritual realm. Once Ramtha's School of Enlightenment was formed, Ramtha began to teach a set of practices that would allow students to access and become directly aware of the spiritual realms. The basic practice termed 'energy and conscious-ness' involves controlled breathing and kundalini yoga, in which latent energy believed to be located at the base of the spine is allowed to rise up the spine and bring its energy and enlightenment to the self.

Ramtha describes the universe as divided into seven levels, at the center of which is the Void (Pure Potentiality) out of which the other levels are derived. The seventh level is the visible world, into which individuals as spiritual entities have come. The spiritual entities cre-ated this world, but then they became trapped in it and forgetful of their spiritual origin. Enlightenment comes as one is able to remem-ber and experience one's spiritual origin and can freely navigate the several levels.

The school is organized as an Esoteric mystery school. Students initially pass through a graded curriculum before being admitted to the larger student body of those who continually work on their self-awareness as spiritual beings. The larger student body gathers at the headquarters twice each year for advanced retreats, at which time new teachings and perspectives are released by Ramtha.

Some three thousand students are active (2002) in the school. Dur-ing the 1990s, all events were held at Yelm, but at the close of the decade Knight began to travel again and introductory sessions con-cerning Ramtha are now being held annually by senior students at locations in Europe, South Africa, and Australia. Literature is pub-lished in Spanish, German, Italian, French, Japanese, and Norwegian.

During the early 1990s, Knight and the school passed through a period of intense controversy, much of which was related to the se-cretive esoteric nature of the school's work. In the mid-1970s she opened up the school to a group of scholars, including several psy-chologists who ran a set of tests on Knight and some of her leading students. Their positive reports concerning her psychological health and the extraordinary nature of her channelling activity largely end-ed the attacks she had previously experienced.[1]

*   *   *   *

1. The foregoing description is taken from J. Gordon Melton & Martin Bau-mann (eds.), *Religions of the World. A Comprehensive Encyclopedia of Beliefs and Practices*, ABC-Clio, Volume 3, Santa Barbara, 2002, p. 1062. The edi-tors of the present volume wish to thank our colleagues for providing this opportunity.

This chapter summarizes findings from questionnaires completed by a sample of 540 intermediate and advanced students in Ramtha's School of Enlightenment (RSE), and in-depth interviews conducted with ten advanced students. The questionnaire yields a demographic profile, including age, gender, place of residence, marital status, occupation, education, and income. Questionnaire narratives and interviews yield information on religious experience, including religious socialization in childhood, religious activity as a child, conversion to new religions, and orientation to religion. A summary reports experiences with RSE and offers analysis of the function of a Gnostic school in contemporary America.

Method

Questionnaires were administered to intermediate and advanced residential groups at RSE. The rate of return was quite high and the returned questionnaires (N'540) were largely complete. Approximately ten questionnaires with complete demographic items but no responses to experiential questions were omitted from the sample. Demographic items were largely self-coding and, therefore, objective. Experiential items were phrased to elicit narrative responses, written in the respondents' own words, and were, therefore, subjective. Experiential responses were coded by a team of three researchers who are familiar with RSE practices and literature. A number of variables, selected from the teachings and literature of RSE, were chosen for initial coding. The team coded several hundred questionnaires and met again to revise the coding procedure and to refine categories and variables of interest. Questionnaires were then reviewed and often recoded according to the refinements of collaborative research. The team is confident that it has gleaned a great deal of valuable information from this research technique and that the respondents' experiences are well represented in the following analysis.

In addition, after attending an introductory weekend and reading extensively in the RSE literature, the author conducted in-depth interviews with ten advanced students, all of whom live within or very near Yelm. These conversations yielded extremely rich data from an emic perspective, data that are incorporated into the analysis below.

The Sample: Demographic Profile

The sample consists of 540 respondents, all intermediate or advanced students in RSE who attended one of several residential courses at Yelm during the last months of 1994. The sample is 80% female (N'431) and 19% male (N'103) with 6 respondents not specifying gender. Mean age is 41.14 (s.d. 16), ranging from 14 to 83 years of age. Age distribution approximates a bell-shaped curve around the mean of 41.

Marital status is almost evenly divided among single (N'128, 23.7%), married (N'175, 32.4%), and divorced (N'129, 23.9%) respondents. 24 respondents (4%) are widowed and 77 (14%) are living with a significant other.

The questionnaire asked about current residence only, not place of residence before joining RSE. Thus, all of the following descriptors relate to present status. Most of the sample (N'450) are residents of the U.S., although significant numbers of respondents reside in other English-speaking and Western European countries (see Table 1). Within the U.S. population, most (N'352, 65.2%) reside near Yelm, either in Washington state, Oregon, or other states in the Northwest or West (see Table 2).

Current residence is preponderantly rural (N'390, 72.2%), as compared to urban (N'74, 13.7%) and suburban (N'61, 11.3%), especially among those living adjacent to Yelm. (See Table 3.) Most rural residents have moved from urban areas and have not lived in rural areas throughout their lives. They have chosen intentional migration from urban centres to accommodate a shift in values and priorities. Most have located near the school, and have made other shifts in their lifestyles, preferring to live closer to nature with fewer resources:

I am now receiving some of the things I wanted when I first started the school six years ago. Now six years later I wonder why I wanted them. They don't mean anything now. What I truly want is to realize the God in me.

Socio-economic status is measured here by three indices: occupational prestige ranking, educational attainment, and income. These variables considered together indicate a great degree of status inconsistency among the sample. Occupational prestige is quite high, with large numbers in the most prestigious categories of profession-al/technical and administrative/self-employed (see Table 4). A large percentage (N′ 99, 18.3%) of the sample is not active in the paid labour force, holding statuses of student, homemaker, retired person, or unemployed.

Educational attainment is also quite high and is positively corre-lated with occupational prestige. The modal category for education is 'some college' (N′168, 31%) with an additional 37% in the combined categories of 'college graduate' and 'graduate school' (see Table 5).

While occupational prestige and education are both consistently high for the sample as a whole, income is quite inconsistent with these two variables. The modal category for income, which repre-sents almost half of the sample, is 'less than $20,000', the lowest cate-gory on the questionnaire (see Table 6). This status inconsistency is consonant with the pattern of migration discussed above. The sample consists of a large number of individuals who have grown up in urban centres, have been well educated, and work in relatively pres-tigious occupations, but who, because of a shift in priorities and values, have opted for geographical mobility to rural areas and, thus, report incomes well below what would be expected given their educa-tional and occupational profiles.

Religious Socialization and Background

The sample is characteristic of American socialization to religion, in that all major Western religious traditions except Islam are represented. As expected, the largest category is that of Protestant, including Mor-mon (N′223, 41%). Also expected is the large category of Roman Catholics, including Eastern Orthodox (N′184, 34%). But, given the high representation of Jews among non-Christian religious move-ments, especially movements with Eastern philosophical orientations such as RSE, the sample's participation in socialization to the Jewish tradition (N′13, 2.4%) seems quite low. Interestingly, the younger members of RSE report childhood socialization to a variety of non-traditional religious orientations, including new age/occult groups, Eastern religions, and atheist/humanist groups (see Table 7). But when all of the non-traditional religious socialization categories are combined, the sum is less than 20% of the sample, as compared to

78% of the sample socialized into traditional Protestant, Catholic, and Jewish religions.

Respondents were asked specifically if they were active or not in a church or synagogue during childhood. Almost half of the sample (N'260, 48%) reported that they were active during childhood.

Thus, we see a not untypical representation of American religious practices in this sample. Few were raised outside the 'mainstream' religious traditions of this country and approximately half were active as children in their respective faiths.

Other measures of religious background are gleaned from narratives and, as such, are not as definitive as the measures above. The research team looked for themes and reportage that would indicate religious experience during adulthood when religious and philosophical questions can be examined independently and life affords more personal choices.

First, we wanted to know if RSE students consider themselves 'seekers' in religious terms. Thus, we coded the respondent as a seeker if the respondent's biographical statement contained any mention of an extended personal quest to find truth or spiritual meaning beyond what life had shown them. We found that less than half (N'236, 43.7%), but very close to half, of the sample could be considered seekers. Many see themselves as different from most other people since childhood, in that they are aware of a greater reality and they are searching for an understanding of that reality. One respondent's remarks are representative,

'I have always known there was something more in life than the mundane existence offered most human beings. I knew this at a very young age, so was considered odd or different, not of the 'in' crowd'. In another respondent's words, 'I feel like I've waited all my life to learn what he [Ramtha] is teaching and continues to teach'.

Next, we were interested in finding out what religious experience, beyond childhood socialization, would be mentioned in the biographical statements. We particularly wanted to know how varied this experience had been. Had respondents had past exposure to and study of several religious orientations other than the religion of socialization? Had they joined two or three groups before coming to RSE? Had they experienced a 'career' of exploration into religious questions or a series of conversions to different religions?

We were surprised to find that few individuals demonstrate any-thing approximating a conversion career, i.e., having studied deeply three or more religious groups in their adult years. Of those who had investigated other groups, most had participated in Western religious groups, particularly New Age groups. Quite a range of Western movements were mentioned, including Lifespring, A Course in Mir-acles, and New Thought churches. Eastern influences include sever-al types of yoga and a number of teachers, including Paramahansa Yogananda, Haryakhan Baba, Ram Dass, Bhagwan Rajneesh, Satya Sai Baba, Krishnamurti, Buddha, and Swami Rama. Several had studied indigenous religions such as Huna and North American shamanism.

A few had studied or been affiliated with all of these types of religious groups; these respondents were grouped under the rubric 'eclectic'. One woman reports, 'I had been a Roman Catholic, had studied Mormonism, Judaism, Hinduism, been baptized as a Jehovah's Witness, yet only Ram gave me freedom from lies, the abil-ity to be me freely, without guilt or shame'. The few who reported ex-tensive 'careers' in new religious movements had studied and joined a number of religious and meditation groups and had participated in sophisticated practices for extended periods. Even though there are few in the sample that have experienced conversion 'careers', the quality and extent of these careers are remarkable in their depth and discipline. Only a few mentioned having seen any other channelled entities before meeting Ramtha (see Table 8).

Experiences with RSE

Respondents heard of Ramtha from a variety of sources, not always through a personal referral from a friend. Some report dreams in which Ramtha or Ramtha's name was introduced; when Ramtha's voice was heard on tape or video, they recognized the person as one who had been in an earlier dream. Others were taken to RSE events by friends or family. Others grew up with parents who regularly at-tend RSE courses. But the most common introduction to Ramtha's message is through books and other published material, video pres-entations, and advertisements of events. The most cited sources are the 'White Book' and the Hawaii video (see Table 9).

Upon seeing Ramtha in person or on video, 174 respondents say that they were deeply touched and spontaneously knew that his teaching was important for them. Consistently, these narratives report that an initial encounter with Ramtha in person, through video tapes, or through reading, brought a certain 'knowing of the truth' and a recognition of Ramtha as a personal teacher. In the words of one woman, 'The new element that Ramtha introduced into my life was in no way connected with dogma, but rather a truth that rang out loud somewhere deep in my being. It was the truth that I sought.' Many narratives include an assurance that being brought to Ramtha was not accidental, but part of a larger plan, 'Something beyond me led me here in the beginning this I know'. We tried to discern the nature of most conversions, by classifying them as spiritual, emotional, and intellectual. We found that most statements of initial contact with Ramtha contained elements of all three dimensions.

Years in attendance at RSE vary from 2 to 16, with a mean of 5.5 years (s.d. 2.9). Thus, the sample as a whole is well acquainted with the school and its teachings, all respondents being either intermediate or advanced students. 39 respondents were 21 years old or younger, largely children who have grown up in the school. As families increasingly enrol in RSE, we can assume that the student population will become progressively more intergenerational.

After association with RSE, respondents report a variety of healthy and pleasant, if not supernatural, benefits. Some respondents wrote detailed descriptions of the advantages they had received after study and practice at RSE. The overall impression from these descriptions is of extreme happiness, even joy, derived largely from a cognitive and spiritual knowledge of how the universe is constructed, how one fits into that construction, and how one can gain further understanding of self. Well-being is rarely identified with success in the outer world of career, financial success, and power in the world, but is often described as a result of learning more about self. Ten major themes have been extracted from personal accounts and are discussed below, ordered with most mentioned first and least mentioned last. (See Table 10.) In addition to these major themes, three minor themes, relating to miracles, lucid dreaming, and finances and material prosperity, were also discernible. These minor themes are incorporated into the major themes for clarity in presentation.

Most respondents write in the language of Ramtha, using his phrases and rhetoric, as when they describe 'finding God within' and 'breaking out of the limits of social conditioning'. One is impressed by the clear exposition in almost all narratives. Students have indeed learned the language of their teacher and most are able to explain in considerable depth Ramtha's teaching on the complex relationships among brain function, creation of reality, and levels of being.

1) Self-Development

Almost 70% of the sample reports some form of self-development as a result of association with RSE, including 'breaking through limitations and boundaries', 'major changes in personality', and 'learning to be very allowing and non-judgmental'. Personal narratives contain many incidences of growth in self-empowerment, self respect, emotional well-being, and inclination to be consciously moral, ecological, and humane.

Ram showed me that I came here to see Me not him, to learn to be a lover of self within.

I learned from the Ram that I am responsible for *everything* in my life.

I am more in tune with my feelings. I have much more compassion in dealing with others.

I realize my limitations and can persevere to get beyond them.

I feel a sense of internal strength and balance after a lifetime of none and always running.

Ramtha has taught me how to control the events in my life.

As part of self-development, recognizing and breaking out of the limits of social conditioning play important roles in the lives of these respondents. Most are quite articulate about how to find God within, how to be in analogical mind, and how to analyze the self's discovery of its true nature.

The new elements in my life are being able to apply my thoughts into [sic] a deconditioned aspect of our modern culture, including religious, genetic, and social programming. I understand what is mind, its nature, and how it's created and how it influences every aspect of our reality in life. Now I know how to make the awareness of this knowledge be used as a tool for our evolution into something of greater substance.

The most extraordinary part is that I unfolded my own value…and gave up the desperation.

Also, part of the discovery of self is the significant change in lifestyle and values. Many find new priorities in their lives as they understand more about themselves and move toward a new purpose:

I have gotten in touch with a deep-seated anxiety from infancy and I am finally slowing down, becoming more peaceful. My health is improving, my lifestyle and my values have dramatically changed and those who worry about me being in the school also seek my counsel. I have peace and purpose. After years in New York living and traveling the fashion world, I had grown highly superficial, unhappy, and drug addicted.

I always knew there was purpose to my life, but could never express myself in that way. Since I've been in the school my life is whole, it's in progress everyday. I learned how to be determined, to have self-respect, solve my own challenges and lost a lot of fear and guilt. I am very powerful and follow the God within me.

Joy has replaced a somewhat too serious nature and I can 'boogie' with the best of them now. Ramtha's way of teaching and what he teaches has helped me put many puzzle pieces together about life, how it works and relationships. I am more of what I have endeavoured for years to become because of these teachings.

2) Healing of Self or Other

Healing from many types of diseases, varying in severity from corns to cancer, is reported in the narratives. Respondents describe healings from acute pleurisy, allergies, depression, broken bones, diabetes, neurological and disc damage after surgery, cysts, sciatic nerve dysfunction, bulimia nervosa, genetic deformity, intestinal blockage, severe internal bleeding, ruptured appendix, lupus, adenocarcinoma, breast cancer, prostate cancer, liver failure, and cataracts. Healing occurs both spontaneously and over time, but always faster than expected, based on diagnoses and clinical predictions. In addition to healing themselves, RSE members report being instrumental in healings of other people, particularly close friends and relatives, of their pets, and of objects, e.g., automobiles. Most accounts of healings involve either consciousness and energy (C & E) exercises, moving into the blue body,[2] or focusing as the means for overcoming disease.

I have had an elbow injury that would not heal for ten years heal in one night.

The most important healing I have done was with a friend. He was taken to the hospital with congestive heart failure. I touched him and spoke to the Lord of my being and I saw him whole and getting out of bed. Three days later he was released from the hospital and is doing great.
I helped heal [my brother of] a serious cancer of the lymph nodes.

I have healed several parts of my car, including the spark plugs, the battery and the starter. I notice that the starter won't work if I am in a negative thinking mode. I fix the car in consciousness and it starts in a few minutes.

3) Intuitive, Spiritual Sensitivity
Whereas the first category relates to personal well being and the second category to physical healing, this category includes accounts of spiritual or intuitive knowing. Most accounts in this category centre around identification of self and God and a consequent expansion of self into wider realms of possibility.

God lives within me.

I know that I am God and I can do and be anything.

2. A 'body of energy vibrating in the ultraviolet range' symbolized by the blue Hindu god Shiva. An esoteric concept associated with Ramtha's gnostic teachings.

God is truly within each and every one of us.

I have found courage within myself.

He taught me the value of me; he has provided me with an opportunity to be free of the rigors of social life and answered why I'm here.

Other reports centre on finding love, compassion, and acceptance within self as well as in interpersonal relationships.

Ramtha's techniques have brought tremendous healing, rebirth, and a deepening sense of self-love and self-value.

A new love for myself was developed and consequently a new love for others. The new element that was added to my life was true joy from within!

The greatest effect is the tremendous presence of love and acceptance.

I find my whole life changing into one of joy, power, self-respect, and love for all.

Ram changed my attitudes of bitterness, anger, and resentment to understanding and compassion.

4) Paranormal

Experiences beyond the normal were common, yet they are not easily defined. In some narratives, individuals see UFO's, as discussed below. In other narratives, intrapsychic states are induced which open students to experiences of 'holographic views of the blue realm' or 'the eye of Horus appearing like a clearly defined drawing on the clouds above my house'. One woman discovered '...fourth dimensional sight when I view the sun. I see what normal sight does not see. This proves that the mind sees reality; the eyes only accommodate light'. A number of respondents report increasing sensitivity to nature, especially communication with undomesticated animals.

Aside from healings and a few reports of being in several places at once, paranormal experiences consist largely of visions, apparitions, and perceptions of another reality. As such, paranormal experience within this sample is largely a matter of perception. This intrapsychic emphasis is consistent with the other themes that comprise the first seven themes, in that all are focused on individual experience not shared with others.

While wearing blinders, the history of all mankind and all knowledge passed in front of me in pictures.

I was wanting to work with fairies. The field was full of tall clover. I said that there were clover fairies and I wanted to experience them. I received three four-leaf clovers and one five-leaf clover, each with a separate message.

My original contact with Ram was when I had a near death experience at the age of five and encountered him out of body [She is 45 at present]. I was in touch with 18 past lives with his teaching and was able to remember my life with him 35,000 years ago.

I have experienced out-of-body, x-ray vision, 360 degree vision, holographic images, past life memories, music from other dimensions, lucid dreams, prophetic dreams, and understanding foreign languages that I have never studied.

I have seen other dimensions, other beings, and conversed mentally with them.

5) Cognitive Understanding

Many of the reports centre on a growing awareness of one's real nature as divine. In these accounts, the teachings of Ramtha relating to consciousness, energy, focusing, and manifestation are clearly claimed as one's own understanding. Often a life experience is recounted to demonstrate how the abstract teaching has been concretized in personal life.

Ramtha has given me the answer and made my life have meaning.

Ramtha has taken my knowledge and understandings from other teachings to a new level, added new depth. Also, Ramtha has brought new possibilities of what life can be about, e.g., moving into new dimensions, living forever, etc.

A great number of respondents mention their discovery of 'truth' through RSE: 'I felt a knowing and knew that it was truth', 'I discovered that I live forever', and 'Ramtha answered all the questions I had'.

Many narratives speak of previous religious affiliations that had not 'made sense' and of Ramtha as the teacher who can put prior teachings into some reasonable and effective system.

Understanding through knowledge has been my greatest quest.

I am learning the answers that the church never gave me.

Ramtha brought all the pieces together to clarify my own personal beliefs with religious dogma. I discovered what Christ meant.

6) Manifestation

Because one of the central tenets of Ramtha's teaching is that one's thoughts are made manifest in the physical world, we looked for instances of individual creation through thought. Manifestations include finding a sought-for job, creating money, and calling hummingbirds on command. Most examples in this category are of healings, in which respondents visualized a state of health. Other examples centre around constructing a card for fieldwork,[3] finding the card in the field, and later manifesting the desired object or state.

A card that I drew — and found in the field that I focused on — of a dream vacation home, became a reality within six months.

I did a card on getting a job with a partnership and manifested it three weeks later without an interview. Perfect job — exactly what I focused on!

I have manifested major things in my life — a move from another country, a beautiful piece of property, a loving spiritual partnership, a new career, and I am healthier and happier than I have ever been in my life.

3. Index-type cards with texts or drawings are used as a divice during 'fieldwork', a ritual based on intuitive movement designed to improve the student's spiritual skills.

I was able to manifest the relationship of my dreams.

Last March I created a card representing a new business and, through a series of unusual circumstances, I was able to buy a new business. I had very little money, yet it all worked out. All circumstances were very similar to the symbols on the card.

7) Intervention by Ramtha.

Most reports of conscious interventions by Ramtha consist of simultaneous events, synchronicity to some, to which respondents attribute a common purpose. For example, during an event, a 48-year-old man reports that Ramtha created lightning at a climactic moment. Later, he found that Ramtha had predicted that he (Ramtha) would bring thunder and lightning to the event. Coincidentally, the man's card also had a lightning bolt on it.

I was catching a baby a while back. [She is a midwife.] I called on the Ram for healing. I got an idea to do something new and it worked. Ram inspired me to do it.

Ram became the wind, deftly using the corner of my sweater to break the fire off my cigarette, the message being 'you smoke too much, and you should quit'. I was later able to quit and this ex-perience empowered me (after 47 years as a smoker).

Ramtha at one event said, 'I will see you in a dream and when you wake you will feel as if the dream were real and the waking state is really the dream'. I dreamed I was pure light and whatever I wanted, it was so. I moved by thought in a split second. When I thought of the dream, it was the reality.

While wearing a lot of expensive jewelry, I saw Ram. He looked at me. I became immediately aware of how shallow my values are. Later, after receiving a lei from someone, Ram commented, 'I would rather have this than all the expensive jewelry in the world'. I realized that he was speaking directly to me. This began a journey of deep self-transformation, which continues today.

In all of these perceived interventions, the common element is the meaning that respondents attribute to events.

8) Family and Relationships

Interestingly, the eighth category in order of magnitude is the first clearly social category, relating to position in the world and relationships to others. In these narratives, respondents experience improvement in interpersonal relations not because of some general rule gleaned from Ramtha's teaching, but rather because of their own self-development that enabled them to see their situation more clearly and to act upon that vision. Consequently, what was gained from RSE led both to strengthening and dissolving relationships.

Ramtha's teachings have enabled me to regain my power. I got myself out of an abusive relationship.

I left my husband of 20 years and have a new relationship which is very special.

I was close to a divorce and now our relationship has healed.

My husband and I were headed for divorce. I had even called the moving van. I put the following on my list — my husband — and I joyously celebrate the evolution of our marriage.

I feel more in control of my life, work, and relationships.
I created a card to help me fully understand myself through a mirror. I met a man immediately after and I'm with this person now.

9) Experience of the Void

Ramtha's teaching concerning the void is central to his cosmology, yet few mention experiences with the void. Narratives about the void, however, though few in number, are quite dramatic. To experience the void, by all accounts, is to enter into another reality, perhaps the genuine reality, where several truths are evident. First, manifestation is possible from the void, as described below. Second, the nature of the universe as plastic is made clear. And third, ordinary life is made more bearable because one knows that another reality exists and that one can return to it.

In seeing other realms, I realized that this realm is insignificant in many ways.

I take the list into the void. I leave my body regularly and learn from masters in the void. What I take into the void becomes a part of me. When I take a concept into the void, it becomes tangible.

I became the void, lost all sense of body and could move freely about the void and whatever I thought of I experienced, i.e., a palm tree, a brook. I experienced the living of what my focus was.

10) Experience with UFO's

We assumed that a considerable number of narratives would contain mention of UFO experiences, because Ramtha himself has mentioned UFO's in his teaching. Actually, few respondents spoke about experiences with UFO's and these instances did not contain genuine dialogue between aliens and respondents. Instead, UFO's or aliens were merely observed or information from them was channelled.

One 41-year-old woman who expressed an overwhelming desire to visit a spaceship recounted, 'The next thing I knew, I was in a huge spaceship with very tall, blonde, very beautiful, very kind people. I didn't say a word, but understood everything they 'said' — telepathically'.

The most important thing to happen to me is my ability to remove myself from an alien ship, because of the Blue Star and my knowledge and awareness being expanded.

I was in my office one afternoon and I suddenly started receiving channelled transmissions from a spaceship. I recorded the pictures. I drew pictures of rams, JZ, and the days to come. Several months later I saw a video and realized Ram sent the channelled transmission. I became a 7-foot being, vaporizing into nothingness, re-forming in an alien world and dimension, unvaporizing back into this one. It felt like ecstasy.

Practices and Techniques

We reviewed all narratives to ascertain how the practices of RSE affected the lives of students. These practices, ordered by magnitude of incidence, are included in Table 11. By far, the most reported influence is that of the teachings themselves, mentioned in many of the categories above. Next, the disciplines and fieldwork in general are thought to provide a number of benefits, both on the field and away from the field.

I have discovered, with the help of the disciplines, that I have externalized unhappiness, jealousy, and deceit. The disciplines show me what I can't accept in myself.

Fieldwork has taught me perseverance, sensing beyond my physical senses, patience, tolerance, forgiveness, worthiness, and surrender of the body so that it is moved by my greater knowledge.

The more I do the disciplines, the less problem there is with life. Permeating the day is the knowing that the primary reality is a breath away.

If you can focus on the field very deeply, you are healing yourself.

Working with blue body is associated with extraordinary benefits, primarily healing of the physical body, awareness of a greater reality, and protection from danger.

I broke my nose five years ago and continued to suffer pain and discomfort until the '94 retreat. I blue bodied it and that day I felt it crack and straighten. All pain and discomfort were gone two days later.

I have had blue body protect me during an incident when I got my thumb caught in a three-ton wench cable. It would have totally cut off my thumb, yet blue body flashed and protected it just like a shield. When I reversed the wench and removed my thumb it came out unhurt. There were 2000 pounds on the wench cable at the time of the incident.

The greatest thing the blue body has given me is that I gained the knowledge and power and confidence that I can heal myself and that a miraculous healing is really just a change of mind.

Often what happens after I have drawn and then focused on the Blue Body, I will wake up the following morning with burns on my right arm which simulates a web.

Although fewer in number, experiences with the dance have evoked mystical states and an understanding of a deeper reality.

When Ram taught the sacred dance, I lost self-sense of ego and lost touch with this dimension. Space and time disappeared. The experiences from the dance awakened me to know that this is accessible to me and accessible to anyone. When I came back, I was no longer me as a personality. I was like dust, which precipitated into a body and took on the ego again.

Students also write about the importance of the list and C & E exercises in their lives, as they use these practices to move into analogical mind. All of the techniques seem to provide a sense of confidence and an experiential knowing of Ramtha's teachings.

The analogical mind is a totally different place from this one. Negative emotions disappear there.

If I can survive the tank, I can survive anything.

Analysis

A host of interpretations of the Ramtha phenomenon exist, from theoretical tracts on his teachings about quantum physics to comparative papers that place his teachings in a historical context. What this paper offers is a venue in which RSE members speak for themselves. As such, this analysis speaks to the wide spectrum of complaints about how new religions affect psychological welfare. Granted, this research does not include responses from former members, or 'defectors' as we could call them. And for this omission we can only plead expediency. Perhaps former members can be surveyed in the future. But, given what we have, we see a remarkably 'normal' set of people that have gained a great deal from their association with Ramtha and report that their lives are, without exception, better after their association with RSE.

Demographically, RSE members are primarily mid-lifers who have made their way in the world, achieving high levels of education and occupational prestige. Having reached mid-life, in which they are freer to make choices about their lives, many have chosen to reorient themselves to a new set of values and to make a commitment to live near the school. Many of them display status inconsistency because they have chosen to live near the school, where their skills are not as marketable as in urban areas. They voice a significant change in values in which striving for material prosperity via the American Success Ethic is supplanted by a personal striving for self-development and mastery of the human condition. Even though the average age is above 40 years, we can see the evolution of Ramtha's school toward a denominational status, as the children of students begin to enrol as students themselves. Of course, denominational religion often becomes nominal over time as successive generations identify with religious labels, but commit to little else. Gnosticism, in its very demand that teaching be incorporated into being, should be antithetical to nominal religion. It will be interesting to see if the Gnostic rigor of today's RSE will be maintained in the face of institutional pressure to appeal to larger audiences by making fewer demands.

Certainly, the degree of commitment shown by those who have left comfortable niches in society in order to be near the school is one indication of rigor that should not be underestimated. Students who have moved to Yelm from urban centres around the country have transferred their considerable achievements in administering governmental and educational systems to proficiency in using solar power and maintaining root cellars. Others have left families that did not see the value of Ramtha. One man relates,

I suffered because I left my family. I was a victim because my family didn't want me to do what I needed. There was much animosity. I made the change and created the split with them. Families don't like change. But when I am with members of my family, they pick up my consciousness. They were all upset with me, but there is no harm. I have changed tremendously.

The shift in values and priorities is unmistakable. It is this shift and subsequent sacrifices which most distinguish RSE students from the hosts of New Agers who strive for evermore prosperity, even while in the midst of plenty. This sample seems genuinely not to be interested in material advance or prestige in the larger world and some speak eloquently of the joy they have found after leaving their former lives to assume the responsibilities of being a student at RSE.

The previous religious experience of RSE students approximates a profile typical of the larger American scene, as discussed above. A large number were 'seekers', individuals who take religious questions seriously and go beyond the nominal sphere to inquire into meaning and to seek experience. But, an equal number were not seekers, finding Ramtha and his message compelling even after expending little effort in contemplating religious questions.

What can we make of this split between the sophisticated and the unschooled? I would suggest that Ramtha's message, while religious and philosophical to its root, is more appropriately viewed as a psychological, developmental message that speaks to the human condition in quite effective, though not theological, terms. Those who have pursued organized as well as new religions came to define their search in more radically personal, not institutional, terms. They had found out from experience the difference between 'spirit' and 'letter' as delineated in Christian thought. When they encountered Ramtha, they experienced 'spirit' and were compelled to investigate further. Those who had not pursued religion experienced a similar compulsion because Ramtha spoke to the issues of life in a pragmatic way.

Of particular note in any consideration of the issues of life is the role of gender. It is important that 80% of the respondents are women, that Ramtha's cosmology includes levels of being in which gender is transcended, and that Ramtha does not reinforce a patriarchal system, either in his cosmology or in his personal style. These latter two considerations seem to go a long way toward accounting for the first consideration. All respondents agree that, in both the message and the practice of RSE, gender is irrelevant. Even when women did not openly label their previous experience as oppressive, they, more often than men, spoke of the benefits of RSE in terms of 'finding value within myself', 'learning to love myself', and 'giving me permission to be myself'. Even the most cursory reading of these narratives yields a strong theme of gender emancipation and personal acceptance. Of course, Ramtha's teaching about the ultimate nature of all humans is the same for women and men, but women seem particularly affected by Ramtha's proffering of hope for finding power within and genuine transformation, because they have experienced a greater social and cultural conditioning to inferior status and self definition.

I am very happy and not afraid to express it now. I have confidence that I can be powerful inside, even though I am female. The Ram is even in his teachings and thinks women are no different than men. Gender means nothing in this school. This is freedom for me because I always felt I was powerful but most of my unhappiness and depression was based on the squashing of self by others and me. My family was based on the Muslim beliefs of squashing females; subservient females were to glorify males whether they had virtues or not.

C & E itself enables me to tap into a personal power that is usually trapped below the surface because of being a woman, because of social conditioning over this lifetime and many others.

I have erased 'victim' from my personality.

Who wouldn't want to believe that they are god and have all the power in the universe available to them?

Women's narratives speak of acceptance, participation, and freedom to be independent. Their relationship with RSE is not organized around affiliation with an institution, but rather self-reliance in a spiritual sense. At once they are claiming their humanity — and their divinity — by understanding and participating in what they perceive to be an egalitarian ethic. Marital status is almost evenly distributed across the sample and few women speak of being in the midst of raising children. Thus, we assume that RSE is speaking to women in general, not to specific categories of women who are suffering from the well-documented trials of a woman's life cycle. Women comment on their struggles with sexism and stereotyping and assert that the school gives them new options for defining their lives.

I put loving myself on the back burner, because I had to care for others. Now I see that I have to love myself and look inside. Ramtha helps me do this.

I am God. Being raised LDS, God has always a male and the best I could do would be to marry a man and he and I could be god and goddess together. Since we are made in the image of God, it makes sense that we are God — not perfected to his form, but can become so.

Before, I couldn't say the Lord's Prayer because it was a lie for me: MALE, JUDGMENT, STERN, the way I thought my father was.

I realize that I cannot be sovereign if I am still owned by a man and his sexual needs.

Women in this sample are not unsuccessful in life; they are not down-and-out or recovering victims trying desperately to cope with life. They may be defeated and discouraged, perhaps even cheated, by the dominant culture, but they are intelligent and are asking great questions of life. Thus, these women are representative of women in the larger society who seek personal authenticity and freedom. Culturally bound perspectives have limited their life's choices, their self-respect, and their opportunities for playing the real game of life — the game of self-acceptance and transformation. But not all have broken free from the societal pressures that compel women to internalize an inferior image of themselves. Women, more often than men, faulted themselves for not having enough belief to do more and more miracles.

Lastly, although this paper has focused on the characteristics of RSE students and the nature of their experiences, a word must be said about the perceived nature of Ramtha among the sample. Clearly his teachings stand out as the most important aspect of RSE for most respondents, yet these teachings are recognized by many as common fare, taught by previous as well as current teachers. Ramtha is considered unique because of his combination of teaching and practice, because of the deepening of spiritual truths that he fosters, and because of his unconditional love.

He turns my soul outside. He reflects hope and joy and always fearlessness.

Ramtha is really just a porthole through which I can open to an even larger reality. Universal consciousness focused inward is Ramtha. For us, he is our oversoul.

What is so different with Ramtha is that other groups provide theory and abstract thought, but Ramtha provides the experience, the effective techniques for manifesting spiritual reality into form.

Ramtha brought the living truth into my life, plus the experience — without experiences the teachings would be just another book. My brain has expanded!

The Ram is a real teacher, pushing and loving us all the way 'home'.

In true Gnostic form, narratives downplay the value of dogma, belief, and abstract theories, concentrating instead on the practical and technical abilities that give realization and power through direct experience. More than rejection of previously acquired teaching, Ramtha's benefit appears to be fulfilment, clarification, and experiential understanding of past teachings Part of this experiential emphasis is the rejection by respondents of the label 'follower'.

I have to take responsibility for myself. I still have to battle thoughts of wanting help from outside, but now I know the difference between being a follower and becoming a master.

Although the ancient wisdom is touched on by many different religions, teachers, etc., Ramtha will not allow followers — he creates a stimulating environment wherein the student learns by individual experience and gains wisdom and joy because of it.

He is an example of what I feel my life always was about. His footsteps are wonderful for me to pattern my life after. I refuse to follow but rather lead myself back home to the place from which I came.

Summary

Ram has empowered me to empower myself, to have joy, virtue, forthrightness, honour, impeccability, deep thought, courage, freedom of expression, the will to live, peace.

This statement of Ramtha's influence is an apt summary of what these data relate about the many functions of RSE in the lives of its students. While many reports are not extraordinary in any supernatural sense, all statements are remarkable in their witness to a profound, though often subtle, evolution toward greater self-awareness and expanded consciousness. The narratives speak in a number of voices about a single phenomenon — the transformation of self. Each respondent has encountered this transformation in some degree or another. Each has tasted, according to the needs of her or his palate, what we call the Gnostic quest.

Table 1. Country of Residence

Country	N	%
U.S.	450	83.3
Canada	38	7.0
Australia	29	5.4
South Africa	4	0.7
Europe	16	2.9
South America	2	0.4
Asia	1	0.2

Table 2. Residence within U.S.A.

U.S. Region	N	%
Northwest	352	*Mode* 65.2
West	29	5.4
Mid-West	20	3.7
Northeast	15	2.8
South	8	1.5
Southwest	1	0.2
Other	3	0.6

Table 3. Rural-Urban Dimension of Residence

Urban Dimension	N	%
Rural	390	Mode 72.2
Urban	74	13.7
Suburban	61	11.3
Unspecified	15	2.7

Table 4. Occupation

Occupation Category	N	%
Professional/Technical	157	Mode 29.07
Administrative/Self-Employed	85	15.74
Sales/Clerical	48	8.9
Skilled Labour	63	11.7
Unskilled Labour	36	6.7
Farming	3	0.6
Unemployed*	99	18.3
No answer	49	9.1

*Includes: homemakers, students, unemployed, and retired

Table 5. Education

Level of Education	N	%
Graduate School	103	19.1
College Graduate	97	17.9
Some College	168	*Mode* 31.1
High School Graduate	92	17.0
Less than High School Graduate	63	11.7
No Answer	17	3.1

Table 6. Yearly Income

Income Range	N	%
Over $65,000	48	8.9
$50-65,000	31	5.7
$40-49,000	37	6.9
$30-39,000	45	8.3
$20-29,000	102	18.9
Less than $20,000	235	Mode 43.5
No answer	42	7.8

Table 7. Religious Socialization

Religion	N	%
Roman Catholic	184	34.1
Jewish	13	2.4
Protestant	223	Mode 41.3
New Age/Occult	22	4.1
Eastern	8	1.5
Atheist/Humanist	6	1.1
Other	9	1.6
None	70	12.9
No answer	5	0.9

Table 8. Religious Experience in Adulthood

Type of Religion	N	%
Western Religions	140	25.9
Eastern Religions	105	19.4
New Age Religions	191	35.3
New Thought Religions	53	9.8
Eclectic: three or more groups	93	17.2

Table 9. Introduction to RSE

Source of Introduction	N	%
Self	29	5.4
Other person	148	27.4
Published material	260	Mode 48.1
Other	6	1.1
No answer	97	17.9

Table 10. Life Experiences after Association with RSE

Experience	N	%
Self-Development	373	Mode 69.1
Healing of Self or Other	316	58.5
Intuitive/Spiritual Sensitivity	312	57.8
Paranormal	214	39.6
Cognitive, Understanding	211	39.1
Manifestation	187	34.6
Intervention by Ramtha	68	12.6
Family and Relationships	51	9.4
Experience of the Void	24	4.4
Experience with UFO's	7	1.3

Table 11. Reports of RSE Practices

Practices	N	%
Teachings	292	Mode 54.1
C and E	212	39.3
Field	205	37.9
Blue Body	185	34.3
Tank	111	20.6
List	45	8.3
Dance	23	4.3

Bibliography

http://www.ramtha.com

Knight, J.Z. 1997. *A State of Mind*. New York: Warner Books.

Melton, J. Gordon 1998. *Finding Enlighenment. Ramtha's School of Ancient Wisdom*. Hillsboro: Beyond Words.

Contributors

Judith Coney, Professor, Dr.
Department of the Study of Religions
School of Oriental and African Studies
Thornhaugh Street
London WC1H OXG
England

Jean Duhaime, Professeur Titulaire
Faculté de Théologie
Université de Montréal
C.P. 6128, succ. Centre-Ville
Montréal, Quebec
H3C 3J7 Canada

Robert Ellwood, Emeritus Professor
10 Krotona Hill
Ojai, CA 93023
USA

Liselotte Frisk, Associate Professor, PhD.
Högskolan Dalarna
791 88 Falun
Sweden

Massimo Introvigne, Dr., Director
Center for the Study of New Religions (CESNUR)
Via Confienza 19,
10121 Torino
Italy

Constance A. Jones, Ph.D.
California Institute of Integral Studies
1453 Mission Street
San Fransisco
CA 94103
USA

Reender Kranenborg, Professor
Faculteit der Godgeleerdheid
Vrije Universiteit Amsterdam
De Boelelaan 1105
1081 HV Amsterdam
The Netherlands

Albertina Nugteren, Associate Professor, Dr.
Phenomenology and History of Indian Religions
Faculty of Theology
Tilburg University
Tilburg
The Netherlands

David Piff, Ph.D.
P.O. Box 155
Haifa, Israel 31 001
Israel

Mikael Rothstein, Associate Professor, MA & Ph.D.
Department of History of Religions
University of Copenhagen
Artillerivej 86
2300 Copenhagen S
Denmark

Mark Sedgwick, Dr.
Department of History
American University in Cairo
Cairo
Egypt

Christine Steyn, Dr.
Department of Religious Studies
University of South Africa
P.O. Box 392
UNISA 0003
South Africa

Jan A. M. Snoek, Professor, Dr.
Institut für Religionswissenschaft
Ruprecht-Karls-Universität Heidelberg
Akademistrasse 4-8
69117 Heidelberg
Germany

Margit Warburg, Associate Professor, MA.
Department of History of Religions
University of Copenhagen
Artillerivej 86
2300 Copenhagen S
Denmark

Index